Qamishli

□ Moqebleh

*IRAQI
KURDISTAN*

Hasakah

Erbil

• Raqqa

Deir Ezzor •

S Y R I A

I R A Q

Baghdad

0	50		100 mi
0	50	100	150 km

A U D I   A R A B I A

"Fascinating and full of insights. . . . A welcome antidote to the flood of ill-informed blather that has deformed our understanding of this alarming crisis."
—Stephen Kinzer, author of *Overthrow* and *All the Shah's Men*

"Journalist Reese Erlich guides the reader through the labyrinth of Middle East history and politics that led to the Syrian Civil War. Since the fallout from that conflict has global ramifications, this well-written book is a must read."
—Conn Hallinan, columnist for *Foreign Policy in Focus*

"Read this book and you will receive an in-depth, objective, and truly fair understanding of what is taking place in the Middle East at this moment. We need Reese Erlich in the mass media."
—Peter Coyote, actor, author of *Sleeping Where I Fall*

"Well before the US invasion of Iraq, Reese Erlich's firsthand reporting challenged the official justification for that effort—and the mainstream media's failure to report on it accurately. Since then, Erlich has combined independent reporting with straightforward political analysis and expert media criticism. *Inside Syria* continues that important work. It parses that region's conflicts, considers the historical and geopolitical forces at work, and skips the usual forms of demonization and mystification. If the news from Syria doesn't make sense to you, read this book."
—Peter Richardson, San Francisco State University, author of *A Bomb in Every Issue: How the Short, Unruly Life of Ramparts Magazine Changed America*

"Erlich's work is a reliable astrolabe and an essential guide in navigating the shifting political winds of the Syrian war and regional conflict. Meticulously investigated."
—Meghan Nuttall Sayres, editor of *Love and Pomegranates: Artists and Wayfarers on Iran*

"The strength of the work lies in the interviews and firsthand observations that other types of analyses may lack."
—Dr. Amir Sharifi, Department of Linguistics, California State University, Long Beach

INSIDE
SYRIA

INSIDE
SYRIA

The Backstory of Their Civil War and What the World Can Expect

Reese Erlich

FOREWORD BY NOAM CHOMSKY

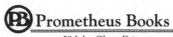 Prometheus Books

59 John Glenn Drive
Amherst, New York 14228

Published 2014 by Prometheus Books

Top cover image © Media Bakery
Bottom cover image © Shutterstock
Jacket design by Grace M. Conti-Zilsberger
Unless otherwise specified, all images in the photo insert are by Reese Erlich
Maps by William L. Nelson

Inquiries should be addressed to
Prometheus Books
59 John Glenn Drive
Amherst, New York 14228
VOICE: 716–691–0133
FAX: 716–691–0137
WWW.PROMETHEUSBOOKS.COM

18 17 16 15 14   5 4 3 2 1

Library of Congress Cataloging-in-Publication Data

Erlich, Reese W., 1947–
    Inside Syria : the backstory of their civil war and what the world can expect / Reese Erlich ; foreword by Noam Chomsky.
        pages cm
    Includes bibliographical references and index.
    ISBN 978-1-61614-948-2 (hardback) — ISBN 978-1-61614-949-9 (ebook)
    1. Syria—History—Civil War, 2011– 2. Syria—Politics and government—2000– 3. Protest movements—Syria—History—21st century. 4. Political violence—Syria—History—21st century. I. Title.

DS98.6.E75 2014
956.9104'2—dc23

2014015840

Printed in the United States of America

To the people of Syria

CONTENTS

FOREWORD

The Arab Spring uprisings of early 2011 were highly exciting events of historic importance. Despite setbacks, significant gains have been achieved, and I suspect they will be lasting—very likely a prelude of more to come.

In Tunisia, France was the dominant imperial power and supported the dictator strongly in ways that were a considerable embarrassment. A French cabinet minister was even vacationing in Tunisia while the popular uprising was expelling Ben-Ali. In Egypt, the dominant influences were the United States and the United Kingdom. Both supported the dictator, General Hosni Mubarak, until the very end.

They then followed the standard script when a favored dictator faces internal problems: support him as long as possible, and when it no longer is—particularly if the business classes and the army turn against him—ship him off somewhere. Then be sure to issue ringing declarations about your love of democracy, and try to restore the old system as fully as possible.

The United States supported the elected Muslim Brotherhood government of Mohammed Morsi, which, crucially, left the military pretty much in charge. When the military overthrew the government and took full control in July 2013, the United States supported it with the usual formulaic comments about democracy.

I was also excited about the uprising in Syria, although the vicious reaction of the Assad regime turned the early nonviolent demands for reform into a murderous civil war that is destroying the society. In chapter 5, Reese Erlich shows that the conflict remains one between the Assad regime and major sectors of the Syrian people. But the war has become much more complicated because of intensified fighting between Sunni, Alawites, Shia, and other religious and ethnic groups, and the intervention into the conflict of jihadi groups with their own varying agendas.

11

The Sunni-Shia split, of course, goes back to the founding days of Islam. The Alawites were an early offshoot of Shia Islam. Ottoman Turks and French colonialists sought to exploit religious differences to maintain their rule. When the United States invaded Iraq in 2003, the occupation exacerbated low-level religious tensions, which have since been tearing Iraq apart and spread to the entire region—Syria in particular.

There is perhaps some hope for a negotiated, political settlement of the Geneva type. Russia and the United States could bring pressure to bear to end the civil war. It is a very slim possibility, but it is actually the only one that I can see that has any hope of saving Syria.

From the beginning, as Erlich shows in chapters 10–11, the United States and Israel have been wary of the Syrian uprising. Assad had, in fact, been relatively cooperative with the United States in recent years, sharing intelligence, absorbing huge numbers of people fleeing from the wreckage of the US invasion of Iraq, and generally conforming to US demands.

Interestingly, the United States and Israel did not undertake one fairly straightforward action that could have significantly helped the rebels. Israel could have mobilized its forces on the occupied Golan, which would have compelled Assad to move forces to the south, relieving pressure on the rebels. Israel is quite happy to see Arabs murdering each other, as Erlich documents in chapter 10 by interviewing Israeli analysts.

The United States has been helping expedite some arms flow to the rebels from the Gulf states and directly training selected rebels in Jordan, but otherwise not intervening extensively. The United States offered lukewarm support for UN negotiator Lakhdar Brahimi's Geneva peace initiative, the one (very thin) reed that might offer some hope of arresting Syria's plunge to catastrophe.

The US failure to bomb Syria after the chemical-weapons incident in August 2013 was highly significant. The Obama administration was unable to obtain virtually any international support. Even Britain wouldn't support it. Congress wasn't going to support the attack either, which would have left Obama completely out on a limb. So the Russian plan to dismantle Syria's chemical weapons was a godsend for Obama. It saved him from what would have been a very serious political defeat.

This would have been a perfect opportunity to ban chemical weapons in the entire Middle East. The Chemical Weapons Convention, contrary to the Obama administration position, does not refer just to use of chemical weapons; it refers to production, storage, or use of chemical weapons. Well, Israel has chemical weapons and has refused even to ratify the Chemical Weapons Convention.

The appropriate response would be to call for imposing the Chemical Weapons Convention throughout the Middle East, which would mean that any country that is in violation of that convention, whether it has accepted it or not, would be compelled to eliminate its chemical-weapons stores. Just maintaining those stores, producing chemical weapons—all of that is in violation of the convention. Of course, that would require that a US ally, Israel, give up its chemical weapons and permit international inspections. This should apply to nuclear weapons, as well.

The United States hasn't given up on possible future military action in Syria. In chapter 11, Erlich describes the various justifications offered for "humanitarian intervention." Advocates argue that the Syrian Civil War is so horrific—with the possibility of hundreds of thousands of civilian deaths—that the international community must intervene with bombs and troops, though there is every reason to expect that as in other cases, the intervention would not be in the interest of the Syrians, but of those intervening, and would make the tragedy even worse.

Syria is a terrible atrocity. But there are much worse ones in the world. The worst atrocities in the past decade have been in eastern Congo, where maybe five million people have been killed. And the United States is indirectly involved. The government of Rwanda, which is a US client, is intervening massively, as is Uganda to an extent. It's almost an international war in Africa. How many people know about this? It's barely in the media. No one is calling for US humanitarian intervention to save people in the Congo.

The concept of "humanitarian intervention" is very old, and to find genuine cases is no easy task. In the 1990s, the concept became very fashionable in the West. The jewel in the crown was Kosovo, but the traditional victims were unimpressed. The summit of the Global South, usually ignored or ridiculed in the West, condemned "the so-called 'right' of humanitarian intervention" as another face for imperialism.

The outcomes of these grand enterprises and the reactions led to development of a new concept, "Responsibility to Protect," or *R2P.* There are two crucially different versions of this doctrine. One was adopted by the United Nations in 2005. Apart from a shift of focus, it barely goes beyond well-established international law and practices.

A radically different version was produced by the commission headed by Gareth Evans, former Australian prime minister, who has since been hailed in the West as the guardian angel of R2P. The Evans version departs from the UN version in authorizing military action by regional groupings in the area of their jurisdiction, subject to subsequent acquiescence by the UN Security Council. The main regional grouping that can act this way is NATO, and it officially takes its area of jurisdiction as virtually the entire world.

It comes as no surprise that the traditional imperial powers adopt the Evans version and justify it on the grounds that the United Nations adopted R2P, concealing the fact that it is a crucially different version.

Finally, I would like to mention that Reese Erlich's reporting and investigative journalism around the world have been highly enlightening and, speaking personally, have been of great value to me in my own work on global issues and current affairs.

Noam Chomsky
May 27, 2014
Boston

CHAPTER 1

THE UPRISING THAT
WASN'T SUPPOSED TO BE

About seven months into the Syrian uprising, I arranged to meet with opposition activists in Damascus. It wasn't easy. We had made a rendezvous at a large traffic circle where cars careened about, competing with motorcycles for space on the small streets. Many dozens of people were hanging out. Some looked like secret intelligence officers, wearing leather jackets and aviator sunglasses—even at night.

Finally I met my contact, and we made our way to Old Damascus. We walked through the narrow, cobblestone streets where no cars would fit and anyone tailing us could be spotted.

I was meeting with leaders of the Local Coordinating Committees, the loose-knit group then spearheading the uprising against the government of President Bashar al-Assad. The activists I met represented one sector of the protestors: mostly young, secular, and middle-income.

Demonstrators wanted to establish a genuine parliamentary system and hold free elections. An activist leader named Ahmad Bakdouness said that at first the demonstrators called for reforms when they came out into the streets in March 2011. They wanted free elections, a parliamentary government, release of political prisoners, and the right to organize peaceful protests. The government rejected these demands and responded with violent attacks. Within weeks, protestors were demanding the government's overthrow. "When they [the government] started killing people," Bakdouness said, "people increased their demands. No one accepted how they killed us and arrested us for nothing."[1]

At the beginning of the Arab Spring, Assad bragged that his country would never see a popular uprising because of his nationalist

15

credentials. History has rarely delivered a more stunning and immediate rebuttal. Over 150,000 Syrians have died in the civil war since the beginning of the uprising, with thousands more dying every month. Several thousand army and police personnel have been killed. Over nine million Syrians have fled the country or been internally displaced.

Another activist, who used the name "Leen," said everyone is taking sides. She said her country had become much more dangerous than Tunisia or Egypt at the height of their revolutions. "In Egypt and Tunisia they can demonstrate showing their faces, take photos, and put them on Facebook," she said. "We can't do that." Leen said demonstrators faced the possibility of death at each confrontation. "When we ask someone to come to the streets, they say, 'you are asking us to commit suicide.'"[2]

Gradually, the liberation movement shifted from demonstrations to armed attacks. But unlike movements in Latin America or Africa in earlier decades, the Syrian uprising lacked cohesive political or military leadership. Young men from the same village or town grouped together to form ad hoc local militias. They armed themselves with homemade rifles or supplies captured from the Syrian military.

By the beginning of 2012, foreign powers were arming the rebels, each seeking groups that would carry out its political goals in post-Assad Syria. Adventurers, journalists, and spies prowled the Syrian–Turkish border, seeking contact with militias. I visited one such hotbed of international intrigue—Antakya, Turkey, close to the northwestern border with Syria.

During the Islamic holy month of Ramadan in August, Syrian Muslim insurgents in Antakya weren't supposed to eat or even drink water during the day. Instead, they stayed up all night so they could eat—and even drink alcohol. That pretty much describes the role of religion for some armed groups participating in the Syrian uprising. Some of the insurgents are ultraconservative Islamists. But many of the Free Syrian Army guerrillas grow beards, pray five times a day, and observe Ramadan—not out of religious conviction, but in order to appear pious. To get funding from Saudi Arabia and other Gulf states, groups must appeal to religious sensibilities.

To the pious go the guns.

While the United States claimed to be promoting moderate, secular rebels, in fact the strongest groups held rightist, Islamic views. In part that's because Saudi Arabia had been supplying arms to both the Free Syrian Army (FSA) and rebel groups that follow an ultraright, Islamist ideology. Groups such as the al-Nusra Front and the Islamic State of Iraq and al-Sham (ISIS) wanted religion to play the leading role in government, claimed their holy book should be the basis of the legal system, held other religions in contempt, and opposed women's rights. In short, their ideology was similar to ultraright groups in the United States and Europe, except they carry out activities in the name of Islam, not Christianity.

Meanwhile, the CIA had posted agents along the Turkish–Syrian border to check on which militias would receive arms from Saudi Arabia and Qatar. The CIA later poured more resources into training selected guerrillas in Jordan. The FSA rebels have to appear superpious to the Saudis but as moderate Islamists to the CIA. It's not easy being a Syrian insurgent these days.

I met one such chameleon group. This FSA brigade of 150 men is called Ahrar Syria (Free People of Syria). It is only one of many dozens of groups loosely affiliated with the FSA. When I interviewed them at two in the morning, eight men crowded into a sparsely furnished living room, tapping on laptops and answering e-mails on smartphones. Ahrar Syria even has its own Facebook page.

As brigade leader, Abdul Salman nervously pulled on newly minted facial hair; he told me they grew beards in order to look more religious. Members of Ahrar and other armed opposition groups are angry at the United States for not giving them enough backing. "We haven't gotten any arms from the United States," Salman complained. "If we had arms, Assad would have fallen by now." He also favored establishing a no-fly zone over parts of Syria as the United States and NATO did in Libya.[3]

At the same time, Ahrar and other opposition groups strongly oppose US policy in the region. They want the return of Syria's Golan, seized by Israel in the 1967 war. They support Palestinian rights and oppose US aggression in Iraq and Afghanistan.

Syria's uprising will impact the entire Middle East. But the United States faces a major contradiction. Many Syrians in the opposition want Washington to offer stronger support for their cause, yet their plans for Syria's future diverge significantly from US strategic goals.[4]

The Washington debate about Syria is strangely detached from the reality on the ground. Doves favor tough economic sanctions and arming "moderate" insurgents. Hawks advocate sending even more arms to guerrillas accompanied by US military bombing. Syrian opposition leaders I met said those differences are only tactical. Both hawks and doves want to replace Bashar al-Assad with a pro-US strongman. "The Americans haven't supported the revolution strongly enough because they are still looking for someone who can ensure their interests in the future," Omar Mushaweh told me.[5] He was a leader of Syria's Muslim Brotherhood living in Istanbul.

While US officials helped create opposition coalitions, ordinary people didn't accept US goals, he said. Mushaweh pointed to Iraq and Afghanistan as examples of US military intervention that produced political disasters. He doesn't want Syria to follow that path. That could be one reason the United States cooled on the Muslim Brotherhood and sought to back other armed groups that it trained in Jordan.

The Obama administration and major US media portray Syria as a quagmire of religious groups fighting centuries-old battles. The reality is quite different. For many years, Syrians lived peacefully with one another. Syria was a secular dictatorship where dissidents faced torture and jail for criticizing Assad, but people largely ignored religious differences. Once the fighting began, however, leaders on both sides used religion to rally their troops. Rebels relied on the Sunni Muslim majority. Assad appealed to minority groups such as Alawites, Christians, and Shia Muslims.

When the US government and media start to bewail the quagmire of centuries-old disputes, it means the United States hasn't figured out how to win the war or its plans have gone askew. And so it is with Syria.

Oddly enough, we can learn a lot about US and Syrian politics by looking at the country's seat belt laws. Wearing a seat belt is mandatory in Syria. But a taxi driver, when approaching a traffic policeman, drapes the seat belt over his chest without buckling. It looks like it's on, but he has no need to actually benefit from the belt's safety. This practice continues even now, when military checkpoints are common in Damascus.

Seat belts are so seldom worn that people actually look strangely at you when you put them on. One day I found out why. I was given a ride back to my hotel in the personal car of a very high-ranking government official. This guy had a car and driver at his disposal anytime. I got in the front passenger seat and reflexively strapped up. The driver looked strangely at me but said nothing. Even if he had said something, it would have been in Arabic. I interpreted his look to mean, "What? You don't trust my driving?"

We made the uneventful drive back to my hotel. Then, I went to my room on the eighth floor and passed a mirror. The dirty seat belt had made a perfect black sash across my chest and shoulder. Having never been used, the belt had simply been collecting dust and dirt for the past four years.

The civil war stalemate in Syria is a lot like my seat belt experience. Syria's government pretends to provide security for its people, but the seat belt is dirty, dusty, and seldom used. Extremist rebels offer security through the piety of Islam, but in reality pursue dictatorial power. Meanwhile, the United States pretends to uphold the rules but can't figure out why the seat belts don't work.

I had another seat belt experience in Damascus when an official car and driver picked me up. This time the seat belt was scrupulously clean. I was about to meet President Bashar al-Assad.

Strange as it may sound, I first met Assad as part of a delegation of visiting Americans from South Dakota in 2006. Former US Senator Jim

Abourezk had organized people from his home state to tour Syria. His wife is Syrian, and the Abourezks periodically visited relatives in the western part of the country. Because of his long history as a progressive politician and leader in the Arab-American movement, Abourezk had won Assad's respect. In fact, every time Abourezk came to Syria to visit his in-laws, the president invited him over for a chat.

We filed into a huge meeting hall and sat on the ubiquitous overstuffed chairs popular throughout the Middle East. Assad is tall and thin with an angular face. He sports the mandatory mustache and short haircut of the model Arab leader. He was charming, personable, and fluent in English. He won over many in the group as being a reasonable leader seeking normal relations with the United States.

After the meeting, I approached him to ask if I could get a one-on-one interview for public radio. He immediately agreed and said Bouthaina Shaban, a presidential advisor and spokesperson, would make the arrangements.

Shaban is one of the few women in high government positions and always objected to the rampant corruption in Syria. At the time, she appeared to be a moderate in the country's ruling elite. Once the uprising began, however, she remained a public spokesperson, staunchly defending Assad's repression.

Bashar's father, Hafez al-Assad, seized power in a military coup d'état in 1970 and ruled with an iron fist. Bashar was not supposed to follow in his father's footsteps. That role was set aside for Basil al-Assad, Hafez's eldest son. Bashar had become an ophthalmologist and was doing advanced studies in London when his brother died in a car crash. Bashar was called home in 1994 and groomed for the presidency.

Bashar's familiarity with the West, high level of education, and natural charm convinced many that he would be a reformer. Western leaders also praised Assad's neoliberal economic policies. He sold off state-run enterprises and encouraged private sector, capitalist development. But none of these changes resulted in significant reform, let alone an end to Syria's highly centralized, authoritarian system.

A few days after my initial meeting with Assad, that government car with the clean seatbelt showed up at my hotel. I was driven up a long, winding road to the presidential palace. Assad normally works out of his downtown office and uses the palace only for formal events. I must have been considered a formal event. I walked through enormous red-carpeted rooms to a set of eight-foot-high double doors. The doors parted, and there stood the president.

I unpacked my radio recorder and short, shotgun microphone. It's shaped like a very short, single-barreled shotgun barrel with a foam covering, a standard mic for radio and TV. For some reason, Assad was intimidated by it. He fidgeted uncomfortably and kept looking nervously at the mic. Perhaps it looked too much like a real shotgun.

I had asked opposition activists all over Damascus what questions I should ask their president. So I came not just with the usual list of questions about US-Syrian relations but also with many questions about domestic issues. When would Syria have free elections for a parliament? When would opposition parties be allowed? Why hadn't 300,000 Syrian Kurds been allowed citizenship? When would Syria end the state of emergency in effect since 1963?

Assad bobbed and weaved around these and other questions. He claimed calls for democratic change were really efforts by the United States to weaken his government. He claimed to be creating a dialogue with Syrian intellectuals to discuss domestic reform.

"It takes about a year of dialogue to define the frame" for negotiations, he told me.[6] That was in 2006. Five years later, no meaningful dialogue had taken place, let alone reform.

In March 2011, the Arab Spring came to Syria, and people raised many of the issues I had asked about in the interview. It's not because I had a crystal ball; large numbers of Syrians had been raising those issues for decades. In a panic, Assad implemented some reforms. He lifted the state of emergency, gave citizenship to most of the disenfranchised Kurds, and opened a dialogue with moderate opposition leaders. Had he made such reforms in 2006, Assad would have been hailed as a farsighted leader.

By 2011, it was too late. The uprising against Assad and his entire regime had begun, and there was no turning back. Syria's ruling elite became increasingly isolated, internationally and domestically. The Arab League—composed of twenty-two states from the Middle East and North Africa—voted unprecedented sanctions against Syria and later voted to recognize the Syrian opposition and eject Assad's government. The United Nations sent several observer missions and tried to broker a peace agreement. All the efforts failed.

The regime has suffered a number of high-level defections, including the Syrian ambassador to Iraq, a Republican Guard brigadier general, and the prime minister. Every week saw desertions by lower-level military. Syria faced serious economic problems as well. But as ultra-right-wing rebels gained strength within the opposition, Assad rallied some Syrians to his side, arguing that a secular strongman is better than Islamic rule.

A big question remained: Will the Syrian people blame the country's crisis on the Assad government or the rebels?

I received a partial answer during a very unusual trip. Syrian authorities organized a media visit to an elementary school in the southern city of Daraa, where the uprising began. Government officials wanted to show that life had returned to normal. All was going according to plan when the children came out for morning recess.

Then, spotting the TV cameras, the children suddenly began chanting, "Freedom, freedom," one of the main antigovernment slogans. Then others chanted "Syria" and similar progovernment slogans. Government officials leading the delegation went pale. Here, in front of the whole world, stood the divided Syria.

"The political chasm has reached the schools," said my translator, who was assigned by the government to accompany me on this visit. "First graders are now politically motivated."[7]

The fact that students dared to chant antigovernment slogans during an official visit did not bode well for Assad and the future of the Syrian government.

Uprisings aren't new in Syria. To fully understand the revolt that began in 2011, we need to look at the country's tumultuous history.

CHAPTER 2

LAWRENCE OF SYRIA

I f Americans know anything about twentieth-century Middle East history, it's likely gleaned from watching reruns of *Lawrence of Arabia*. The 1962 epic film featured an all-star cast riding camels across the desert while fighting the evil Ottoman Turks during World War I. I enjoyed watching the film as a teenager, particularly Peter O'Toole's heroic portrayal of T. E. Lawrence. Later, as a college student and anti–Vietnam War activist in the 1960s, I wondered if the film accurately portrayed history. It took me years to find out.

Peter O'Toole has become the iconic image of Lieutenant Colonel Thomas Edward Lawrence: tall, lanky, and blond. The real-life Lawrence stood only five feet five inches tall, so short that he didn't even look like a British Army officer. But the two men did share fine blond hair and very blue eyes.

The life of T. E. Lawrence was inextricably intertwined with the modern history of Syria. He was born in 1888 and entered Oxford University in 1907. Lawrence began his early career in 1909 with a walking tour of Syria, then part of the Ottoman Empire. He made two more trips to Lebanon and Syria after graduation to work on archaeological digs overseen by the British Museum. Lawrence had learned to speak colloquial Arabic and wrote his PhD thesis about Crusader castles in Syria.

Lawrence became a quasi–Indiana Jones by using his archaeological travels as a cover to spy for the British military, although history does not record his owning a bullwhip. Some historians dispute whether Lawrence spied for the British before the war. But without doubt, British intelligence was very interested in the area being studied by Lawrence because of the nearby bridges and a new railway line being built by the Germans.[1] Lawrence's mentor, who got him the archaeological job, worked for British intelligence. And, without doubt, Lawrence in his early travels did carry a 9mm Mauser pistol.

After the outbreak of World War I, Lawrence officially joined British Army intelligence and was posted to Cairo. He developed both a respect for and a romantic affinity for Arabs, a marked departure from the colonial arrogance of the times. His fellow colonialists suspected him of being too sympathetic to the natives.

Lawrence sought to distinguish himself from the typical British colonial. At the same time, he realized the contradiction of being British in an Arab land, an issue that would plague him throughout his life. "Some feel deeply the influence of native people, and try to adjust themselves to its spirit," Lawrence wrote. "To fit themselves modestly into the picture, they suppress all in them imitate the native, and so avoid friction in their daily life. However, they cannot avoid the consequences of imitation, a hollow, worthless thing. They are like the people but not of the people . . ."[2]

But the Arab leaders of the revolt against the Turks had a decidedly different perspective on Lawrence. Most saw him as a minor British liaison officer who became famous only after the war. Abdullah ibn al-Hussein, one of the leaders of the Arab revolt, had to convince his followers of Lawrence's usefulness in military matters. He forbid Lawrence from making direct contact with tribes under his control.[3] Lawrence's seemingly contradictory role became understandable in the context of his political goals. He favored independent Arab states, but only to be governed by friendly Arab monarchs who supported Britain and opposed France. Lawrence was an advocate of neocolonialism.

The Ottoman Sultans ruled the area that is now Syria from 1517 to 1918. The provinces that are now Syria, Lebanon, Jordan, and Palestine included numerous tribes, ethnicities, and religious groups. The Ottomans allowed some local autonomy to feudal Arab tribal leaders. Local noblemen ruled in rural areas so long as they paid taxes to Constantinople (Istanbul). They allowed Christians, Jews, and Muslims to control their own personal-status laws, such as marriage and divorce.

Both conflict and cooperation had historically existed between Christians, Muslims, and Druze, a distinct ethnic group that split off from Shia Muslims nearly one thousand years ago. The Ottomans played one group off another to maintain their rule. To further complicate matters, European powers sought to extend their influence by supporting certain groups. The French backed the Christians, and the British supported the Druze.

Like all colonialists, the sultans also used brute force. In those days the Ottoman Empire extended into southern Europe. The sultans brutally suppressed an 1875 rebellion in Bosnia and Herzegovina (Yugoslavia), the 1876 rebellion in Bulgaria, and an Armenian uprising from 1892 to 1893. The Ottoman Empire was impacted by the same nationalist and democratic movements as other countries around the world. Around the turn of the twentieth century, revolutions had erupted in Russia (1905), Iran (1906), China (1911), and Mexico (1910).

With the outbreak of World War I, the Ottomans sided with Germany and the Austro-Hungarian Empire against Britain, France, and Russia. The British, and to some extent the French, hoped to use the war as a means to divvy up the Ottoman Empire, as well as seize control of German colonies. Not surprisingly, the British Empire and French colonial empire were happy to use Arab nationalism to help defeat their enemy. While paying lip service to Arab independence, however, both powers planned to extend their colonial empires at the expense of the local populations.

Lawrence of Arabia more or less accurately portrays how the British sought a wartime alliance with Sharif Hussein ibn Ali, governor of Mecca, and his sons. Alec Guinness portrayed Faisal bin Hussein, one of Hussein's sons, although the real Faisal was twenty-nine years old when the war began and Guinness was forty-eight when the film was shot. As the official who governed Islam's most holy city, Sharif Hussein represented a political alternative to the Ottoman Turkish Sultan Mehmed V, who was then the recognized leader of the Muslim world. Hussein, the patriarch of the Hashemite family, claimed to be a direct descendant of the Prophet Mohammad and thus offered a credible case for an alternative, pro-British leadership of the Muslim world.

Hussein offered to support the British in return for a guarantee of a postwar independent Arab nation under his rule that would encompass virtually the entire Middle East. His vision of an independent state was decidedly conservative, opposing many of the reforms imposed by the Turks. He would not allow women to work. Hussein favored a strict version of Islamic Shariah law, including amputations of thieves' limbs.[4] Such views didn't stop Sir Henry MacMahon, the top British diplomat in the region, from responding favorably to Hussein's offer. Even then, Western empires feared the power of Islamic movements. Lawrence prophetically sought to divide the Muslim world by promoting pro-British Sharif Hussein against Sultan Mehmed V.

Referring to the violence needed to overthrow the Ottoman Empire, Lawrence wrote, "If we can arrange that this political change shall be a violent one, we will have abolished the threat of Islam, by dividing it against itself . . ."[5] MacMahon wanted to leave the impression that he supported Arab independence, but he intentionally clouded his support with opaque and ambiguous diplomatic language. The British government had no intention of actually granting independence.[6] But Lawrence's Arab allies knew little of Britain's long-term plans. Hussein, his sons, and other nationalist leaders trusted that the British would carry out their promises. Auda Abu Tayi was one of them.

An old color-tint photo showed Auda dressed in a plain, white keffiyeh, brown robes, and carrying both a curved dagger and a sword. He had dark skin, a black mustache, and goatee. He looked the part of a fierce desert warrior. Anthony Quinn portrayed Auda in *Lawrence of Arabia*.

Auda led the Huwaytat clan of Bedouin nomads who roamed the deserts of what is now Saudi Arabia and Jordan. In 1908, Auda became a thorn in the side of the Ottomans when he killed two government officials in a dispute over tax collection. They tried to hunt him down but never succeeded.

When World War I broke out, Auda and his kinsmen became key participants in the Arab revolt. He joined Lawrence in the very first military campaign against the Turks. Auda and his clan were known as skilled fighters, with each man functioning as an independent fighting unit. Such initiative ran counter to British military doctrine that relied on massing troops. But it proved perfectly suited for guerrilla warfare in the desert.

Lawrence of Arabia portrayed Auda as boorish, greedy, and loyal only to his own tribe. When there was no loot to be found, Quinn's character threatened to abandon the struggle. The real Auda was a desert intellectual and fierce supporter of the Arab cause, not just his tribe. According to Lawrence, "He saw life as a saga, all the events in it were significant: all personages in contact with him heroic, his mind was stored with poems of old raids and epic tales of fights."[7] Auda was a charismatic fighter who also helped unite the other tribes against the Ottomans. He was a key fighter in the Arab revolt's capture of Aqaba and Damascus. Auda is "the greatest fighting man in northern Arabia," Lawrence once said.

The British were happy to use Auda and other Arab leaders to win the war but relied on other aristocratic families to eventually rule the region. After the war, British officials installed the Hashemites as rulers in Iraq and Jordan. The Ibn Saud family conquered the holy cities of Mecca and Medina in Saudi Arabia, and the British ultimately made an alliance with them. The Saud family rules Saudi Arabia today. The British were perfectly willing to ally with ultraconservative, religious rulers so long as they politically supported British rule. That policy was promoted by a British leader who would become world famous only a few years later.

My image of Winston Churchill is an elderly man wearing an ill-fitting three-piece suit and chomping a cigar, which for some reason was called a "Churchill." (In the 1950s, a Cuban cigar company named a particularly large cigar a "Churchill," and it subsequently became the generic name for that size stogie.) That was the iconic image of Churchill as British prime minister during World War II. But he had a long history as a controversial member of Parliament and cabinet minister dating back to the early 1900s.

Churchill was a political conservative and proponent of expanding the British Empire. The British Navy, the largest and strongest of its era, played a crucial role in maintaining that power. From 1911 to 1915, Churchill became first lord of the admiralty, the cabinet member who oversaw naval affairs. He favored development of airplanes for use in war and wanted to convert the navy from coal to oil. Oil was more efficient, lighter weight, and provided a speed advantage over the coal-fired German fleet.

The British faced one very ticklish problem, however. At the time, Britain had no known domestic oil supplies. The United States was the world's largest producer of petroleum back then. But the United Kingdom didn't want to be dependent on any other major power, even an ally. It wasn't sufficient to buy oil on the open market at a fair price. Britain had to guarantee strategic control of oil supplies on favorable terms—and deny oil to its enemies.

"This control must be absolute and there must be no foreign interests involved in it of any sort," said one British admiral at the time.[8] Imperialist powers, including the United States, have been carrying out a modernized version of that policy ever since. A privately owned British company had already struck oil in Iran in 1908 after establishing a sweetheart deal with the corrupt Shah (emperor). By 1911, Churchill arranged for the British government to secretly buy a majority stake in the company, which would eventually become known as British Petroleum (BP). The British Navy was guaranteed an oil supply for twenty years on very favorable financial terms.

But they needed more. Before World War I, the British had started a joint company with Germans and Turks to pump oil in what is now northern Iraq. Four days after the end of the war, on November 3, 1918, British troops occupied Mosul in northern Iraq. The British produced their first gusher in October 1927 in nearby Kirkuk, after seizing German and Turkish investments and dividing the oil concession among British, French, and American oil companies.

But that was nearly ten years away. Back in 1914, oil was a long-term dream; the Suez Canal was an immediate reality. It was vital for

British worldwide trade, particularly for accessing India, which had become the number one importer of British goods. So the British wanted to protect the canal by controlling areas near Egypt: Sinai, Gaza, Palestine, and Jordan.

The French had their own colonial ambitions, often in fierce competition with the British. They had lost wars to Britain during the 1700s and early 1800s and continued to compete for spheres of influence into the early twentieth century. Although they were allies during World War I, the French never really trusted the British—and vice versa. France entered the competition for oil a few years after the British. France was late in converting its military and industries to oil and was still searching for oil-producing colonies when World War I began.

France, like Britain and the United States, wanted its own oil company, unsullied by foreign ownership. At the behest of the French government, in 1924 French capitalists formed the Compagnie Française des Pétroles (French Petroleum Company), CFP, the antecedent to today's Total. The privately owned company initially joined the British in developing the oil fields in Iraq. It later developed oil fields in France and Algeria. But CFP never achieved the international dominance of British or US oil companies.

France also wanted control of Syria as a gateway to Europe. "The region controls Mideast access to Europe," government advisor Mudar Barakat told me in Damascus. "Now as then, it's all about location."[9] France had direct economic interests as well, including connections with the valuable silk trade in Syria and access to the Mediterranean port of Beirut. France justified its claims with a selective reading of history. In 1536 the Ottoman Sultan made France the "protector" of Christians living in the Holy Land. The French consolidated ties with Maronite Christians in Lebanon. The Maronites are a Christian sect who have lived in Syria and Lebanon since before the Arab conquest and have their own patriarch living near Beirut.

French became the most widely spoken language in the Ottoman Empire after Turkish and Arabic. The French built Syria's railway system, as well as the gas and electricity companies in Beirut. The French even argued they had a right to the colony because they built crusader castles there hundreds of years earlier. From the outset of World War I, the British and French competed for control of the postwar Middle East. But during the war years, they kept secret their plans to divvy up the spoils.

In *Lawrence of Arabia*, Peter O'Toole found out very late in the film about the secret British-French Middle East deal. In a classic scene, Claude Rains, portraying a British official, explained that a "British civil servant" named Sykes and a "French civil servant" named Picot sat down and drew a line on a map to determine the borders of the new colonies. In real life they were a lot more than civil servants, and the division of territory they influenced was to cause violent conflict in the region down to the present day.

Sir Mark Sykes had a great mustache. It was thick and bushy, with hair drooping ever so slightly over the upper lip, the epitome of the British military officer of that era. Sykes not only looked the part, he walked the walk. He had attended Cambridge, joined the British Army in 1897, and briefly fought in the Boer War in South Africa. Sykes was posted as honorary consul to Constantinople from 1905 to 1907. Sykes wrote two books on the Middle East, including *The Caliphs' Last Heritage: A Short History of the Turkish Empire*. He was heir to a baronial estate in East Yorkshire and won election to Parliament from that area in 1911.

When war broke out, Sykes helped form the Arab Bureau under Lord Horatio Kitchener, then secretary of state for war. Kitchener had an even more famous mustache, with its thick middle tapering to points on each end. His mustache and grim visage graced the famous World War I British recruitment posters. With his finger pointed outward, the poster beseeched, "Britons: Your Country Needs You."

Sykes quickly impressed colleagues with his supposed comprehensive knowledge of the region. He couldn't speak Turkish or Arabic, although he wanted his superiors to think he did. Nevertheless, he became known in government circles as an expert on the Ottoman

Empire. Working under Kitchener, Sykes did make some oblique historical contributions. He designed the black, green, red, and white "Arab Revolt Flag." The flag had three horizontal stripes with a triangle on the right with the point facing inward. Variations of that flag were later adopted by governments in Iraq, Syria, and Jordan.

In December 1915, Sykes met secretly with Prime Minister Herbert Asquith and his war cabinet to propose a deal with the French for dividing up the Ottoman Empire after the war. Sykes stated the British position succinctly. Referring to the Palestinian city of Acre along the Mediterranean and the northern Iraqi city of Kirkuk, Sykes said, "I should like to draw a line from the *E* in *Acre* to the last *K* in *Kirkuk*."[10] That would give Britain control of oil-rich Iraq, along with Palestine and Jordan. The French would get Lebanon and Syria and a strip of southern Turkey called Hatay Province. Neither power cared about how their division would impact the local populations. The cabinet authorized Sykes to hold secret talks with the French government, and they ended up negotiating for ten months before reaching agreement. Sykes was to meet his match in a dapper Frenchman, another diplomat far more important than a mere civil servant.

An early sketch of François Georges-Picot shows a thin young diplomat with a stylish upturned collar and silk cravat. Picot was as serious about his diplomacy as his couture. He was a member of the Comite de L'Asie Française, a group that pushed for expansion of French rule in Syria and the Middle East. Picot served as a French diplomat in Beirut prior to the outbreak of the war. He had arranged to supply Lebanese Christians with fifteen thousand modern rifles to spark an uprising against the Ottomans. The uprising failed, at least in part, because Picot might have left files identifying Lebanese rebel leaders' names when he fled for France at the beginning of the war. The Ottomans rounded them up, put them in jail, and executed many.

In August 1915, Picot took a secret boat ride across the English Channel for what would be a series of fateful meetings with Sykes. They argued bitterly over a number of issues. Who would control oil-rich northern Iraq? Would Jerusalem be ruled directly by Britain or brought under international administration? The final agreement, signed on May 16, 1916, reflected a compromise among the imperialist powers. Sykes's line on the map prevailed, with some exceptions. France got Lebanon, Syria, southern Turkey, and parts of northern Iraq. Britain got the rest of Iraq, Jordan, and full control of Palestine, including Jerusalem.

The Sykes-Picot Agreement rhetorically supported the creation of independent Arab states. But clause 2 makes clear its real intention: "France and . . . Great Britain shall be allowed to establish such direct or indirect administration or control as they desire and as they may think fit to arrange with the Arab State or Confederation of Arab States."[11]

Sykes-Picot remained secret for a time because of its imperialist audacity, even by the standards of the time. Both sides also sought to expand their region of control while supposedly sticking to the agreement. Britain and France wanted Arabs to revolt against the Ottomans but knew they would never fight just to become colonies of another power.

Lawrence of Arabia accurately reflected that Arab sentiment in scenes where Omar Sharif and Anthony Quinn, playing Arab leaders, first learned of betrayal by the British. In the film, Lawrence hears about Sykes-Picot very late in the war. In reality, he knew about the skullduggery very early and made false promises to his Arab allies nonetheless.

After the war, Lawrence admitted, "[N]ot being a perfect fool, I could see that if we won the war, the promises to the Arabs were dead paper. Had I been an honourable Adviser, I would have sent my men home and not let them risk their lives for such stuff. Yet the Arab inspiration was our main tool in winning the Eastern war. So I assured them that England kept her word in letter and spirit . . . but, of course . . . I was continually bitter and ashamed."[12]

Picot also understood that the British were making promises they would never keep. He justified colonialism because of the so-called backwardness of the Arabs. "To promise the Arabs a large state is to throw dust in their eyes," wrote Picot. "Such a state will never materialize. You cannot transform a myriad of tribes into a viable whole."[13] Picot admitted that the French were also lying. "What the French want is only to deceive the Arabs. They hope to accomplish this by offering them a lot while admitting that the building they are constructing will probably not last beyond the war."[14]

After the 1917 Russian Revolution, the Bolsheviks published various secret European treaties, including Sykes-Picot. The release caused international outrage, but no change in colonial policy. In postwar peace treaties, the Ottomans were forced to give up all their Arab land. The British and French proceeded to set up "mandates," as the colonies were called, and deny self-determination to the Arabs.

Sykes did play another significant role. He facilitated meetings between Zionist leader Chaim Weizmann and important British leaders. The growing, mutual support of British colonialism and the Zionist movement were to have earthshaking consequences for Syria and the entire Middle East.

Chaim Weizmann was born in 1876 in a small village in Belarus, Russia. He escaped small village life and received a PhD in Switzerland. He moved to Manchester, England, to become a chemistry professor in 1906. Weizmann had already committed to Zionism, a secular nationalist movement calling for Jews to leave their countries of birth and immigrate to a Jewish homeland. In those years, the Zionist movement had little popular support. Most Jews either stayed in their homelands or immigrated to countries with greater political and economic opportunities. Many joined unions and leftist movements.

That lack of support was reflected in Weizmann's correspondence lamenting the reception he received from working-class Jews in Manchester. "You are dealing with the dregs of Russian Jewry, a dull ignorant crowd that knows nothing of issues such as Zionism," he wrote to a friend. "You cannot imagine what it means for an intellectual to live in the English provinces and work with the local Jews. It's hellish torture!"[15]

While alienated from working-class Jews, Weizmann did become friends with local businessmen, including Simon Marks and Israel

Sieff, who later built Marks and Spencer into a national retail chain. And from the beginning, Zionist leaders worked with colonial powers to sponsor a Jewish state. Britain was the most responsive. But the path toward supporting the Zionist endeavor was a winding one.

In 1903, the British foreign office suggested a Zionist settlement in the British colony of East Africa, in what became known as the Uganda Plan. The World Zionist Organization (WZO), the main Zionist group, sent a small delegation to what is modern-day Kenya to check out the proposed homeland. Some Zionists argued that Kenya "overlooked" the promised land of Palestine and thus should be accepted as a Jewish homeland.

The British clearly wanted to deposit yet another oppressed group in the middle of one of their colonies as part of a divide-and-rule strategy. The British had successfully used that ploy by sending East Indians to the Caribbean and whites and Indians to South Africa. Ultimately, the WZO rejected the Uganda Plan, but a group supporting the effort split off to form a new Zionist organization. The Zionists had to wait another twelve years before seeing their efforts bear fruit.

Meanwhile, small numbers of European Jews settled in Ottoman-controlled Palestine. In 1907, Weizmann visited there and helped start the Palestine Land Development Company, which bought land for Jewish settlement.

Many in the British ruling elite were anti-Jewish bigots on both institutional and personal levels. They allowed only a limited number of Jews to attend elite universities and prohibited them from joining their private clubs. A British aristocrat certainly wouldn't want his daughter marrying a Jew. So why would they even consider supporting Zionism? The answer is simple: geopolitics. The issue came to a head with the outbreak of World War I.

Creating a dependent Jewish settler minority in Palestine had several advantages. It would help in the defense of the British-controlled Suez Canal. The British also hoped that supporting Zionism would gain them kudos from American Jews, who would then help pressure President Woodrow Wilson into joining the war. The British wanted to establish a pro-British settler colony as a buffer against the French. Herbert Samuel, a Zionist and British high commissioner for Palestine, wrote, "We cannot proceed on the supposition that our present happy relations with France will continue always."[16]

For many years, Weizmann had befriended Arthur Balfour, an ambitious member of Parliament from the Manchester area. Balfour was part of a coterie of Christian leaders who came to accept Zionists as legitimate, if unequal, allies of the British Empire. Balfour was a deeply religious Christian. He and future prime minister David Lloyd George were some of the first Christian Zionists, a right-wing trend that exists to the present day.

Christian Zionists believe that Jews returning to the biblical land of Israel will precede the second coming of Christ. They support populating Palestine with Jewish settlers to hasten that process. However, if the Jews and every other religious group don't convert to Christianity, they will perish in the fires of hell. Zionist leaders embraced these Christian allies, despite the blatantly anti-Jewish theology that requires Jews to give up their faith.

One morning in 1915, Chancellor of the Exchequer David Lloyd George had breakfast with Chaim Weizmann to discuss British support for the Zionist cause. While Lloyd George was partially motivated by Christian Zionism, geopolitics played the decisive role. He later presciently wrote that the Jews "might be able to render us more assistance than the Arabs."[17] Weizmann later met with Arthur Balfour, who in 1917 asked the World Zionist Organization to draft a declaration of British support for Jewish settlement in Palestine.

I first learned about the famous Balfour Declaration while studying for my Bar Mitzvah at age thirteen. I learned it was a major breakthrough for Jews everywhere, the first step on a long road of establishing a Jewish state. I was surprised years later to see that the Balfour Declaration consists of three paragraphs, with only the one paragraph containing any substance. Issued on November 2, 1917, the message declared:

His Majesty's Government views with favour the establishment in
Palestine of a national home for the Jewish people, and will use their
best endeavours to facilitate the achievement of the object, it being
clearly understood that nothing shall be done which may prejudice
the civil and religious rights of existing non-Jewish communities in
Palestine, or the rights and political status enjoyed by Jews in any
other country.[18]

The Balfour Declaration was deeply rooted in the arrogance and
racism of the imperial powers toward Syria, Palestine, and the entire
region. Britain didn't even pretend to consult the opinion of local
Arabs. For someone who was supposedly a devout Christian, Balfour
disregarded the opinions of the local Palestinian population, at least 10
percent of whom were Christians. It was not a religious decision but a
calculation of power.

Lord Balfour admitted as much, writing in 1919, "The four great
powers are committed to Zionism and Zionism, be it right or wrong,
good or bad, is rooted in age-long tradition, in present needs, in future
hopes, of far profounder import than the desires and prejudices of the
700,000 Arabs who now inhabit that ancient land."[19]

The Balfour Declaration and subsequent British policy are the
cause of strife to the present day. British foreign secretary and Labour
Party leader Jack Straw said in 2002, "A lot of the problems we are
having to deal with now, I have to deal with now, are a consequence
of our colonial past. . . . The Balfour Declaration and the contradictory assurances which were being given to Palestinians in private at
the same time as they were being given to the Israelis—again, an interesting history for us but not an entirely honourable one."[20]

During World War I, both major colonial powers claimed historic ties to
Arab land. The French argued they had rights in Syria because of their
crusader castles built centuries before, and now the British could claim
they were supporting the Jewish people who lived in Palestine two thousand years ago. Neither argument carried much weight with the people
of Syria and Palestine. Uprisings would soon flare throughout the region.

The larger-than-life, World War I–era political characters are etched in the history books. David Lloyd George became prime minister and later the chief British delegate at the Paris Peace Conference. By 1922, however, he was involved in a scandal for selling knighthoods. He became politically marginalized and died in 1945. When Arthur Balfour died in 1930, major newspaper obituaries made no mention of the Balfour Declaration. Chaim Weizmann served as the first president of Israel from 1949 until his death in 1952. Sir Mark Sykes died of influenza in 1919 while a delegate to the Paris Peace Conference.

I was initially drawn to *Lawrence of Arabia* because of its magnificent desert cinematography, the exciting battle scenes, and Lawrence's support for the Arab cause. Only later did I understand that a crucial scene distorted history. Toward the end of the film, the Arab armies have occupied Damascus and set up a governing council in city hall. The scene is based on a description in the *Seven Pillars of Wisdom*. But unlike Lawrence's version, the filmmakers have Arab leaders bicker and show no understanding of electricity generation, water works, and other modern technology. They blame each other for the city's problems and threaten one another with violence.

The British stand aside and wait for the Arab disunity to consume them. Eventually the Bedouins depart, leaving the British to take power. Peter O'Toole is distraught as he learns that the Arabs are not ready for self-government. In reality, the British Army under General Allenby tried to assert control but was rebuffed by the General Syrian Congress. The congress elected King Faisal ruler of the new Arab kingdom liberated from the Turks. The congress governed Damascus for nearly two years, until the British turned over Syria to the French, thus carrying out the Sykes-Picot accord.

There certainly was quarreling, infighting, and even a short-lived rebellion. But the Arabs were able to restore electric power, provide clean water, and establish police and other vital services using the former Ottoman Empire employees and technicians. Lawrence, in the last chapter of *Seven Pillars*, defended the congress. "Our aim was an

Arab Government with foundations large and native enough to employ the enthusiasm and self sacrifice of the rebellion."[21] Lawrence added that the Arab government "endured for two years, without foreign advice, in an occupied country wasted by war, and against the will of important elements among the Allies."

Despite Lawrence's opposition to direct British colonial rule, his legacy remains controversial among Arabs, according to Elie El-Hindy, chair of the Political Science Department at Notre Dame University outside Beirut. "People in the region look at this as the time of high manipulation by Western countries," Professor El-Hindy told me. "They look at Lawrence and other British, French, and American agents as manipulators who tried to grab whatever was left from the Ottoman Empire and [bring it] into their own area of control."[22]

El-Hindy did admit one glaring irony. The main reason people of the Middle East know about Lawrence is because of the 1962 movie. They just interpret it differently than Western audiences. The film helps perpetuate the myth of Arabs as unable to govern themselves because they suffer from centuries of religious and ethnic divisions. The same myth continues to the present day.

Lawrence of Arabia ends with an unhappy Peter O'Toole driving out of Damascus to return to London. In real life, Lawrence did return to London—not despondent, but to continue his fight for neocolonialism. Within a short time, T. E. Lawrence would become a household name, thanks to a little-known American war correspondent.

CHAPTER 3

TREATIES, REBELLIONS, AND INDEPENDENCE: 1919–1946

Reporter Lowell Thomas interviewed T. E. Lawrence for only about a week, but in the years that followed, he managed to create the myth of Lawrence of Arabia, promote his own career as a daring foreign correspondent, and spread myths about Arabs. Lawrence wasn't riding a camel in the desert when they met. They were in Jerusalem and Aqaba after the British had occupied those cities and the fighting had stopped. But Thomas was intrigued by the short British officer wearing a *keffiyeh* head scarf and an embroidered traditional robe, and sporting a curved dagger in his belt. Thomas was searching for an American war hero, but British citizen Lawrence would do. Thomas was to transform this little-known liaison officer into a world-famous figure.

Thomas created the romanticized version of Lawrence that was later maintained in the 1962 film. A fictional version of Thomas, played by Arthur Kennedy, even showed up in the movie. Thomas almost single-handedly created the myth of Lawrence of Arabia while perpetuating many of the modern-day prejudices about Muslims and Arabs. Those prejudices would impact Syria and the entire region for years to come. Thomas was a twenty-two-year-old reporter and adventurer when World War I broke out. He had already produced one of the first filmed travelogues and was a fervent supporter of the Great War at a time when many Americans opposed it. His love of film and war were to come together in an unusual way.

In 1917, President Woodrow Wilson's administration put together a fact-finding team supposedly to report on developments in the war. In reality, the trip was intended to promote the war effort to the American public. Thomas was happy to join the group.

Already a talented orator and an endless self-promoter, Thomas understood the impact of movies as propaganda. But he faced the problem of freelancers everywhere: he had no funding. So Thomas contacted old businessman friends in the meatpacking industry in Chicago, where he had been a reporter. Executives at Armour, Swift, and other beef processors were anxious to support the war effort, in no small part because of the profit they could make selling meat to the military.[1]

So eighteen meatpacking executives raised $100,000 to finance Thomas's trip, a huge budget in those days. Thomas, his wife, Fran, and skilled cameraman Harry Chase went first to the European front and then to the Middle East. When Thomas met Lawrence in Jerusalem, Thomas found what he considered the perfect combination of war hero and mysterious denizen of the Arab world.

Thomas interviewed Lawrence for a total of a few days (according to Lawrence) or a few weeks (according to Thomas). In 1919, Thomas returned home to put together his material.

He eventually developed the world's first multimedia lecture show. Thomas used three projectors, slides, stage props, dancers, and live music. His florid rhetoric conjured up scenes of endless desert sands, veiled women, and Bedouins carrying curved swords.

Thomas's stage show was a huge hit. He played to overflow crowds in Madison Square Garden in New York and the Royal Opera House in London, among other venues. Here's how Thomas modestly described his extravaganza:

> When I opened in London I used the sixty-piece Welsh Guards Band in their scarlet uniforms. On stage, the Moonlight On the Nile scene, as the curtain opened on the Nile set, the moon faintly illuminating distant pyramids, our dancer glided onstage for a two-minute Dance of the Seven Veils accompanied by an Irish tenor in the wings, singing the Mohammedan Call To Prayer, which Fran had put to music. At

the end of this I emerged in a spotlight and without even saying Good Evening Ladies and Gentlemen, I started my show with the words: "Come with me to the lands of mystery, history and romance." The first prologue ever used in connection with films. This again was one of my wild ideas. Then the pictures began to roll.[2]

Thomas never explained what the slinky "Dance of the Seven Vells" had to do with the Arab revolt.

That dancer and similar irrelevant scenes cleverly played to Western stereotypes of Arabs and Muslims. They were to have a long-term impact on Americans' view of Syria and the entire region. Thomas promoted Lawrence as the white savior of the Middle East. Lawrence biographer Richard Aldington noted that Thomas's British and American audiences understood little about the Middle East. Thomas "doubtless calculated that what little they thought they knew came from hazy memories of the Arabian Nights and the Bible [and] a reading of sensational novels of 'The Sheik.'"[3]

Thomas quickly became the latest in a long line of Orientalists, intellectual dilettantes who seemingly explain the mysteries of the Middle East while patronizing Arabs and promoting the supe riority of Western culture. For example, Thomas wrote in his 1924 book *With Lawrence in Arabia* that Muslim leaders had sought to unify Arabs. "None was successful, but where they failed, Thomas Edward Lawrence, the unknown unbeliever, succeeded. It remained for this youthful British archaeologist to go into forbidden Arabia and lead the Arabs through the spectacular and triumphant campaign."[4] In reality, as explained in the previous chapter, Arab nationalists unified themselves and helped defeat the Ottoman Empire.

Thomas's characterization of Islam as a violent, intolerant religion echoes contemporary, right-wing views. "Mecca and Medina, its sister metropolis, are the two most mysterious cities in the world," Thomas wrote. "Any man in the vicinity of either who declared that Christ was the son of God would be torn to pieces."[5]

And Thomas was not above lying to embellish the Lawrence myth.

In a 1919 magazine article, he claimed to have been with Lawrence when he dynamited a Turkish railway line behind enemy lines. Thomas wrote "about the expedition in vivid detail—but it never took place," according to historian Jeremy Wilson. "Thomas's diaries, together with other contemporary documents, show that he and Lawrence were together for only a day or two in Aqaba, during one of the quietest periods in the Arab campaign."[6]

After the war, Thomas performed his multimedia show in the United States, Europe, and Asia, eventually playing to an estimated four million people. Lawrence went to see the performances several times in London, professing not to like them. But Lawrence posed for additional Thomas photos dressed in Arab garb. Clearly, Lawrence's career benefited from the publicity. Thomas later said of Lawrence, "He had a genius for backing into the limelight."[7]

Thomas earned millions from his performances and launched his career. He went on to become a famous travel writer and radio newscaster. He was an early pioneer in newsreels and TV. And he continued his pattern of carrying out the needs of big business. During World War I he took funding from the Armour company for his Mideast travels. Later in life he syndicated radio broadcasts to NBC and CBS but collected his salary from the show's sponsor, oil giant Sunoco. In 1947, Thomas cofounded what would become Capital Cities Broadcasting. Although he had left Capital Cities years before, that company later bought ABC in 1980 and grew to be one of the biggest media conglomerates in the world. Thomas died one year later in 1981.

At the end of *Lawrence of Arabia*, Peter O'Toole leaves Damascus despondent and disillusioned with the failures of the Arab revolt. In real life, he did depart Damascus for London, but far from being alienated, he immediately plunged into imperialist politics. Lawrence met with Prime Minister David Lloyd George and members of the cabinet. He promised that his wartime ally Faisal bin Hussein, and other Hashemite allies, would support the British if French power was reduced or eliminated altogether from the Middle East. Lawrence attended the

Paris Peace Conference, working as an undersecretary for Winston Churchill, who was then the secretary of war.

The Paris Peace Conference opened January 18, 1919, and closed one year later. It resulted in the Treaty of Versailles, which was most famous for imposing harsh sanctions on Germany to cover the costs of the Allied war effort. But Paris was also abuzz with discussions of how to carve up the old Ottoman Empire—an argument that was not fully resolved for another four years. Britain and France competed fiercely to set up new colonies and spheres of influence. Each had its allies among the Arabs and Zionist leaders.

Since the end of the war, Emir Faisal had headed the Arab Kingdom of Hedjaz, encompassing much of the former Ottoman Arab territories. Lawrence translated as Faisal gave a famous speech at the peace conference, calling for Arab independence. Faisal received strong verbal backing from Britain and the United States, who supported his claims to Syria and Lebanon. But Faisal's views angered the French, who coveted that region for themselves.

Since the British issued the Balfour Declaration supporting a Jewish presence in Palestine, Zionist leaders had become important new players in the Middle East. At the behest of the British government, Lawrence brought Faisal from Paris to London just before the opening of the peace conference. The British brokered a secret meeting with Zionist leader Chaim Weizmann.

Faisal was receiving £150,000 a month from the British.[8] The Zionists were sending Jewish settlers to Palestine. The British hoped to use both sides to keep populist and nationalist Arabs in check.

On January 3, 1919, Faisal and Weizmann agreed on a border that would create Jewish and Arab countries. They agreed to establish a Zionist-controlled state in Palestine, leaving the rest to the Hashemite monarchs. The Zionists were to get land and peace. The monarchs got a vastly larger territory and promises of Zionist help with economic development.[9]

The Zionist movement sometimes points to this agreement as an indication of early Arab acceptance of a Jewish state. But Faisal attached a handwritten addendum that made clear that the deal would go through only if the British followed up on their wartime promises of an independent Arab state. The addendum read: "If the Arabs are established as I have asked in my manifesto of 4 January, addressed to the British Secretary of State for Foreign Affairs, I will carry out what is written in this agreement. If changes are made, I cannot be answerable for failing to carry out this agreement."

In addition, the General Syrian Congress, which briefly ruled postwar Syria and Lebanon, issued a declaration renouncing the agreement and censuring Zionism. British officials had never intended to establish a truly independent Arab state nor to recognize a Zionist state. The Weizmann-Faisal agreement was a dead letter within days of its signing.

But the methodology lived on in Israeli policy. When Israel was established in 1948, the Zionists allowed King Abdullah of Jordan to seize the West Bank in hopes that the Hashemite monarch would cooperate with Israel. Abdullah was King Faisal's older brother, and his family rules Jordan to this day. For many years Israel made deals with corrupt Arab monarchs rather than respond to Palestinian demands for sovereignty.

While the colonial powers were wheeling and dealing, there was one effort to determine popular opinion in the region. The British, French, and Americans initially agreed to set up a commission that would survey public opinion in the Arab region of the former Ottoman Empire. Did the people favor independence, colonial control, or something in between? The other powers dropped out of the project, but the United States forged ahead. President Woodrow Wilson formed the Inter-Allied Commission on Mandates in Turkey, better known as the King-Crane Commission. It produced some surprising results.

Henry Churchill King, born in 1858, was a theologian and an academic when chosen to cochair the commission. Photos show a handsome man wearing a clerical collar, a stylish suit, and the round glasses favored by intellectuals of the time. King had studied at Oberlin College in Ohio and went on to graduate school at Harvard. He went back to teach mathematics and philosophy at Oberlin before becoming its president.

King was sensitive to the views of Protestant missionaries who were lobbying hard for greater US involvement in the Middle East. Missionaries had established American schools, churches, and hospitals with the aim of finding new converts to Christianity. The missionaries wanted to expand their presence but needed more active US government participation in the region.

Charles R. Crane, also born in 1858, was a wealthy industrialist and heir to the Crane plumbing fortune (think Crane toilets). Crane had developed a great interest in international affairs. He had been appointed US envoy to China in 1909 and participated in a US delegation to the new, revolutionary Soviet Union in 1917. Crane was also an anti-Jewish bigot who later wrote favorably about Hitler's policy toward the Jews.[10] In the 1930s Crane helped finance the first oil exploration in Yemen and Saudi Arabia.

Back in 1919, when the King-Crane Commission was appointed, Crane represented the kind of activist businessman who advocated that international policy decisions should be driven by the corporate profit motive. King, Crane, and a group of advisors set out for a long journey through the Middle East in the summer of 1919. They traveled by boat to Jaffa (now incorporated into Tel Aviv) and then by car over the rutted roads of the Arab lands.

Commission members conducted interviews in thirty-six towns and cities in what is today Syria, Lebanon, Jordan, Israel, and Palestine. People in each region submitted a total of 1,863 petitions listing their demands, and the commission staff conducted in-person, follow-up interviews. It wasn't a scientific survey because the commission couldn't get proportionate responses from the region's various groups. The commission acknowledged, for example, that opinions of Sunni Muslims were underrepresented.[11] In addition, many of the petitions were suspiciously similar, indicating an organized effort to affect the data.

Given the lack of other broad-based exploration of local views, however, the commission produced an interesting snapshot of public opinion. The survey reflected the depth of opposition to any colonial rule in the region.

Seventy-three percent of the people favored "absolute independence" for Syria and Iraq. When forced to choose among colonial powers that might "assist" them until independence, 60 percent chose the United States and 55 percent chose Britain. In a fascinating footnote, the commission admitted, "The high figures given for American and British assistance . . . are because the people ask first for complete independence."[12]

Seventy-two percent opposed the creation of a Zionist state in Palestine. The report noted that Zionist leaders, far from planning to live in peace with the Arabs, planned to dispossess the Arabs through land purchases and Jewish immigration: "If the American government decided to support the establishment of a Jewish state in Palestine, they are committing the American people to the use of force in that area, since only by force can a Jewish state in Palestine be established or maintained."

Despite the overwhelming Arab desire for independence, the commission accepted the colonial myth that the Arabs were not ready for self-governance and needed assistance from an outside power. It then humbly suggested that the United States provide that assistance not only to the Arab Middle East but to the defeated nation of Turkey as well. The commission report stated that the United States has a "special fitness . . . for the particular task in hand—a fitness growing naturally out of her experience as a great growing democracy, largely freed hitherto from European entanglements."[13]

Not surprisingly, neither the European colonial powers nor the Arabs accepted this American "special fitness." The report was highly controversial, and it wasn't made public until 1922. The commission's report, while never considered an important document, reflected part of the upheaval in US ruling circles at the time over how best to expand the US empire.

The United States had only seriously entered the empire game in 1898 with its colonization of Puerto Rico, Cuba, and the Philippines. Some leaders wanted to expand US domination to the Middle East. But in 1919 the United States lacked the military, economic, and political heft to establish additional direct colonies. American interests in the region included access to oil for US corporations, freedom for Protestant missionaries to operate in the region, and maintenance of US institutions such as hospitals and schools.

In words, President Wilson supported "self-determination" for the Middle East. In reality, the United States sought to extend its domination by establishing nominally independent client states under US control, a model it used in Latin America. For example, Wilson favored an independent Syria under the rule of King Faisal, who was pro-Britain and pro–United States.

But other powerful Americans argued for a different imperialist policy. Henry Cabot Lodge, a conservative Republican and chair of the Senate Foreign Relations Committee, became one of Wilson's most famous opponents. Lodge had supported the Spanish-American War and World War I. But he strongly opposed the Treaty of Versailles and the League of Nations, arguing that they would allow European powers too much influence and limit the United States' ability to pursue its own interests.

Cabot formed an alliance with isolationist senators who opposed any US intervention in the Middle East or elsewhere. As a result, the United States focused less on Europe and the Middle East and more on the Western Hemisphere. In November 1919, the US Senate voted against joining the League of Nations. The Senate never ratified the Treaty of Versailles. By then the British and French had permanently installed their troops in the Middle East. That combination of domestic and international events relegated the United States to a secondary role in the region until after World War II.

At the end of World War I, while imperial powers feuded among themselves, Arabs were busy exercising their independence. The General Syrian Congress elected Emir Faisal king of the Arab nation with its headquarters in Damascus. The Arabs had governed their newly liberated land—but by 1919 the colonial powers were ready to divvy up the colonial spoils. The results were bloody indeed.

On November 21, 1919, French general Henri Gouraud landed in Beirut as head of the French Army of the Levant. He had already become famous in 1894 for putting down an anticolonial uprising in French Sudan. He lost an arm fighting in World War I. He wore a crisp uniform and Van Dyke beard and mustache. General Gouraud quickly set about conquering inland Syria, extending French colonial rule. It wasn't easy. Faisal's government controlled Syria and part of Lebanon while Britain controlled Iraq, Jordan, and Palestine. In early 1920, the British decided to pull back their troops, conceding the eventual control of Damascus and Lebanon to France.

Faisal hoped to cut a deal with French prime minister Georges Clemenceau to keep himself in power, but Syrian nationalists opposed him. Faisal's government prohibited the French military from using rail lines in Aleppo and other regions under his control. Anti-French nationalists blew up other rail lines. The anticolonial war was on.

The Arab forces were weak politically, economically, and militarily. They lacked a stable source of income and fought without heavy weapons. On July 25, 1920, French troops entered Damascus. Faisal fled to Palestine, then controlled by the British. General Gouraud installed himself as the military and political leader of the French mandate. But first, with colonial swagger, he entered the old city of Damascus to visit the tomb of the Arab leader who had driven out the Crusaders.

"Saladin, we're back," he said.[14]

Faisal's forces were defeated because of the overwhelming French military superiority but also because Arab nationalism was still in its infancy. Many Arabs identified with their tribe, ethnic group, or region more than with their newly emerging nation states. Various ideologies competed for support on the Arab street. Pan-Arabists called for a single Arab nation made up of people from throughout the region. A few Islamists called for a unified Muslim emirate, and still other nationalists wanted to build independent countries.

Arabs included people from the Arabian peninsula, Palestine,

Mount Lebanon, Syria, Iraq, and North Africa, and they often fought among themselves. "They were very disunited," political scientist Elie El-Hindy told me in an interview. "The people of the Near East, they had so many diverging opinions about who they were and what was their nationalism."[15]

France and Britain took advantage of the disunity. Both powers "did not care what people thought," said El-Hindy "They did not care about the best interest of these people. They simply cared about their division. They applied it by force. They [the French] had to bomb Damascus to make Faisal move out."

By 1920, the colonial powers had seemingly resolved their differences over how to divvy up the Middle East. On August 10, they signed the Treaty of Sevres, which allocated Lebanon and Syria to France and the rest of the Arab areas to Britain. France was also given control over Hatay Province in what is today southwestern Turkey, along the Syrian border.

But Turkish military officers under Mustafa Kemal Ataturk rejected the Treaty of Sevres on the grounds that it gave too much land to the colonial powers. Ataturk led a military campaign that took back territory and established the Republic of Turkey.

The Treaty of Lausanne, which took effect August 6, 1924, replaced the previous treaty and established most of the borders of modern Turkey. Turkey officially gave up territorial claims to the Arab Middle East, which, in any case, had already been seized by Britain and France. Hatay Province remained part of the French mandate of Syria and Lebanon. In 1938, residents of Hatay separated from Syria and then joined Turkey in 1939. Hatay has long-standing cultural, linguistic, and economic ties to Syria. So the split-off was controversial.

"Hatay was stolen by the Turks," Mudar Barakat told me in a Damascus interview.[16] As an economist and a government advisor, he reflects the common view among Syrians on this issue. "The Turks disenfranchised the Christians and Alawites and replaced them with people from Turkey."

Succeeding Syrian governments have claimed Hatay as part of Syria.

Official Syrian maps don't recognize the de facto border. The border dispute remains an irritant between modern-day Turkey and Syria.

During all these conferences and treaty signings, the colonial powers never allowed local people to decide their own fate. The results became strikingly clear when the French tried to govern Syria and Lebanon.

Soon after marching their troops into Damascus, the French faced the problem of how to keep themselves in power. General Gouraud's secretary, Robert de Caix, wrote that France had two choices. It could "build a Syrian nation [state] which does not yet exist." Or it could "cultivate and maintain all the phenomena . . . that these divisions give. I must say that only the second option interests me."[17] In short, the French chose to divide and rule.

French officials carved up the old Ottoman territory with the aim of exacerbating ethnic and religious tensions. France demarcated separate administrative regions named State of Greater Lebanon, Aleppo, Damascus, State of the Alawites, and State of the Druze. Greater Lebanon included many Maronite Christians, whom the French favored. The French discriminated against the Muslims, Alawites, and Druze, thus maintaining a cheap labor force while sowing religious division.

Syrians were never happy with the new colonial occupiers. France boasted of bringing civilization to Syria in the form of new railroad lines and roads. But peasant farmers were forced to build the roads for no pay.[18] The French administrators were notoriously corrupt, expecting bribes to carry out even minor government tasks.

A new group of nationalists emerged in Syria during and after World War I. They didn't come from the traditional wealthy clans like King Faisal and his brothers. They arose from among the petit bourgeoisie, the merchants, the well-to-do farmers, and the Arabs who served in the Turkish Army. The man who would become known as Sultan Pasha al-Atrash was one such army veteran.

Sultan al-Atrash cut a dashing figure sitting astride a white stallion. He wore a traditional robe and a tightly wound keffiyeh, and he sported a large, tapered mustache favored by Arab sheiks and Ottoman bureaucrats. In a photo, Atrash stood in front of his rebel army with banners and flags raised high. In 1925 he became one of the top leaders of a massive Syrian revolt against French rule.

Atrash was born in 1891, the son of a local sheik, or village headman, and grew up in a rural Druze community. He was conscripted into the Ottoman army at the age of twenty, where he learned to read and write. The army, and its military academies in particular, offered opportunities for village Arabs to gain a formal education. Some Arab officers were exposed to the nationalist thinking being spread by fellow students at the academies. One day, Atrash came home to find that Turks had hung his father and four other sheiks for antigovernment activities. Atrash became a committed revolutionist.

Atrash fought alongside T. E. Lawrence and Auda abu Tayi during the World War I Arab revolt. He helped liberate Damascus from the Turks in 1918. In recognition for his military prowess, Emir Faisal made Atrash a *Pasha*, an honorific denoting high military rank. But Atrash clashed with Lawrence and Tayi and was sent home to the Jabal Druze area, what is the Golan today. The Druze are an ethnic group that practice their own form of Islam that dates back to the tenth century. They lived in isolated, mountainous regions of what is now Lebanon and Syria's Golan. They earned a justified reputation as fierce fighters.

The 1925 revolt started in Druze villages but quickly spread to all parts of the country. It ultimately included at least some fighters from all of Syria's religious and ethnic groups, reflecting a nascent Syrian nationalism. The uprising bears a striking political similarity to the early days of the 2011 Arab Spring when young people rebelled against the established regime and defied their elders. In both cases, the country's economic elite sided with the governing authorities. And the government tried to divide the insurgents while brutally suppressing them with the most modern weapons available.

The 1925 anticolonial rebellion began when the Druze in one village held a demonstration that led to an exchange of gunfire with

French authorities. Atrash, leading a group of armed men on horse-back, forced the French *gendarmes* to retreat.

Atrash soon issued a statement demanding an end of colonial rule and "to liberate the homeland from the foreigner."[19] At the time, France had only seven thousand troops in Syria, so rebels met little initial resistance. They seized a series of towns and villages by riding into the central square, calling for the end of French rule and recruiting followers on the spot.

On July 22, Bedouin and Druze rebels attacked a French military camp in Suwayda and wiped it out in a thirty-minute battle. Almost no French troops survived.

The rebels sought support in the big cities as well. They distributed leaflets in Damascus with the headline, "To Arms Syrians!" It began, "At last the day has come when we can reap the harvest of our struggle for liberty and independence . . . Let us seek death so that we win life."[20]

Sultan al-Atrash sought support among all religious and ethnic groups, saying they were all sons of the Arab nation. He sent letters to Christian and Muslim villages, calling for solidarity against the French. The revolt also got support from leftists in France. The Communist Party mailed prorebellion letters to thousands of Syrians and Lebanese using the French postal system.

While the rebels' nationalism was pragmatic, it lacked ideological consistency. As historian Michael Provence wrote in *The Great Syrian Revolt and the Rise of Arab Nationalism*, "They focused on expelling the French from Syria and sometimes mixed in popular Islamic religion, anti-Christian agitation and . . . class warfare against urban landlords and notables."[21]

The French government claimed the revolt was led by Druze feudal chiefs trying to reinforce reactionary customs. The French, by contrast, were bringing progress through modern infrastructure and French education. They denounced the rebels as backward and anti-Christian.

In fact, the rebels had support far beyond the Druze community. But the revolt became complicated because many Christians did side with the French and were therefore attacked by the rebels. Some Syrians also saw the revolt as benefiting only Druze because they would have a disproportionate share of power. The ruling authorities played Sunni, Shia, Alawite, and Christian against one another to maintain power. And the fragmented rebels lacked a common plan for the future beyond eliminating French rule.

Interestingly enough, some of the same cities that strongly backed rebels in 1925 did so again in 2011. Maydan, a southern suburb of Damascus, was a hotbed of rebellion in both uprisings. Hama was a conservative, deeply religious city in 1925 when it backed the rebels and strongly supported the rebels again in 2011.

The events of 1925 were well known to the rebels of 2011. "They were both popular rebellions," said Bisher Allisa, an exiled leader of the Syrian Non Violent Movement. "Assad used the same strategy as the French to manipulate religious groups."[22]

After initial successes in rural areas and smaller cities, the 1925 rebels faced a massive influx of French troops armed with the most modern weapons at the time: heavy machine guns, artillery, and airplanes. The rebels successfully seized Damascus. But the French mercilessly bombed the city by air, one of the first such attacks on civilians in history.

By the spring of 1927 the rebels were defeated and Atrash fled to Jordan. He returned home in 1937 after being pardoned by the French. He received a massive hero's welcome. Atrash again fought for Syrian independence in 1946, remaining a secular pan-Arabist. Atrash stuck to the slogan developed in the 1920s: "Religion is for God, the fatherland is for all." He died of a heart attack in 1982 in Syria at the age of ninety.

Atrash remains a national hero today for Syrians. A bronze statue of Atrash and his followers bedecks the central plaza in Majdal Shams in the Golan, which is currently occupied by Israel. But in a reflection of modern-day politics, he remains controversial.

"For the Druze and Syrian nationalists, they see him as a hero who fought with all he could against the French mandate," said El-Hindy. "The Christians in Lebanon would look at him with a more careful eye. [Because of] his attempt to unify Lebanon and Syria, they would be more hesitant to consider him a hero."[23]

I asked El-Hindy the age-old question that has vexed Arabs for decades: What if the colonial powers had not arbitrarily drawn lines on maps to create the modern Arab states? Could Arabs have done a better job?

He said that after a few years of preparation, people could have voted on a referendum on self-determination, creating their own nation states. He said Syria and Iraq could have become independent countries using a federal system with far more rights for ethnic and religious minorities.

I asked if that process of self-determination would have created more equitable and secure borders. With a shrug and a smile, he said, "I have no idea."

We do know, however, that when the colonialists drew arbitrary maps and intensified ethnic/religious tensions, they sowed problems that continue to this day. While various kinds of nationalism dominated the anticolonial struggle, another kind of opposition was brewing in nearby Egypt.

Just a year after the defeat of the Syrian revolt, Hassan al-Banna founded the Muslim Brotherhood in Cairo in 1928. Banna never visited Syria, but his influence there would be profound. Banna was born in 1906 into a devoutly religious family. His father was a clockmaker and an *imam* (prayer leader), and Banna followed in his footsteps to become a school teacher and an imam. He sported a neat beard and wore the traditional fez. By all accounts Banna was a charismatic leader who eventually developed a loyal following in Egypt and elsewhere in the Arab world. His ideas would make their way into Syria.

The Muslim Brotherhood combined a populist anti-imperialism with Islamic conservatism. While nationalists such as Atrash focused on the political and economic oppression, Banna put more emphasis on colonialism's cultural and religious impact.

Banna wrote, "Western civilization has invaded us by force and with aggression on the level of science and money, of politics and luxury, of pleasures and negligence, and of various aspects of life that are comfortable, exciting, and seductive."[24] Banna called on Arabs to reject the sin and corruption of Western civilization and return to the roots of religion. "Islam is the solution" became the brotherhood's motto.

In those years, the brotherhood sought to create an Islamic state. The new state would be tolerant of other "people of the book," Christians and Jews. But the Muslim brothers were intolerant of non-Sunni Muslims, including Shias, Alawites, and Sufis.

By the 1930s, some Sunnis in Tripoli, Lebanon, and other parts of the French mandate were drawn to Banna's ideas. But Sunni Muslims were much more likely to support nationalist and leftist ideologies at that time, according to El-Hindy. "They didn't think of Islam as their primary identity. They thought about their national identity and regional identity."[25] The movements influenced by Banna wouldn't gain a mass base of support for years.

Meanwhile, the imperialists worked assiduously to secure their oil profits. After the French deposed Faisal in Syria, the British installed him as king of the newly created nation of Iraq. The British rigged a plebiscite to legitimize Faisal's rule, but the British military retained real power. In 1927, Iraqi oil fields near Kirkuk began producing oil, continuing the scramble for black gold throughout the region. The imperial powers formed an international oil company, the Iraq Petroleum Company, to pump and market the oil. The ownership was split among British, French, and US oil companies.

World War II put a temporary stop to the anticolonial uprisings in Syria and Lebanon, but not to anticolonialist sentiment. The British and French sought to mobilize Arabs against the Germans once again. Many Egyptians joined the British Army, while Arabs in Lebanon and Syria opposed the Vichy French.

When the Nazis occupied France in 1939, they established the Vichy government supported by the conservative French military. Vichy continued to administer the French colonial empire. Perhaps the most famous Vichy military officer in popular American culture was the character played by Claude Rains in the film *Casablanca*. He was the one shocked to discover gambling at Rick's. At the end of the film,

Humphrey Bogart and Claude Rains plan their escape to the Congo, then under control of the "Free French" loyal to Charles de Gaulle.

Such films helped bolster the popular impression that the pro-American Free French were better than the evil, pro-German Vichy colonialists. The colonized people didn't see much difference, and in the case of Syria and Lebanon, the Free French were worse than the short reign of the Vichy.

In 1941 the British occupied Lebanon and Syria and expelled the Vichy forces. The Free French guaranteed independence for Lebanon and Syria, but their promises would prove as reliable as the British declarations during the Arab revolt of 1915. De Gaulle was a political conservative and a staunch defender of the French empire. Once Nazi Germany was defeated, he planned to reassert French colonial rule in Asia, Africa, and particularly in the oil-rich Middle East.

With the arrival of British troops, the Vichy colonial administrators in the French mandate changed sides and declared their loyalty to de Gaulle while intensifying their repression of the local populations. De Gaulle opposed independence and in 1943 publically refused to allow parliamentary elections in the French mandate.

British officials worried that barring elections would drive Arabs into the hands of Hitler. The British also had postwar aspirations to dominate the entire region. At the time, de Gaulle was living in London and was completely dependent on the British. Under orders from Prime Minister Winston Churchill, the British withdrew de Gaulle's telegraphic links with his Free French operatives around the world. Within a week, de Gaulle relented. Elections were set for the fall of 1943.

De Gaulle and his Free French administration were not prepared for the results. Independent nationalists opposed to French colonialism won the August 1943 elections in Lebanon. The Lebanese parliament immediately amended the constitution to establish Lebanese independence. That assertion of sovereignty infuriated de Gaulle and the other Free French colonialists.[26]

On November 11, 1943, the French arrested Lebanese president Bishara al-Khoury and his cabinet. Gendarmes broke into the president's house, held a pistol to the head of Khoury's son, and demanded the president's surrender. French colonial administrator Jean Helleu immediately announced suspension of the new constitution.[27]

Lebanese poured into the streets of Beirut and Tripoli in mass demonstrations, which sometimes turned violent. French troops attacked the protestors with live ammunition, killing and wounding over a hundred. The British realized the destabilizing effect of the Free French crackdown and threatened to impose martial law if President Khoury and cabinet were not released immediately. On November 22, the French reinstated the elected government. Forty thousand people demonstrated joyfully in Beirut.

Meanwhile in Syria, the National Bloc handily won parliamentary elections in 1943 and advocated independence policies similar to the nationalists in Lebanon. Shukri al-Quwatli, a wealthy landowner from Damascus and leader of the National Bloc, tried to negotiate independence with the French, but de Gaulle demanded that he sign a colonial treaty that would maintain de facto French control.

In May 1945, mass demonstrations broke out in Damascus and that city became the center for anticolonial activity for all of Syria. The French launched a vicious air and artillery attack on Damascus, eventually killing over four hundred. Once again, the British intervened to stop the fighting.

The brutality of the attack on Damascus only hardened the determination of the independence forces and led to the capitulation of France. By the end of 1945, France had given up control of Syria. Both Lebanon and Syria were able to join the newly formed United Nations in 1945. France withdrew all its troops from its mandate in 1946.

Syrian and Lebanese independence was a stinging defeat for France. It spelled the beginning of the end of the French empire, presaging later French defeats in Vietnam, Tunisia, and Algeria.

While the Syrian independence movement dealt a serious blow to France, it would not bring stability to the country. The battle for control was just beginning.

CHAPTER 4

WARS AND COUPS—
THEN THE ASSADS ARRIVE:
1947–2011

The newly independent Syria soon faced a major crisis that would engulf the entire Middle East: the formation of Israel. For years, Syria had strongly opposed the creation of a Zionist state. In 1945 it was one of the founding members of the Arab League, which also included Egypt, Iraq, Lebanon, Saudi Arabia, Jordan, and Yemen. The league called for expelling Zionists from Palestine, and Syria pushed hard for military action.

In 1948, Britain still maintained colonial rule in Palestine. The United Nations had voted to create Arab and Jewish states in Palestine with Jerusalem under international control. Many Zionist leaders were unhappy with the plan because they wanted more land and opposed creation of a Palestinian-Arab state. Arabs opposed the plan because Zionists would gain control of half of Palestine although they owned only 7 percent of the land. Surrounding Arab countries sent in armed groups to blockade Jerusalem. By May 1948, Jewish military forces launched a full-scale attack on British forces and the Arab armies.

Syria sent troops against the Zionists and encouraged other Arab countries to fight, even knowing that the Zionists were much stronger militarily. Joshua Landis, director of the Center of Middle Eastern Studies at the University of Oklahoma, wrote:

> We now know that early military assessments by the Arab League and individual states of their ability to defeat Zionist forces in the impending conflict were unanimous in warning of the superiority of the Zionist military, which outnumbered the Arab forces at every

stage of the war. Certainly, the Syrian leadership was painfully aware of the weakness of the Syrian army and had little or no faith in the ability of the Arab leaders to cooperate effectively against the Jews or win the war in Palestine.[1]

Within two to three months of fighting, the superior Zionist militias had turned the tide on the Arabs, and the war formally ended in March 1949. The Zionists drove out the British, defeated the Arab armies, and expelled large numbers of Palestinian civilians. It was a humiliating defeat for Syria and all the Arab countries involved. The defeat had a devastating impact on Syrian politics and helped precipitate the overthrow of Syrian president Shukri al-Quwatli in a 1949 military coup. Syria agreed to an armistice with Israel but never recognized its legitimacy as a nation state. The conflict continued.

The battle with Zionism and Western imperialism had given rise to intense Arab nationalism throughout the region. In the 1940s a group of middle-class intellectuals came together to form the Syrian Baath Party. *Baath* means "rebirth" in Arabic, and leaders such as Michel Aflaq created a leftist, secular movement within the party that would eventually come to power in both Syria and Iraq. As a youth, Aflaq wore an oversize fez, a sartorial holdover from the Ottoman days. Later he was a handsome man with a pouting look, wearing a double-breasted suit. He was to become one of Syria's best-known political philosophers and leaders.

Born in 1910 in Damascus, Aflaq attended the Sorbonne in Paris from 1929 to 1934. He became an independent Marxist and organized his fellow intellectuals upon his return to Syria. They combined Marxism with pan-Arabism, calling for a single, socialist Arab nation. They opposed both the colonial powers and the *comprador bourgeoisie*, or local Syrian elite.

Aflaq cofounded the Arab Baath Party in 1946. The Baathists later merged with another party to become the Arab Baath Socialist Party. Their new slogan became "Unity, liberty, socialism."

The Baathists enjoyed electoral success in the early 1950s, becoming

Syria's second-largest party. The Baathists, Communists, and other parties on the left enjoyed widespread support among intellectuals, peasants, workers, and even sections of the military. But that popular support was put to the test by developments in Egypt.

In 1956, Egyptian president Gamal Abdel Nasser nationalized the Suez Canal, angering Britain, which had controlled the canal since 1888. Syria and the Arab world sided with Nasser. But Israel, France, and Britain invaded Egypt with the goal of ousting Nasser and returning the canal to British control. The United States pressured all three countries to stop fighting. Nasser stayed in power, and the Suez Canal has remained under Egyptian control.

Nationalist Arab countries concluded that the United States would continue to back Israel, while the Soviet Union did not. So immediately after the Suez War, Syria signed a military agreement with the Soviet Union. The Soviets began shipping planes and tanks to Syria. Their alliance survived the collapse of the Soviet Union and continues with Russia today.

Michel Aflaq and other pan-Arabists then instituted the first and only merger of modern Arab states. In 1958 Egypt and Syria formed one country, the United Arab Republic (UAR). The Baathists assumed they would be the ruling party in the Syrian part of the new country. But Nasser sought to dominate the entire UAR and tried to crush the Baathists.

Baathist military officers in Syria didn't like the power divisions in the UAR; they instigated a coup, and Syria seceded in 1961. Syria maintained subsidized healthcare, education, and other social services adopted under the rubric of Arab socialism. Important industries were nationalized, but workers had few rights and certainly no control of the factories. Syria remained a capitalist country under military domination. The Baathists moved to the Right politically as the military wing of the party expelled the Marxist faction. In 1963 the Baath Party seized power in a military coup. Internal disputes led to another coup in 1966 and yet another in 1970. The military officers who ruled Syria for the next fifty years maintained the same Baathist rhetoric but few of its early ideals.

By 1967, both Israeli and Arab governments were preparing for war once again. Arab leaders never accepted the existence of Israel, and Israeli leaders were dissatisfied with their country's borders. A military clash was coming, but neither side wanted to be blamed for firing the first shot. Then Nasser closed the Straits of Tiran to Israeli shipping. Those thirteen-kilometer-wide straits controlled access to the Red Sea. Egypt also concluded military pacts with Syria, Jordan, and Iraq. The Lyndon Johnson administration suggested sending US and Israeli warships through the Straits of Tiran in order to get the Egyptians to fire first. But US congressional leaders balked at the plan.[2]

So, on June 5, Israel launched a massive first strike. It claimed self-defense against an enemy seeking its extinction as a nation. Israel occupied Syria's Golan, arguing that the area gave the Syrian military free rein to fire artillery into Israel. The Israelis also seized the West Bank of the Jordan River from Jordan as well as the Gaza Strip, a thin piece of land along the Mediterranean coast belonging to Egypt. The occupied land held at least one million Palestinians.[3] The war lasted six days and ended in another humiliating Arab defeat.

Officially, Israeli leaders promised to follow UN Resolution 242 by trading occupied territory for recognition of Israel—what they called "land for peace."[4] But successive Israeli governments sent settlers onto Palestinian land, occupied East Jerusalem, and eventually annexed the Golan. Israel never intended to return all the occupied land.

For the United States and Israel, the 1967 war was a swift victory over Arabs intent on wiping out the Jewish state. For one young Syrian living in the Golan, it was just incomprehensible violence. That year, Taleb Ibrahim was four years old, living in the city of Quneitra, not far from the Israeli border. "We had been awakened very early in the morning listening to the airplanes," he told me. "I saw airplanes at a very low height. I was happy to see airplanes. I said, 'Look.' My uncle said, 'No, they will bomb.' After a while I heard a massive explosion. I couldn't hear anything in my ears."[5]

During the 1967 war, Israel captured Quneitra, part of an area Israel said posed a military threat. In 1973 Syria, Egypt, and Israel fought another war in which Syria recaptured some of the Golan, including Quneitra. I drove through the rubble of Quneitra in 2006. It looked much as it did after the last war because the Syrian government never rebuilt the city. The roofs were intact, but the structures had collapsed. The hospital and churches were ransacked. Mohammad Ali, a Syrian government spokesperson, admitted that some of the city was damaged by military battles. But he told me Israeli soldiers intentionally destroyed much of the city before their withdrawal.

"Concrete buildings were destroyed by bulldozers," he said. "The bulldozer pushes or pulls a corner of the building. So the roofs collapse down. We made a complaint to the UN. An investigation committee came here. This committee found that the destruction was systematic and intentional."[6]

The Israeli officials have an official explanation. They said Quneitra was destroyed in fighting between the two sides and deny any intentional destruction.[7] However, an official UN report contradicts those assertions.[8] It also states that the Syrian government prohibited families from returning to rebuild Quneitra, keeping it as a historical showcase. Ever since 1967, Syria steadfastly demanded the return of all of the Golan. For all its bellicose rhetoric, however, Syria maintained a secure border with Israel, which no soldier or insurgent crossed until the 2011 uprising.

During my interview, Taleb Ibrahim, who is now fifty, admitted that the Arab-Israeli conflict had gone on for too many years. Military actions by both sides had not solved the problem. "Let us reject violence from all sides," he told me, saying the dispute must be solved politically, not militarily. "Israelis, do you want to be recognized and be safe? OK. Arab: You want to coexist with Israel without any power dominance? Let us try to achieve this. Without this it's impossible to reach a peace." Unfortunately, Syria and Israel remained far apart on that all-important political settlement.

Syria's military defeat in 1967 shook the country's Baathist leadership. Air force general Hafez al-Assad overthrew the civilian Baathist dictator Salah Jadid in 1970. No one knew it at the time, but Assad would bring a long period of relative stability to coup-prone Syria using an astute combination of political deal making and harsh repression.

Hafez al-Assad was tall with a hawklike face, an angular nose, and a neatly clipped mustache. He lacked the polite manners of his university-educated son, Bashar, but he was a street-smart politician and military ruler. Born in 1930, Assad grew up in a poor Alawite family. Following the tradition of ambitious Alawite youth going back to French colonial days, Assad attended a military academy. He spent three years at the Homs academy beginning in 1952, where he became a student activist in the Baath Party. Assad eventually rose to the rank of air force general and, after the 1966 Baathist coup, was appointed defense minister. Assad firmly believed in pan-Arabism, which called for the unification of the Arab world. But in practice, Syria and his own career came first. He stayed in power as president until his death in 2000.

US senator James Abourezk, who represented South Dakota from 1974 to 1980, met Assad many times starting in 1973. "I found him to be extremely intelligent, to the extent that various governments beat a path to his door during the many efforts to make peace between Israel and the Arab countries," Abourezk told me.[9]

Assad also had tremendous endurance. "American diplomats once told me that meeting with Assad was called bladder diplomacy. Assad could sit and discuss issues for eight or nine hours without any physical discomfort, while at the same time, the American diplomats sat, squirming in their chairs, fearful of getting up to go to the bathroom."

Political scientist Elie El-Hindy said Assad's long rule reflected his ability to play religious and ethnic groups against one another. "Hafez al-Assad had a very special character, a special charisma, and a special intelligence that enabled him to control Syria," El-Hindy told me.

"Some people said we're better off in Syria with a dictator than with internal conflicts or Israeli occupation." El-Hindy noted that Assad convinced religious minorities that he was their protector against the Sunni majority. "Assad was clever to play on the divergence in society and make people scared of each other."[10]

Assad also played a clever Cold War chess match with the United States and the Soviet Union. For years, he continued Syria's alliance with the Soviets. As the Soviet Union headed toward implosion in 1990, Assad switched sides and briefly allied himself with the United States. Syria joined in the invasion of Iraq during the US-led Gulf War in 1991. The United States, Soviet Union, and Israel were willing to temporarily cooperate with Syria in this era. "It was much easier for the two superpowers and Israel to have one person in control," explained El-Hindy. "That is what facilitated military guys getting control of most Arab countries."

Some Arab nationalists in that era believed that the military generals ruling Syria, Iraq, Libya, and other countries in the region were more steadfast in the Arab cause. El-Hindy said history proved them wrong. "The myth that these military guys were going to be better than kings and presidents in fighting against Israel and creating Arab nationalism quickly faded. Arab military leaders were as big a failure as any other leader during that time." That myth becomes clear when looking at Syria's relations with the Palestinians.

Assad and the Baathists proclaimed themselves staunch supporters of the Palestinian cause, but the reality was much more complicated. Compared to other Arab countries, Syria had a more enlightened policy toward Palestinian refugees. After the wars of 1948, 1967, and 1973, successive waves of Palestinians fled to nearby countries. In Lebanon, they were segregated into refugee camps and denied basic citizenship rights. The Syrian government treated them better because they weren't forced into refugee camps. While not allowed to become citizens, the government did allow Palestinians access to education and healthcare. By the time of the 2011 uprising, an estimated 500,000 Palestinians lived in Syria, which included the original refugees and their descendants.[11]

But Syrian leaders also sought to control the Palestinian movement by providing political sanctuary, money, and arms. Prior to the 1967 war, Syria backed Yasser Arafat, while Egypt had created a competing group called the Palestine Liberation Organization (PLO).[12] After 1967, the Palestinians began to exercise more independence from their Arab government sponsors. The PLO expanded to incorporate all the significant Palestinian groups and elected Arafat as chair.

At that time, Palestinians and the leaders of Arab countries considered Israel illegitimate and favored a one-state solution. Israel would have to allow exiled Palestinians to return to their homes, and both peoples would elect a common government. Israelis rejected this solution out of hand, arguing that Jews would easily be outnumbered by Palestinians and the nature of their country would change—even assuming everyone could get along.

But conditions were changing rapidly for Israel. In 1973 Egypt and Syria launched a surprise attack on Israel, seeking to regain lost territory, but Israel won the war because of strong US support. Arab countries launched an oil embargo against the United States, cut production, and raised prices internationally. The resulting gas shortages and high prices caused serious economic disruption in the West. Egypt signed a peace agreement with Israel in 1979; Jordan did so in 1994. But neither agreement returned the Golan nor provided for an independent Palestinian state.

Syria joined with a few other Arab countries and Palestinian groups to reject such agreements with Israel. Assad promoted Syria as leader of this "rejection front." Leaders in Syria, Saddam Hussein's Iraq, and the new revolutionary government in Iran gave fiery speeches against Israel but did little to actually help the Palestinians. In fact, Assad tried to manipulate the Palestinian movement.

In 1982 a top PLO commander, Said Musa Maragha, broke with Arafat. Maragha, better known as Abu Musa, was born in Palestine. He had joined, and later defected from, the Jordanian Army. He became the PLO's top commander in Lebanon, fighting on the side of the leftist and Muslim forces in that country's civil war (1975–1990). Israel had invaded Lebanon in an effort to crush the PLO, but a compromise allowed Yasser Arafat and other leaders to depart for Tunisia where they could reconstitute the group. Maragha declared that the PLO should continue the fight against Israel, not escape to Tunis. He couldn't back up his militant rhetoric, however, and later fled to Damascus.

Hafez al-Assad hoped to use Maragha to establish a pro-Syrian Palestinian coalition. He encouraged Maragha to form a new group, the "Fatah Uprising," to challenge Arafat's leadership of the PLO. Syria used its full propaganda machinery to bolster the image of Maragha while disparaging Arafat, but to no avail. Maragha's group never developed a popular base and he died in obscurity in Damascus in 2013.[13]

Syria would later use similar tactics to back such disparate groups as ultraleftists and Islamist Palestinians who opposed the PLO. The ultraleft groups established headquarters in Damascus, issued press releases, and did little to help the Palestinian cause. Assad, while portraying himself as a staunch supporter of the Palestinians and a fighter against US imperialism, in practice, was always best at supporting himself. Nowhere was that more clear than in Syria's military intervention in Lebanon.

Lebanon had prospered through the mid-1970s with Beirut becoming a financial capital known as the "Paris of the Middle East." But the prosperity of the elite masked deep social inequalities, further complicated by the country's patchwork governing system that allocated power based on religion and ethnicity.

The Lebanese Civil War began in 1975 for a number of reasons, including the large presence of the PLO in the country and the conflict between Muslims and Christians. It pitted the country's poor and underrepresented Muslims against wealthy Maronite Christians, an ancient Christian sect affiliated with the Church of Rome. The French had favored a Maronite elite during colonial times. Distribution of political and economic power hadn't changed a lot since.

Conservative Maronites dominated the government under terms of a 1943 agreement that led to the country's independence. The Muslim population had grown tremendously since then, yet Maronites still held 40 percent of the best jobs—Sunni Muslims held 27 percent and Shia Muslims 3.3 percent. In its early stages, the civil war pitted leftist Muslim groups against right-wing Christian parties.

The PLO had made its headquarters in Beirut and eventually joined the fighting on the leftist side. In 1975 and 1976, horrific war raged among the factions, and Beirut was split into Christian and Muslim areas. The Arab League, which by then included all the major Arab countries, authorized Syria to send peacekeeping troops to Lebanon to quell the fighting. Syrian troops arrived in 1976 and initially sided with the conservative Christians. Assad later shifted allegiance to the leftist side and allied with Shia, Sunni, and Alawite militias. Many Lebanese initially supported the intervention because it significantly reduced the violence. At its height, Syria had forty thousand troops in Lebanon, along with thousands of intelligence agents. It controlled the country politically and militarily. Major roads had checkpoints manned by Syrians in plain clothes and carrying AK-47s. Cronies of the Syrian military made millions of dollars in corrupt government contracts and shady banking deals.

Israel was highly displeased with the Syrian presence in Lebanon and the growing power of the PLO. As a preemptive move, Israel invaded Lebanon in 1978. Then it invaded again in 1982, claiming on both occasions that its action was a limited incursion to stop the PLO from firing missiles into Israel. But in 1982 it quickly sent troops northward to Beirut and sanctioned the massacre of civilians in the Palestinian refugee camps of Sabra and Shatila.[14] Israel destroyed an estimated five hundred Syrian tanks and one hundred planes.[15] The Israel Defense Forces (IDF) occupied part of southern Lebanon. The 1982 invasion appeared to be a major Israeli and US victory, but it failed to accomplish the major Israeli goals of driving Syria out of Lebanon and destroying the PLO. In fact, the war laid the seeds of future defeat.

Anger at the invasion led to the formation of Hezbollah, a Shia insurgent group closely allied with Iran and Syria. The United States holds Hezbollah responsible for the 1983 bombing of the US Marine barracks in Beirut, which killed 241 servicemen. A separate bombing the same day killed fifty-eight French paratroopers. Those attacks forced the withdrawal of US and French troops from Lebanon. Hezbollah went on to wage a guerrilla war against Israeli occupation and forced the IDF out of southern Lebanon in 2000, the first Arab armed group to defeat Israel.

The sectarian strife in Lebanon was also bubbling in Syria. The Baathists tried to run a secular dictatorship. In Syria's big cities, Syrians seemingly lived without outward reference to religious differences. Sunni, Shia, Christian, and Alawite had friendships and did business. Assad's family was Alawite, a Muslim sect that had suffered poverty and discrimination under previous regimes. Alawites practiced a less-strict interpretation of Islam, and many became secular.

Before Syria's 2011 civil war, about 74 percent of Syrians were Sunni Muslim, 10 percent were Christian, and 16 percent Alawite and Druze.[16] But beneath the surface, religion and ethnicity did matter. Kurds in the north consider themselves Syrians, but not Arab, and make up about 10 percent of the population, and they suffer greatly (see chapter 9). Alawites enjoy the top positions in the army and intelligence services. Sunni Muslims are underrepresented in government jobs, which breeds resentment.

In the 1980s, the Muslim Brotherhood took advantage of that resentment, grew in influence, and eventually posed a major threat to the Baathists. The brotherhood gained support by providing food and social services to the poor. But their leadership and strongest support came from urban, Sunni traders. They hated Alawites for religious reasons, claiming they were not real Muslims, but also for class reasons. The apostate Alawites ruled, and the Sunnis didn't.[17]

As its influence grew in conservative parts of Aleppo, Hama, and other cities, the brotherhood also split into different factions. Younger militants began to advocate armed struggle and opposed the traditional leaders' reliance on peaceful tactics. Damascus was the bastion of traditional views while Aleppo and Hama favored militancy. The pro-armed-struggle wing also became increasingly conservative politically, rejecting Arab socialism. A leading brotherhood cleric called for jihad against leftists, Shiites, and Sufis. Sufism is an approach to Islam that can include worship through meditation, music, and dance. The Muslim Brotherhood, on the other hand, encouraged followers not to watch TV or listen to music. Even tambourines were considered un-Islamic.[18]

In 1979 Islamic extremists carried out an attack on the Aleppo Artillery School, killing eighty-three Alawite cadets and wounding scores. The government blamed Muslim Brotherhood leaders. But the brotherhood said the attack was launched by a splinter group called the Fighting Vanguard. The Baathist government took full advantage of the popular revulsion against the attack, however, and started a massive propaganda campaign against the brotherhood. While the insurgents claimed a victory against the Baathist military, many Syrians saw it as an attack on Alawites. The incident foreshadowed how the government and armed rebels would portray religious/ethnic issues after 2011.

After the artillery school attack, many older brotherhood leaders fled the country or went underground, leaving the younger members to make decisions. The young militants stockpiled arms, and the violence increased. In 1980, the brotherhood sponsored a general strike in several cities, and there was an assassination attempt on Hafez al-Assad. The Syrian government retaliated by killing over six hundred political prisoners in Tadmur Prison, many of them brotherhood members and supporters. But even this horrific violence was but a prelude.

In 1982, a general uprising broke out in the city of Hama. The brotherhood's younger militants held sway. Young men with full beards and wearing Muslim skullcaps set up barricades around the city. From speakers atop minarets, imams urged insurrection.

Brotherhood militants killed Baathist officials in their homes. In essence, the brotherhood posed the political question: Do you support the secular dictatorship or ultraconservative Islamic rule? The answer came quickly. Assad ordered army troops into Hama, gave residents a few hours to evacuate, and then shelled the civilian areas suspected of supporting the brotherhood. He eventually sent twelve thousand troops, and the fighting lasted twenty-seven days. While exact figures may never be known, the army may have killed over ten thousand people.[19]

The brotherhood had badly miscalculated their level of popular support. Other cities failed to join the rebellion. Syrians were not ready to rise up against Assad, and they rejected the brotherhood's ultra-conservatism. The Baathists gloated in their brutal victory. Rifat al-Assad, brother of Hafez, was commander of the paramilitary defense forces at the time. He told British newspaper journalist Robert Fisk, "You in the West should be grateful to us. We crushed Islamic fanaticism here."[20]

After the 1982 defeat, the remaining brotherhood leaders were either jailed or exiled. It would be decades before they recovered a popular base of support. While Hafez al-Assad appeared secure at home, international events were once again going to intervene.

In 1990, Saddam Hussein's Iraq invaded and occupied Kuwait. The United States mobilized an alliance of Western Europeans and some Arab states to expel Hussein's troops. Officially, the United States invaded in order to liberate Kuwait and protect Saudi Arabia from a future invasion. The United States actually hoped to overthrow Saddam Hussein and bring a pro-US strongman to power. With that goal in mind, President George H. W. Bush gave a February 1991 speech calling on Iraqis to rise up against Hussein.[21]

The Soviet Union, which in the past would have blocked such efforts, was suffering from internal turmoil that would soon lead to its political collapse. Syria could see the handwriting on the Kuwaiti wall. Assad had no love for Hussein, having supported Iran during the Iran-Iraq War in the 1980s. So, in 1991, Assad switched sides. He joined the Gulf War coalition and sent 14,500 troops to participate in Operation Desert Storm against Iraq.

Always the clever operator, Assad also switched positions on Palestine to curry favor with the West. In 1991 the United States, Israel, Syria, and others met in Madrid to discuss a peace plan that would eventually be known as the Oslo Agreement. Oslo called for creation of a Palestinian state in the West Bank and Gaza Strip and Arab recognition of Israel. Syria and Israel held serious negotiations about the return of the Golan. Assad had rejected his own rejection front; Syria came to accept the two-state solution.

The talks concerning the return of the Golan eventually failed, as did the Oslo process. But Assad's participation took the international spotlight off Syria's role in Lebanon and his repression at home.

Hafez al-Assad had been grooming his son Bashar for several years to take over the family business of running Syria. However, after Hafez's death in June 2000, there were a few technicalities to resolve. The Syrian Constitution specified that the president must be forty years old. Bashar was only thirty-five. It would take a constitutional amendment for him to become president. Government critics noted that when they asked for legalization of political parties, they were told it would take years to amend the constitution. No such problem presented itself with respect to Bashar's succession. Parliament convened and immediately amended the constitution to lower the qualifying age to thirty-four. Bashar al-Assad became president and later ran unopposed in a contrived election, receiving 97.29 percent of the vote.

Nevertheless, Syrians had high hopes that the younger Assad would reform the system. After all, he had an advanced degree in ophthalmology, had lived abroad, spoke fluent English, and had married a seemingly progressive woman. But Assad also inherited a sclerotic and repressive system. He even acknowledged some of these problems during his July 2000 speech accepting the presidency. "Don't depend on the state," he warned. "There is no magic wand. . . . We must rid ourselves of those old ideas that have become obstacles."[22]

Within a few years, Assad did make reforms—the kind that warmed the cockles of international bankers' hearts. He "liberalized" the economy by selling off some state enterprises. He allowed businessmen to start up corporations such as cell phone companies that would have been state-owned in the past. Assad cleverly raised the hopes of Western powers that their businesspeople might benefit from the privatization. US and European officials deferred their criticisms of Syria. But it soon became clear that the privatization mainly benefitted Assad family cronies.

Rami Makhlouf, an Assad cousin, is reportedly the richest man in Syria, worth an estimated $5 billion. He owns a variety of businesses, including tourist hotels, duty-free shops, and luxury department stores.[23] He became infamous for his role as owner of cell phone giant Syriatel. The company grew to control 55 percent of the Syrian market. In the early months of the 2011 uprising, regime opponents accused Makhlouf of financing pro-Assad demonstrations. They later learned that Syriatel was cooperating with the regime to tap activists' phones. Demonstrators burned Syriatel posters and stomped on SIM cards in protest.[24]

Some Syrians benefited from the crony capitalism as wealth trickled down to ordinary people. They could buy cell phones and later got connected to the Internet, albeit with close government monitoring of social media. But trickle-down wasn't enough. Most Syrians were angry at the poor state of the economy.

Long before the uprising, on one sultry evening in Damascus, I met Hamad standing with a gaggle of friends in front of a café. Like many Syrians critical of the government, he declined to use his last name. At age twenty-two, he remained in school to avoid military conscription.

Hamad told me it was "extremely difficult" to find work. "Most of my friends are not working, and those who are working receive a very low salary. The people who have jobs have connections."[25]

Hamad's comments were borne out in the economic statistics. In the 2000s, unemployment went as high as 20 percent and the poverty rate hit 44 percent.[26] I interviewed many young people who were victims of Assad's economic policies. Ayman Abdel Nour, a reform-minded Syrian economist, warned me that unemployed youths posed a big problem for the government. "It's a very dangerous situation," he said. Government officials made "some plans to overcome this problem, like launching a program to overcome unemployment and financing small and medium enterprises. They are trying, but it's all on paper."[27]

Syrians were also disappointed by Assad's failure to loosen the dictatorial political policies of his father. The Syrian Constitution specifies that the Baath Party is the only legal political party. President Assad promised to reform the constitution and allow multiple parties. During the first seven months of Bashar's rule, he released some political prisoners, licensed new newspapers, and allowed formation of nongovernmental organizations (NGOs) critical of the regime. Those months became known as the "Damascus Spring."

But even mild hints of change were threatening to the old-guard, Baathist military and intelligence officers who exercised real power. They had to keep the regime in power at all costs. Political openings and transparency might reveal their history of brutality and corruption. So they exerted pressure on Assad to crack down, and whatever he may have thought personally, he sided with them. That pattern was repeated numerous times during his rule.

In a 2006 interview, Assad said the demands to allow the formation of opposition parties was a plot by the United States. He told me it would take a year of dialogue just to set a time frame for discussion of the issue:

> *Assad:* After the dialogue, then you decide. We're starting to put forward the idea. Some suggestions for intellectuals. We're going to make proposals. The proposals will be the basis for the national dialogue.
>
> *Erlich:* Do you have any idea when the dialogue will start?
>
> *Assad:* When they stop putting pressure on Syria to distract us with trivial issues.
>
> *Erlich:* So the Bush pressure is having the opposite effect?
>
> *Assad:* Definitely. We don't live isolated from our region. We're affected by all the problems in it.[28]

Multiple parties, a free press, free trade unions, lifting the state of siege imposed on the country in 1962, and giving full citizenship to

Kurds were all issues of vital concern to Syrians. But for Assad, they were issues raised by the United States to undercut his regime.

Sheik Nawaf al-Basheer agreed that the United States should have stopped pressuring his country. But that had nothing to do with Syrians' legitimate demands for ending dictatorial rule. The sheik was the elected head of one of Syria's largest tribes, a former Communist, and a leading opponent of the government. "The government has talked about passing a multiparty law," he told me. "But this is premised on the idea that the Baath Party will still control everything. We want a genuine multiparty law."[29]

Assad routinely used torture and arbitrary arrest to suppress any opposition. Ironically, incontrovertible proof came to light because of a rare example of American-Syrian cooperation. In 2002, the Bush administration requested that Syrian authorities interrogate Maher Arar, a Canadian citizen of Syrian origin. The US government had detained Arar at JFK airport in 2002 on suspicion of terrorism and forcibly deported him to Damascus. It became one of the most infamous cases of "extraordinary rendition," in which US authorities kidnap suspected terrorists and send them to secret jails for torture.

Assad's security services brutally tortured Arar for a year before determining he was innocent. An official Canadian government commission investigated the case and exonerated Arar, and the Canadian government awarded him $12.5 million.[30] Neither the US nor Syrian governments apologized or paid compensation. Several members of the US House of Representatives did apologize unofficially.[31]

While discontent about poverty, torture, and the lack of democracy bubbled below the surface, the Syrian government was suddenly confronted once again with an unexpected crisis from next door.

In February 2005, a powerful car bomb exploded on the fashionable Corniche Boulevard in Beirut. It killed former prime minister Rafic Hariri and twenty-one others while wounding another 226. The street full of glitzy night clubs and restaurants once again looked like a war zone. Chunks of concrete, twisted metal, and automobiles were tossed everywhere. It was a professional hit.

US and European officials immediately blamed Assad for the assassination, as did many Lebanese. Hariri had been an ally of Syria, but in the months prior to his death, he had opposed extending the term of the then pro-Syrian president of Lebanon. Assad told me he had no part in the assassination, blaming the murder on other Hariri opponents.[32] By 2005, Assad had reduced the number of Syrian troops in Lebanon by 50 percent, but fourteen thousand to sixteen thousand still remained.

After several years of on-again, off-again investigation, the UN-backed special tribunal for Lebanon indicted five members of Hezbollah for the Hariri murder. While Hezbollah is closely allied with Syria, neither Assad nor other Syrian officials were charged.[33]

Soon after the assassination, the Lebanese held protests in downtown Beirut, demanding the ouster of all Syrian troops. The protests were led by conservative and pro-US factions but reflected a popular feeling that Syria had outstayed its welcome. Many Syrians felt the same. In April 2005, under massive pressure, Assad was forced to withdraw his soldiers, although some intelligence agents remained.

Sheik Nawaf al-Basheer told me that Assad's troops had initially entered Lebanon to stop the bloody civil war. But the presence of Syrian troops on their soil for nearly thirty years made the Lebanese resentful. "We supported the withdrawal of troops from Lebanon because Lebanon is an independent country," he said. "If there is a sick man, the doctor comes to treat him. Does that mean the doctor will live with him in the same house?"[34]

While the Assad government claimed to be maintaining political stability in Lebanon, the occupation had proved profitable. "Lebanon was the main outlet for Syrian trade," said Basheer. "There were more than 800,000 Syrians working in Lebanon, sending money home every month. Now there are many fewer." The forced withdrawal of troops shook up politics inside Syria as well.

After a bumpy car ride in the desert outside the eastern city of Deir Ezzor, the estate of Sheik Nawaf al-Basheer rose in the distance. It included a large house, a huge meeting hall, and a mosque. Syrians took big risks if they sharply criticized the Assad regime. Basheer was willing to take that risk. He welcomed me into his grand meeting hall, with its expanse of upholstered benches along the walls and hand-woven carpets on the floor.

In November 2005, Basheer was among three hundred Lebanese and Syrian intellectuals who signed a controversial declaration criticizing the Syrian government, calling it "authoritarian, totalitarian, and cliquish.[35] The Beirut-Damascus Declaration called for peaceful reform, not revolution. It was signed by Islamist, secular, and Kurdish groups The government ignored their demands and jailed twelve signers. Basheer was questioned but not arrested. "The police asked, why did I sign the Beirut-Damascus Declaration?" he told me. "We were questioned because in the declaration there were sections critical of the Syrian government. They warned me not to make the assassination of former Lebanese prime minister Hariri into an international issue."[36]

President Assad claimed that the declaration—a rather mild assertion of human rights—played into plans by the United States and Israel to destabilize the region. In my interview, Assad denounced the declaration:

> *Assad:* It was written by a group in Lebanon who invited the United
>   States to occupy Syria This was made in cooperation with them.
>   This is treason. By Syrian law, they should go to court.
> *Erlich:* Are they going to be charged?
> *Assad:* That depends on the court.
> *Erlich:* So there are no plans to immediately release them?
> *Assad:* You cannot. When they are under the court authority, nobody
>   can help them.[37]

The jailed Syrians who signed the declaration were eventually released. Basheer was jailed during the early months of the 2011 uprising "for his own protection," according to the government, and he later fled into exile. The controversy over Syrian troops in Lebanon and the Beirut-Damascus Declaration are just two more examples of how

President Assad could have carried out reform in response to popular opinion. Instead, he blamed outside powers for causing the problems.

The United States invaded and occupied Iraq in March 2003. A University of Washington study showed that 461,100 Iraqis died between 2003 and 2011 as a result of the US war.[38] Other studies put the number of civilian deaths in excess of 900,000.[39] During those years, 4,486 American soldiers died in Iraq, according to official statistics.[40] Despite much hoopla in Washington about international support, the vast majority of countries in the world opposed the Iraq War, including such traditional allies as France, Germany, and Turkey.

Syria opposed the war from the beginning, although Saddam Hussein had been Syria's sworn enemy for decades. Assad knew that the war would intensify ethnic and religious conflict and spill over into his country. The government estimated that eventually one million Iraqi refugees fled to Syria, which kept an open-door policy despite the huge economic burden. Syria didn't officially side with the rebels fighting the US occupation but sought to influence whatever government would eventually emerge in Iraq. Assad's intelligence agencies met with Iraqi Sunnis and opposition groups. Some armed rebels slipped across the Syrian border into Iraq, leading US officials to claim Syria was sponsoring the infiltration.

In October of 2008, the United States even sent helicopters inside Syria to attack a supposed terrorist cell in Al-Sukariya. The United States killed six construction workers and wounded two others. It was the US invasion of Syria that almost no one remembers.[41]

Assad said his government had done everything possible to stop cross-border activity. Whether true or not, the infiltration had little impact. The US military was looking for scapegoats to blame for their own losses in Iraq. "Even if Syria had been the most compliant and helpful country on the planet toward the United States, the situation in Iraq would not have been dramatically different," according to David Lesch, a professor of Middle East studies at Trinity University in San Antonio.[42]

The US invasion of Iraq, which was supposed to spread democracy throughout the region, actually had the opposite effect. The Iraq War intensified Sunni-Shia conflicts and general political chaos. In comparison, many Syrians saw their own government as relatively stable and secular.

I interviewed Taleb Ibrahim, who fled Quneitra as a young boy and later became a political analyst in Damascus. He said when US officials talked about promoting democracy and "regime change," many Syrians were skeptical. The United States "found it very easy to change a regime, but it's impossible to force security and stability in the region," he told me. "They are having a hard time in Iraq. The population doesn't trust the United States. When I was in the university, I dreamed of going to the United States. But now, I would never go."[43]

Dr. Mahmoud al-Agassi, an influential Muslim cleric and a critic of President Assad, also told me that US calls for Syrian regime change had backfired. He later died, but his words in 2006 were prophetic. "The pressure exerted on Syria is actually unifying the Syrian people. I do recommend that the US government not impose democracy. Give us the opportunity to make our own democracy. The United States is not aware of the structure of Syrian society and the Arab world."[44]

Prior to the 2011 uprising, the Syrian opposition rejected US interference and called for significant, but peaceful, change. Back in 2006, Basheer emphasized the need for a Syrian solution to Syrian problems.

> We want peaceful change, without any war. We don't want to depend on foreign forces. Reform must come from inside Syria. We can compete with the Baath Party if given a fair chance. We don't want the government to fall; we want it to change from internal pressure. And we want gradual change. The opposition and government must work with each other. Let's learn the lessons from Iraq. We don't want chaos.[45]

Assad rejected such overtures, however, convinced that his brand of secular nationalism would prevail. In January, just two months before the 2011 uprising, Assad said, "Syria is stable. Why? Because you have to be very closely linked to the beliefs of the people. . . . When there is divergence . . . you will have this vacuum that creates disturbances."[46]

Both Assad and the traditional opposition proved tragically wrong in the face of a grassroots movement we now call the Arab Spring.

CHAPTER 5

THE UPRISING BEGINS

A huge sculpture of a food vendor's pushcart stands not far from the town center in Sidi Bouzid, Tunisia. The larger-than-life stone wheels and tilt of the carriage propel the sculpture forward as if it could move without human touch. The artist intentionally spray painted English graffiti at the base: *For Those Who Yearn to Be Free.* The sculpture commemorates the life of street vendor Mohammad Bouazizi, who immolated himself on December 17, 2010, initiating the Tunisian uprising and eventually the Arab Spring.

Bouazizi was protesting the confiscation of his goods and harassment by city officials. His self-sacrifice touched a chord. Workers, intellectuals, small-business people, and other ordinary people had been suffering for decades under the rule of the military dictatorship led by the pro-Western Zine El Abidine Ben Ali. Bouazizi's immolation lit a fire that spread quickly. Within a matter of weeks, mass demonstrations forced Ben Ali from power.

When I visited Sidi Bouzid in 2012, the dictator was gone, but the struggle for economic and political justice continued. On the day of my visit, demonstrators at city hall demanded jobs, a key issue that sparked the original demonstrations. Residents said that although they enjoyed greater political freedoms, they continued to suffer from the crony capitalist economic system. "We're just struggling in the same situation," said protestor Alawi Tahrir. "I have a master's degree in English language, and I'm still unemployed for five years."[1] The demonstrators' chants merged with the muezzin's call to noon prayer in this hardscrabble, agricultural city 175 miles south of the capital, Tunis. Islam has deep roots here, and it's reflected in the politics. Conservative Islamists from the Ennahda Party emerged as the strongest single political force in postuprising Tunisia. Ultra-right-wing Islamists had some popular support. They played a destructive role by blockading streets and assassinating two progressive political leaders.

Unlike other countries in the Middle East, however, Tunisia's leftist trade unions, women's rights groups, and other secular movements also developed a significant political base. They forced the adoption of a constitution that protects civil liberties and restricts the role of Islam in government. While the battle certainly continues, Tunisia has made the greatest strides in the region toward achieving the popular goals of the Arab Spring.

In early 2011, the Tunisian uprising inspired similar protests in Egypt, Yemen, Saudi Arabia, Bahrain, and other Middle East countries. Conditions were ripe in Syria as well. Poverty and unemployment were on the rise, particularly among young people. President Bashar al-Assad had implemented neoliberal economic policies that privatized state-owned businesses for the benefit of a small elite while ordinary Syrians suffered. They lived under a dictatorial regime where criticism of the government meant jail and torture. Assad allowed no genuine opposition parties, functioning trade unions, or opposition media. Facebook and other social media were banned prior to February 2011. Assad lived in a political cocoon, however, absolutely convinced that he was immune from the Arab Spring. He believed his own public-relations propaganda that Syrians would never rebel against a pan-Arabist, anti-Israel, anti-imperialist fighter like himself.

Rarely has a world leader been proven so wrong so quickly.

The antigovernment demonstrations began in the southern city of Daraa in March 2011. Police had arrested several preteen school children for writing antiregime graffiti on walls of a school. As in the past, police beat and tortured the youths. But this time, the people of Daraa reacted angrily and publically. Over six hundred protestors confronted the local governor, demanding freedom for the injured children. Security forces attacked and killed two protestors.[2] Daraa is located in southern Syria near the Jordanian border. Local tribal clans remain strong. Some residents had immigrated to wealthy gulf countries and become prosperous. Residents of Daraa weren't willing to accept the old ways. Word spread quickly via text messaging about the brutality. Syria had its Mohammad Bouazizi, and its Sidi Bouzid was Daraa.

By mid-March demonstrations broke out in Damascus and other parts of the country. The demonstrations were nonviolent and secular. In the northwestern city of Banyas, protesters tried to attract the generally pro-Assad Alawite religious minority by chanting, "Peaceful, peaceful—neither Sunni nor Alawite, we want national unity."[3]

The regime faced the biggest crisis in its history. Assad cracked down mercilessly on peaceful protestors. Police and soldiers opened fire with live ammunition. Security forces arrested and tortured anyone suspected of participating in the protests. Then, thinking it occupied a position of strength, the regime offered the occasional olive branch. In late March, Assad lifted the state-of-emergency law, which was declared in 1962 and implemented at the time of the first Baathist coup in 1963. The law had been used as an important repressive tool by successive governments. Assad also legalized the status of some 300,000 Kurds who had been stateless since the 1960s (see chapter 9).

On July 10, a number of prominent opposition figures from different religious and ethnic backgrounds tested the parameters of the new political openings by holding a conference in Damascus. They were allowed to raise criticisms of the regime, and the state TV network broadcast the conference live. On July 24, the Syrian parliament passed a law allowing additional opposition parties. Since the early 1970s, the National Progressive Front, a coalition of minor leftist parties, had been legalized as a sort of loyal opposition. The regime planned to open this door a bit wider, but the Syrian Constitution still contained a clause stating that the Baath Party was the leading party. So the new parties had little actual power.[4]

Steps that would have been hailed as tremendously progressive a few years prior had no impact in 2011. The main opposition groups rejected the weak reforms and continued to call for Assad's overthrow. In July, 400,000 people rallied in the central Syrian city of Hama after security forces had withdrawn. They put forward a nonviolent message inviting participation by all faiths, and the demonstration had a strong presence of women.

In October 2011 I was able to report from Daraa. The government was in nominal control of the city, but antiregime sentiment remained strong. I tagged along with a group of Ukrainian dignitaries and journalists on a trip organized by the government. We drove out of Damascus at about 9:00 a.m. in a large convoy of buses and minivans, accompanied by a police car lettered *Protocol*. While ordinary cars were stopped at military checkpoints along the way, we sailed right through.

Outwardly, Daraa was calm. Its streets had few shoppers, but there were no outward signs of unrest. We met with Daraa governor Mohammed Khaled Hanos and the local attorney general, Tayseer al-Smadi.[5] These government officials spun a well-developed narrative to explain events. They admitted that people in Daraa and elsewhere began with peaceful protests and legitimate grievances asking for democracy. But almost immediately, extremists seized control of the demonstrations, they claimed. Extremists began a campaign of shooting and violence against security forces.

These agitators were armed and paid by Saudi Arabia and the gulf state of Qatar, according to the officials. The demonstrators were politically and militarily backed by Israel, the United States, and Europe. As a result, over 1,200 police, army, and other security personnel had been killed by demonstrators. The government provided no statistics on the number of civilians killed.[6]

The regime's narrative contained some elements of truth. Syrian demonstrators never adopted a Gandhi-style campaign of nonviolent civil disobedience. When government forces fired live ammunition into crowds, the protestors hurled rocks. On March 20, less than one week into the protests, demonstrators in Daraa burned an office of the ruling Baath Party and the local courthouse. In Damascus I interviewed Mahmoud, a twenty-six-year-old activist in Daraa who asked that only his first name be used. As the repression continued for months, he told me, "People in Daraa used Molotov [cocktails] and rifles. But it was a reaction to the government arresting and killing protestors."[7]

Mahmoud admitted that tribal groups, who are allowed to own personal weapons, also used them against the government after months of nonviolent marches and rallies. "Daraa is known for big tribal clans. When they use arms, it's to defend themselves. They use them when the government arrests people and invades people's houses. The big families of Daraa oppose the government and they use arms." But local people taking up arms in self-defense is a far cry from CIA/Israeli/Saudi-sponsored rebels attacking the Assad government. Officials clearly exaggerated the violence in an effort to discredit the opposition.

While there were sporadic armed incidents during the first eight months of the uprising, protestors predominantly used nonviolent tactics. They held marches and rallies and spread the word through text messages and sometimes with social media. They relayed developments on the ground to satellite TV stations such as *Al Jazeera* and *Al Arabiya*.

The opposition movement grew as new organizations sprang into existence. The Local Coordinating Committees (LCC) developed spontaneously in many cities as the mostly young activists created grassroots groups unaffiliated with the traditional opposition. The activists included leftists, liberal secularists, and conservative Muslims. They developed an alliance similar to the coalition of secularists and Muslim activists in Cairo's Tahrir Square.

The LCC in Syria wanted no hierarchical structures. The movement ostensibly had no leaders, no common ideology, or even a short-term political program. But they all united on the need to overthrow Assad, hold free elections, and establish a parliamentary system with civil liberties. I had a chance to meet some secular LCC leaders in Damascus toward the end of 2011. I had taken a circuitous route through Damascus's old city to a clandestine apartment, as described in chapter 1.

After a long conversation, we took a break to drink tea. I looked around the apartment. The beds were unmade, the dishes unwashed, and dust balls were scattered around the room. It could belong to a single guy in his twenties who hadn't done the housework in a while. I found out later it was an LCC safe house paid for by an upper-middle-class sympathizer.

I asked Ahmad Bakdouness how they continued to organize, given harsh government repression. Bakdouness is a civil-society activist who was later jailed and tortured by police. He told me that demonstrators gathered outside mosques on Fridays because that was one of the few places people could still congregate. They used code words over mobile phones to organize demonstrations. "We say, 'We are going to a party' or 'Come to the wedding,'" said Bakdouness. "People know there will be a demonstration on Friday. They know the mosques where people demonstrate. For demonstrations during the week, we know each other and call on mobiles."[8]

Protestors only occasionally used social networking sites because they were closely monitored by the government. They said theirs is not a Facebook revolution. They used Facebook and similar social networking sites only to alert the outside world that someone famous would be participating in a demonstration. I asked Bakdouness how people can demonstrate in the same location each week without being crushed by the security forces. "In the same area, there are a lot of roads. They can't block every road. For the big demonstrations, the government can't enter."

Protestors adopted innovative tactics to reach the public. One day, activists wrote the word "freedom" on five thousand ping-pong balls. They went to a hilltop in Damascus and dumped the balls on the heavily trafficked park below. Leen, another LCC leader at the safe house, chuckled as she explained that the security forces spent the rest of the day chasing their balls.

The heady, early days of the uprising saw Syrians reexamining many of their political values. But the society remained deeply conservative in cultural matters. Syrians continued to hold antihomosexual attitudes, even among many opposition activists. That didn't stop a few brave gays from joining the uprising, as I found out when I met Mahmoud Hassino.

Hassino knew he was gay at age twelve. He wasn't attracted to girls, but he was very interested in his male friends. Later, as a teenager growing up in Damascus, his mother figured out his sexual orientation and gave him what he later realized was good advice. "Don't admit your homosexuality," she cautioned. "You will have trouble finding work and socializing with people."[9] Despite tight cultural restrictions, Hassino told me, he had no problems finding gay partners. "There are gay men everywhere," he said with a quick smile. "You just had to have good gaydar."

Hassino joined millions of other Syrians in the uprising. He marched in demonstrations and participated in underground meetings. Dozens of gay men and lesbians were killed by security forces during the uprising, but most Syrians were unaware of their sexual orientation. Hassino eventually fled to Turkey because of his antiregime activism. He later got word that his Damascus apartment had been destroyed in a government attack. But he continued to write about his homeland in an effort to shine light on its gay subculture and to support the opposition movement.

Homosexuality remains a criminal offense in Syria despite promises of reform by President Assad when he took office in 2000. In March and April 2010, the government arrested groups of gay men who were having parties at private houses in Damascus. Three of the men were arrested on drug charges. Others were kept in jail for three months "until their families and everyone in the neighborhood knew," said Hassino. After their release, "some had to flee Syria to other countries." Hassino said that while gay men undergo harassment, lesbians face even more difficulties. When the family of one lesbian friend found out about her sexual orientation, they "forced her to marry an older guy," recalled Hassino. "Now she's living like a maid, taking care of him and his children."

In recent years, gays organized in an attempt to change the law and educate their fellow citizens. In 2009 some two hundred gays organized a group called I'm Just Like You. "I'm gay and I have a right to my opinion," gays wrote in an appeal, as quoted by Agence France Presse.

"I belong to this society, and it owes me some respect. I'm gay—I don't come from another planet."[10]

While homosexuality remains illegal and gays must lead double lives in Syria, a 2011 UN Office for Human Rights report noted that other Middle East countries are far worse violators of gay rights. Four Middle East nations proscribe the death penalty for homosexual acts.[11] As a result, Hassino concedes, some gay men and lesbians still support Assad. They fear that if conservative Islamists come to power, they will face even more repression. Hassino wanted to reach out to gays who are pro-Assad or on the fence. He started an online, Arabic-language magazine, *Mawaleh*, which means "nuts"—a reference to the food, not a double entendre. The magazine attempts to reach lesbian, gay, bisexual, and transgendered Syrians regardless of their political views. "We all want a secular Syria," says Hassino. And those who support Assad, he argues, "must have a backup plan" in case he falls.

But as the fighting intensified, the secular forces within the opposition were losing strength. And Hassino's views were very controversial, even among the secular opposition. Miral Bioredda, a secular leader of the LCC in Al Hasakah, a northeastern Syrian city, told me he personally views homosexuality as a private matter, "but Syrian society would say 'no way' if gays rose to claim their rights. Developing a civil society will take time."[12] Others are less tolerant. Interviewed in Turkey, Nasradeen Ahme, who considered himself part of the secular opposition, told me: "If I was in charge, I would enforce tougher laws against homosexuals. If someone said homosexuals should be stoned to death as in Iran and Saudi Arabia, I would not object."[13]

As extremist rebels seized control of some cities, persecution of gays intensified. Rebel leaders from Jabhat al-Nusra and the Islamic State of Iraq and al-Sham, two groups affiliated with al-Qaeda at the time, made homosexuality punishable by lashing or even death. Some fifty gays were executed by those groups, according to Hassino.[14] He had moved to the border city of Antakya, Turkey, but was forced to relocate to Istanbul after extremist Syrian rebels threatened to kidnap him. Hassino acknowledged that homosexuals face an intense challenge, whoever wins Syria's civil war. "This is a bigger problem than the law now," he said. "Social traditions are influenced by the religious traditions. Most people reject homosexuality." Hassino argued that fighting against Assad and for the right to organize will benefit all Syrians and eventually help gays as well. "The intelligence services arrest people if they're discussing any kind of social or political change," he said. "Without freedom of speech, we can't address these issues."

People such as Hassino and the LCC leaders represented only one sector of the opposition in the early months of the uprising. A friend offered to introduce me to another kind of Assad opponent. He typified the shady characters who once supported the government and later joined the opposition. After a few hushed phone calls, we met in an outdoor Damascus café. We sat far away from other customers, and he positioned himself with his back to the wall.

He called himself "Bashar," a pseudonym adopted to mock Bashar al-Assad. His demeanor was half-dissident, half-thug. He represented the opportunist opposition, someone who didn't initially support the uprising, joined it when it seemed about to win, and might just return to the Assad camp if the wind changed. With a thick neck and bushy mustache, Bashar looked like a bodyguard. That's because he used to be one. He was vague about whom exactly he guarded, but he bragged of close ties to Syrian security agencies and the police.

To prove his opposition bona fides, Bashar opened his camera phone and showed me photos of him with a very famous exiled Syrian leader. Other photos showed him at Damascus demonstrations. "I'm an agitator," he told me proudly. When I pointed out the questionable practice of keeping a cell phone full of incriminating photos, he said, "I don't care."[15]

Beginning in the fall of 2011, he said, some opposition activists armed themselves with hunting pistols and rifles, which they use when police come to make house arrests. He denied that demonstrators shoot during demonstrations: a foolhardy act given the superior weaponry of the army and police. Some sectors of the opposition were now carrying out targeted assassinations of Mukhabarat (Military Intelligence Directorate) agents, informers, and government supporters, Bashar said during our interview in October 2011. Islamist forces in the city of Homs had set up roadblocks and created areas where the security forces dared not enter.

I obtained confirmation of the difficulties facing the Mukhabarat from an unexpected source. I visited a friend of a friend in Tartus, a city on Syria's western coast near Lebanon. One man turned out to be a member of the feared Mukhabarat. He was a staunch supporter of Assad but admitted that even eight months into the uprising, the security forces had lost control of some cities.

"We can only go to parts of Homs in large numbers," he told me.[16] He asked to remain anonymous, fearing possible reprisal by the rebels. He told me the conservative Muslim rebel forces controlled the Sunni neighborhoods at night. They knew where police and secret police agents lived and weren't afraid to assassinate them. He had been based in Homs and admitted that the opposition was so well entrenched it might take a year for the government to prevail. That was a stark admission coming from a member of the security forces. Two years after our conversation, the rebels continued to control parts of Homs.

The shift away from nonviolent protest and toward armed struggle took place gradually. Peaceful protest became increasingly difficult. Security forces surrounded mosques on Friday afternoons to prevent marches. Any attempt to hold a rally was quickly and violently dispersed. Some in the opposition accused the regime of intentionally releasing Islamic extremists from jail in hopes they would take up a divisive, armed struggle.

In July 2011, defectors from Assad's army announced formation of the Free Syrian Army (FSA). Both sides began to engage in targeted assassinations. On October 2, 2011, the government accused extremist members of the opposition of murdering Sariya Hassoun, son of Syria's grand mufti, the country's most important Sunni religious leader. A few days later on October 7, a government hit squad murdered Syrian Kurdish leader Mashaal Tammo.

In November, the FSA attacked the Harasta Air Force Intelligence Base near Damascus, the first such major battle. By December armed rebels bombed an important security complex in Kafr Soueah Square in Damascus, killing both soldiers and innocent civilians. As armed struggle quickly replaced mass demonstrations, political leadership of the uprising also changed. Political Islam came to the fore. The uprising was becoming a civil war.

In current discourse in the United States, Islam is often equated with extremism and terrorism. "Not all Muslims are terrorists," goes the often repeated maxim, "but all terrorists are Muslims."[17] My, how we show our ignorance. Terrorist tactics have a long history that has nothing to do with Islam. The first modern-day suicide bomber detonated a hand grenade to kill the Russian czar in 1881. The assassin was Christian. The first car bomb was exploded by extremist Zionists fighting the British occupation of Palestine before 1948. The same group, known as *Lechi* or the Stern Gang, also had the distinction of mailing the first letter bombs in an attempt to kill members of the British cabinet.[18] The list goes on. But you get the idea.

Islam is a religion of peace, as is Christianity, Judaism, and all the religions I know of. Some extremists in the United States have murdered abortion doctors or blown up a federal building in the name of Christianity, but we know their actions are anti-Christian. And so it is with political Islam. Opportunist leaders try to seize power quoting passages from the Koran, but their actions are anti-Islamic. To analyze Islamic extremists, we must focus on their politics, not their religious rhetoric. So I describe them using political terms such as *progressive, conservative,* and *ultra-right-wing.* I stay away from the term *moderate,* which in translation usually means "acceptable to the United States."

For many years, the Muslim Brotherhood seemed to be the most influential opposition group in Syria. But during the first weeks of the uprising, the brotherhood was caught with its pants down. Its leaders had been jailed or driven into exile during the harsh government repression of the 1980s. The brotherhood was out of touch with the younger generation, whose members spearheaded the events in early 2011. It initially opposed the uprising as being too provocative and likely to fail.

"At the start of the uprising, the brotherhood appeared hesitant to become involved in the conflict," wrote Aron Lund in a publication by the Carnegie Endowment for International Peace. "This probably reflected doubts about the uprising's chances of success, an awareness of the brotherhood's own weakness inside Syria, and a deliberate choice to maintain a low profile while the regime was trying to portray the revolution as led by Islamists."[19]

The brotherhood had transformed itself politically in the 1990s in an effort to reverse its isolation inside Syria and to gain international legitimacy. It wanted to show that it wasn't a terrorist group— particularly after the events of September 11, 2001. It called for Syria to be ruled as a Muslim nation under a modern form of Shariah (Islamic) law but emphasized the need for elections, human rights, and pluralism.[20] Its 2004 program rejected a strategy of armed struggle and called for peaceful political change.

The group's leader at the time, Ali Sadreddine al-Bayanouni, cultivated a modernist image. For example, he disagreed politically with the Egyptian Muslim Brotherhood when it declared that neither a woman nor a Coptic Christian could become president of Egypt. And he rejected the idea of forming a religious council to determine if secular laws adhered to Shariah. At the same time, the brotherhood maintained conservative cultural views on alcohol, women's rights, and popular entertainment. As Arab nationalists, its leaders refused to recognize the rights of Kurds or Assyrians, two minorities with their own particular demands.

The brotherhood leaders hoped to return to Syria as a tolerated opposition group, which made them initially reluctant to endorse the uprising. As the rebellion gathered steam and appeared that it could topple Assad, however, the brotherhood shifted course. In March 2011, it published the Ten Point Pledge and Charter aimed at showing Syrians and the Western powers that it could govern Syria. It mentioned Islam only in the preamble as being a guide. It called for an elected civil state, a pluralist political system, and no discrimination based on religion. Mohammad Farouk Tayfour, a brotherhood deputy, said, "The brotherhood will not monopolize power in the political arena and in managing the coming period."[21]

Brotherhood leaders had cultivated extensive ties internationally, particularly with the Islamist government of Turkey. Those leaders became major players in the formation of the Syrian National Council based in Istanbul. The SNC, which had the backing of the United States and its allies, was supposed to be a civilian coalition representing the entire opposition. As the Assad regime continued its repression and other groups took up armed struggle, the brotherhood created an armed militia, the Commission of the Revolution's Shields, in May 2012. But they failed to gain traction inside the country.

Omar Mushaweh, a brotherhood leader living in Istanbul, told me that his group favored a moderate version of Shariah law. He said the new Syria would model itself on modern Turkey, which is governed by a parliamentary system and respects different religions. Minority and women's rights would be protected, he argued. "We will not force women to wear the *hijab* [head covering]," he said. "It will be by choice."[22]

Some secular Syrians don't trust the brotherhood's rhetoric, however. Miral Bioredda, the LCC leader we met earlier, told me that the "Islamists say they want a democratic country, but I don't believe them."[23] But the ex-bodyguard calling himself Bashar typified the views of many when he acknowledged that the Muslim Brotherhood no longer called for a conservative, Islamic state as they did during the 1980s. "They favor a civic [nonreligious] state," he told me. "People won't accept their old, extremist ideology."[24] The brotherhood continued to be a significant player in the Syrian opposition. Meanwhile, conditions were changing rapidly inside Syria as people took up arms. Let's take a look at some of the major armed groups.

In July 2011, seven Syrian army defectors publically announced the formation of the Free Syrian Army (FSA). In the following months, the FSA tried to bring under its wing the disparate militias springing up throughout the country. The FSA became the armed wing of the SNC and its successor group, the National Coalition for Revolutionary and Opposition Forces.

The United States, Turkey, Saudi Arabia, and Qatar backed the FSA. The State Department officially allocated $15 million to provide nonlethal aid, such as medical supplies and communications equipment, although the actual figure was much higher (see chapter 11). The "nonlethal" category continued to expand until it included pickup trucks, night-vision goggles, and flak vests—a fact exposed when an FSA depot was looted in December 2013.[25]

The FSA had some initial successes. Affiliated militias captured some towns in the northeast, near the Turkish border. They also took control of towns in central Syria around Homs and Aleppo. But it was difficult to assess the actual popular support for the FSA because local militias frequently changed affiliation. We know for sure that ultra-conservative groups grew in strength as the FSA declined.

By the spring of 2012, the FSA faced a crisis. Rebels in the field complained that they lacked effective weapons, such as shoulder-fired missiles capable of bringing down aircraft. The CIA refused to provide such weapons, fearing they would fall into the hands of extremist groups. The CIA and Turkish authorities established a control room in Istanbul to coordinate military activities and funnel arms to favored groups. By controlling the arms flow, the United States hoped to direct the rebellion politically and lessen the influence of the al-Qaeda affiliate Jabhat al-Nusra. The CIA still didn't provide Stinger missiles but did improve the quality of assault rifles, sniper rifles, RPGs, and ammo (see chapter 11).

In December 2012 the Free Syrian Army announced the formation of the Supreme Military Council (SMC), which would try to coordinate all the militias in Syria. It was led by Brigadier General Salim Idris. Idris's plain features and receding hairline make him look more like a professor than a general. That's because he's both. His father was a farmer when Idris was born in 1958 in Mubarakiyah, south of Homs. Idris entered the Syrian army, was sent to study in East Germany, and returned with a PhD to become a professor at the Academy of Military Engineering in Aleppo. He taught there for twenty years and became dean. Idris defected to the rebels in July 2012.

In many ways, Idris fit the profile of a pro–United States strongman who could eventually rule Syria. He was a military man who promised free elections, opposed extremist rebels, and remained vague about what kind of government would replace Assad. He courted some powerful American friends. Senator John McCain (R-AZ) sneaked across the Lebanese border into rebel-held Syria and met with Idris. "General Idris and his fighters share many of our interests and values," the senator said later in a statement.[26] Critics disparaged Idris's fighting skills, noting that he showed more prowess meeting with foreign donors than he displayed on the battlefields of Syria.[27] As head of the SMC, Idris immediately faced problems.

The CIA and Turkey wanted to focus training on defecting Assad's soldiers. Conservative Islamists considered the defectors traitors if they worked with the CIA. The SMC, which was supposed to be a general command, failed to incorporate the other major armed groups. The SMC became just one more fighting group. "Every time they set up a council to oversee the war effort, it turns into a militia," wrote one rebel in Deir Ezzor.[28]

Another group, Jaysh al-Islam (Army of Islam), formed from the September 2013 merger of dozens of smaller militias, mostly in the Damascus area. It was led by Zahran Alloush, son of Sheikh Abdullah Mohammed Alloush, a well-known Saudi-based religious scholar. The Assad regime released the younger Alloush from jail at the beginning of the uprising, along with other ultraconservative political prisoners. Al-Islam received funding from Saudi Arabia.[29]

Leaders of al-Islam claimed to be carrying out the principles of Islam. Military decisions are made by a *shura* (council) consisting of Shariah law specialists, military officers, and Alloush.[30] Al-Islam is one of the extremist groups claiming that Syria is being overrun by Iran and Shia Muslims. In a YouTube video, Alloush said, "The jihadists will wash the filth of the *rafida* [a slur used to describe Shia] from Greater Syria, they will wash it forever, if Allah wills it."[31] Al-Islam refused to negotiate with the Assad regime, a stand consistent with other ultraconservative groups. Al-Islam flies the black flag of jihad rather than the Syrian flag.[32] At the end of 2013, al-Islam helped form the Islamic Front.

Al-Islam and al-Nusra participated in a massacre of dozens of civilians in Adra, an industrial city just outside Damascus. In December 2013, both groups rounded up Alawites, Druze, and other minorities to execute them with pistol shots and beheadings, claiming they were Assad supporters. "Zahran Alloush has committed a massacre," one antiregime activist told Reuters.[33]

Ahrar al-Sham (Islamic Movement of the Free Men of the Levant) was one of the largest militias in Syria. In this context, *Levant* refers to Syria and Lebanon. Founded in 2011 by ultraconservative former political prisoners, it operated mainly in the Idlib Governate (province) in northwestern Syria next to the Turkish border. It also had fighters in the cities of Hama and Aleppo. Al-Sham is led by Hassan Aboud. Another leader, Abu Khalid al-Suri, admitted to being a longtime member of al-Qaeda.

Al-Sham sought to overthrow the Assad regime and establish a Sunni Islamic state. It differed from some of the other ultraconservatives by acknowledging that Syrians weren't currently willing to accept such a state. So al-Sham urged a go-slow approach. It initially cooperated with the SMC but later broke with General Idris and the US-backed militias.

As an indication of how complicated on-the-ground alliances became, some wealthy members of the Muslim Brotherhood funded al-Sham. That helped create a link between the two groups. But al-Sham also received funding from ultra-right-wing religious leaders in Kuwait, Saudi Arabia, and Qatar. By 2012 al-Sham broke with the brotherhood politically and ideologically.[34]

In November 2013, al-Sham joined with other conservative groups to form the Islamic Front, which opposed both the SMC/FSA and the al-Qaeda-affiliated groups al-Nusra and the Islamic State of Iraq and al-Sham. The Islamic Front charter rejected a representative parliamentary system, saying only "God is sovereign." The charter proclaimed that secularism is "contradictory to Islam."[35] By early 2014 the front emerged as one of the strongest rebel alliances and may have caused the Obama administration to recalculate its strategy in Syria (see next chapter).

Another rebel group, Jabhat al-Nusra (The Support Front for the People of the Levant), was initially funded and armed by an al-Qaeda affiliate in Iraq, although that was kept secret at the time. The Islamic State of Iraq, also known as al-Qaeda in Iraq, helped form al-Nusra in an effort to expand its influence into Syria. But al-Qaeda operates more like a franchise system than a centrally controlled group, and as we'll see below, even al-Qaeda's top leader can't control the franchises.

Al-Nusra is led by Abu Mohammad al-Jolani, who had fought against both the United States and the Nouri al-Maliki government in Iraq. Rather than support a parliamentary system, al-Nusra advocated a religious regime that would implement a harsh interpretation of Shariah. Al-Nusra "has a plan to consult Muslim scholars to establish the rule of Islamic law," Jolani told the *New York Times* "We want the Islamic Shariah to prevail."[36] An al-Nusra spokesperson was even more explicit during an interview with CNN: "In the period after the regime falls, our main goal is to create an Islamic state that is ruled by the Koran," he said. "It can have civilian institutions, but not democracy."[37]

In December 2012, the US State Department put al-Nusra on its list of terrorist organizations because of its ties to al-Qaeda. Other rebel groups, including those backed by the United States, strongly objected, arguing that al-Nusra played an important military role in the fight against the regime. The SMC-affiliated militias continued to cooperate with al-Nusra in the field.

But within less than a year, rebel criticisms of al-Nusra began to surface publically. In May of 2013, Ahrar al-Sham issued a statement, posted on its webpage, criticizing al-Nusra for sectarianism and weakening the rebel cause by openly affiliating with al-Qaeda. Al-Sham said al-Nusra was going too fast toward creating an Islamic state and lacked the legitimacy to provide Islamic rule. The statement "is written in the tone of honest advise for an ally who has committed a damaging mistake," according to Syria expert Aron Lund.[38] Within a few months, al-Sham broke with al-Nusra altogether.

By far the most extreme of the major Islamist groups is the Islamic State of Iraq and al-Sham (ISIS), sometimes translated as Islamic State of Iraq in the Levant (known as *Da'aash* in Arabic). It's headed by an Iraqi rebel named Abu Bakr al-Baghdadi and was initially affiliated with al-Qaeda. The group began in 2007 in Iraq as part of the ultra-right-wing movement opposed to the United States occupation of Iraq but also calling for an Islamic state. Al-Qaeda in Iraq (ISI), as it was then known, was largely defeated during the US-Iraqi "surge" in 2007 and 2008. ISI had alienated itself from fellow Sunnis by killing and torturing other anti-US rebels with whom it disagreed. The US State Department labeled Baghdadi a "Global Terrorist" in 2011 and offered $10 million for his capture.

After the US Army withdrew from Iraq in 2011, the Maliki government in Baghdad alienated many Sunni groups by trying to monopolize power. ISI became reinvigorated. When the Syrian uprising turned toward armed struggle in 2012, ISI set up shop on both sides of the porous Iraq–Syria border and changed its name to ISIS.

ISIS had some military successes against the Syrian army. Using fighters and weapons smuggled from Iraq, it was able to capture several towns. It played an important role in overrunning the Mennagh military airport outside Aleppo in August 2013 after a nine-month siege. ISIS received financing from wealthy gulf donors; from businessmen in Anbar, Iraq; from border tolls; and by "taxing" Syrians in areas under its control. ISIS provided protection to Christians, for example, provided they paid money to ISIS leaders.

In April 2013 Baghdadi formally announced the existence of ISIS and claimed that he had merged al-Nusra and ISIS, which would have created one of the largest political-military groups in Syria. Both ISIS and al-Nusra called for a transnational Islamic state governed by a strict interpretation of Shariah law. Both have reputations for opposing criminality and corruption, unlike some of the SMC brigades. ISIS tried to win hearts and minds by, for example, establishing bakeries and selling bread at below black-market prices.

But al-Nusra criticized ISIS's sectarianism and its desire to dominate the entire movement. ISIS saw itself as an established state on the way to forming a united Muslim caliphate in Syria and Iraq, not just one rebel group among many. Al-Nusra took a slower approach, realizing that it had to build support over time to achieve the same goals. Baghdadi's announcement of the proposed ISIS–al-Nusra merger reflected the arrogance and sectarianism of ISIS. "It is time to announce to the Levantine people and the whole world that Jabhat al-Nusra is merely an extension and part of the Islamic State of Iraq," Baghdadi said.[39]

Rifts appeared immediately as al-Nusra continued to use its own name and fight under its own banner. Al-Qaeda leader Ayman al-Zawahri sided with al-Nusra and criticized ISIS. By the end of the year, the proposed merger had fallen apart as al-Nusra and other rebels took up arms against ISIS. In February 2014, Zawahri formalized the split by cutting ties completely with ISIS.[40]

Both al-Nusra and ISIS attracted a large number of foreign fighters, but ISIS has the reputation for being almost exclusively composed of foreigners. While the leaders and special forces are largely foreign, ISIS foot soldiers are mostly Syrian. Nevertheless, ISIS appeared to be fighting fellow rebels more than the Assad regime. In various northern and central cities, as well as in Aleppo, ISIS seized the headquarters of other rebel groups. It detained, tortured, and murdered some of the leaders.

Meanwhile, ISIS stepped up activity in Iraq. It took advantage of the increased unpopularity of Prime Minister Nouri al-Maliki and seized the city of Fallujah. In June 2014, ISIS, along with Sunni allies, took over the city of Mosul and several crossing points near the Syrian and Jordanian borders. ISIS changed its name yet again, this time to the Islamic State (IS), and declared the existence of an Islamic caliphate that stretched from Syria to Iraq. The IS continued its sectarian attacks on other rebels in Syria, insisting that they join IS as the only legitimate revolutionary group. Syria's internecine fighting and extreme right-wing ideology was hurting the rebel cause. But nothing would impact the rebel movement like the chemical-weapons controversy, as we'll see in the next chapter.

CHAPTER 6

CHEMICAL WEAPONS, MILITARY OFFENSIVES, AND STALEMATE

The videos shocked the world. Hundreds of bodies lay on the floor of makeshift morgues in and around the town of Al Ghouta on the southeastern outskirts of Damascus. Early in the morning of August 21, 2013, sarin gas killed hundreds of men, women, and children. Survivors reported seeing rockets hitting the ground and then spewing out a strange, green mist. Victims suffered horrible deaths, going into spasms and gasping for air. The videos, produced by the rebels, blamed the Syrian army.

The world reacted with anger and indignation. The Obama administration strongly condemned the Assad regime and over the next few weeks prepared to bomb Syria in retaliation. The Syrians had crossed the "red line" created by the administration on the use of weapons of mass destruction. The rebels hoped the American bombing raids would destroy Assad's air force and lead to an opposition victory.[1]

But not everyone accepted the administration's claims. The Assad regime argued that the rebels, not the government, had fired the chemical weapons in order to provoke a US assault on Damascus. UN weapons inspectors eventually issued two reports on the use of chemical weapons. Investigative reporters cast doubts on some of the Obama administration's claims. The controversy deepened over time.

So the question remained: Who used chemical weapons and why? First, the official US government version.

On August 30, the White House issued a "government assessment" about the Al Ghouta attack. It stated that the sarin gas killed

101

1,429 people, including 426 children. The White House stated that the Syrian military had used chemical weapons previously. "This assessment is based on multiple streams of information including reporting of Syrian officials planning and executing chemical weapons attacks and laboratory analysis of physiological samples obtained from a number of individuals, which revealed exposure to sarin."[2] The statement went on to say, "We assess that the opposition has not used chemical weapons. We assess that the regime's frustration with its inability to secure large portions of Damascus may have contributed to its decision to use chemical weapons on August 21."

As part of a coordinated effort to sway public opinion, Secretary of State John Kerry gave a series of talks and press conferences. He left no doubt that US intelligence had revealed who was responsible for the sarin attack. "We know where the rockets were launched from and at what time," Kerry said. "We know where they landed and when. We know rockets came only from regime-controlled areas and went only to opposition-controlled or contested neighborhoods."[3]

The US position seemed to gather strength when Human Rights Watch and the *New York Times* indicated they had independently analyzed information that calculated the trajectory of the rockets that landed in the Al Ghouta area. Rick Gladstone and C. J. Chivers of the *Times* wrote, "When plotted and marked independently on maps by analysts from Human Rights Watch and by the *New York Times*, the United Nations data from two widely scattered impact sites pointed directly to a Syrian military complex."[4]

The next day, the *Times* ran an even more detailed analysis showing the rockets were fired from a military complex solidly under government control, some nine kilometers from the Al Ghouta sites. Chivers wrote that the rockets were fired from Mount Qasioun, which he described as "Damascus's most prominent military position. . . . It is also a complex inseparably linked to the Assad family's rule." The article held the top forces of the regime responsible for the attack and discounted the possibility that a rogue officer or a rebel mole carried it out.[5]

Within weeks, the US version of events began to fall apart. First was the matter of civilian deaths. The White House figure of 1,429, a strangely precise number for estimating mass deaths, was nearly three times the size of the highest estimates of other reliable sources. Doctors Without Borders, which had medical personnel on the ground in Al Ghouta, estimated 355 deaths.[6] British intelligence indicated 350, and the pro-opposition Syrian Observatory for Human Rights counted 502.[7] Only the Syrian National Coalition, the opposition group backed by Western powers, agreed with the US estimate. But when pressed by the Associated Press for a list of names, it could come up with only 395.[8]

Ake Sellstrom, head of the UN chemical-weapons inspection team, said the rebels significantly exaggerated the number of dead and injured treated in Al Ghouta hospitals. "We saw the capability of those hospitals, and it is impossible that they could have turned over the amount of people that they claim they did."[9] The discrepancy was explained when the *Wall Street Journal* revealed that US intelligence had scanned the rebel videos with face recognition software to count the number of dead.[10] They made no on-scene investigation.

Second, the White House statement was a "government assessment," not an intelligence assessment or National Intelligence Estimate (NIE). The difference is significant. An NIE, for example, would contain dissenting opinions. And, according to several investigative reports, there *was* dissent. Some intelligence officers thought the report was an effort to help the administration save face for having failed to act sooner. One former intelligence officer told longtime *New Yorker* writer and famed investigative reporter Seymour Hersh that the Obama administration altered intelligence to make it look as if it was collected in real time. In fact, it was retrieved days later. In the *London Review of Books*, Hersh quoted the intelligence officer:

> The distortion, he said, reminded him of the 1964 Gulf of Tonkin incident, when the Johnson administration reversed the sequence of National Security Agency intercepts to justify one of the early bombings of North Vietnam. The same official said there was immense frustration inside the military and intelligence bureaucracy: "The guys are throwing their hands in the air and saying, 'How can we help

this guy'—Obama—'when he and his cronies in the White House make up the intelligence as they go along?'"[11]

Third, serious questions arose about the White House and Kerry statements that the sarin rockets were fired from the heart of Assad-controlled Damascus. The *New York Times* and Human Rights Watch analyses assumed that the rockets were fired from over nine kilometers away. But a report published by missile experts showed otherwise. Richard Lloyd is a former UN weapons inspector and currently works at Tesla Labs in Arlington, Virginia. Theodore A. Postol is a professor of science, technology, and national security policy at the Massachusetts Institute of Technology in Boston. They analyzed the data presented by the UN inspectors concerning the sarin-laden rockets. They concluded that the rockets would have a maximum range of two kilometers. When asked about this issue at a press conference, Chief UN chemical-weapons inspector Ake Sellstrom concurred that the two-kilometer range would be a "fair guess."[12] He later indicated the rockets could have been fired as close as one kilometer.[13]

Lloyd and Postol superimposed the two kilometer rocket range onto the White House maps. Their report said, "These munitions could not possibly have been fired at east Ghouta from the 'heart,' or from the eastern edge, of the Syrian government-controlled area shown in the intelligence map published by the White House on August 30, 2013."[14]

The report noted that these "improvised artillery rockets" could have been constructed by the army or the rebels. "The indigenous chemical munition could be manufactured by anyone who has access to a machine shop with modest capabilities, that is, the claim is incorrect that only the Syrian government could manufacture the munition." The *New York Times* wrote about the report and noted the much shorter range but never retracted its erroneous reports that the rockets must have been fired from the Mount Qasioun military complex.[15]

Meanwhile, other investigative reporters were tracking down the origins of the *Grads*, the two guided rockets used in the chemical attack. Robert Fisk, veteran Middle East correspondent for the London *Inde-*

pendent, discovered that the Grads were apparently made in the Soviet Union in 1967. According to Fisk's Russian sources, the Soviets sold this batch of Grads to Yemen, Egypt, and Libya—but not Syria. The Russians didn't provide documentation, however.[16] Right-wing Islamist groups in Libya have actively supported al-Qaeda-affiliated groups in Syria. So it is possible that al-Nusra or ISIS received the rockets and chemicals from Libya.

Poking holes in the US government's case doesn't automatically mean the rebels were responsible, however. Eliot Higgins, a self-taught, British weapons expert who writes the *Brown Moses Blog*, said the Al Ghouta massacre was beyond the capability of a group like al-Nusra. Producing over fifty gallons of liquid sarin and loading it into rockets in the midst of a war zone is a massive undertaking. It requires huge amounts of specialized precursor chemicals and produces a toxic acid runoff. "Where is this factory?" he wrote. "Where is the waste stream? Where are the dozens of skilled people—not just one al-Qaeda member—needed to produce this amount of material?"[17]

Were the rebels militarily capable and politically willing to carry out a massive war crime against their own supporters? To find out, we must first take a look at sarin itself.

Sarin is a nerve agent first developed in 1938 Germany as a pesticide. The Nazis soon realized it was also a potent chemical weapon. In liquid or gaseous form, it can be deadly on contact. Sarin is a "clear, color-less, and tasteless liquid that has no odor in its pure form," according to the Centers for Disease Control and Prevention. But when mixed in battlefield conditions, in which the chemical precursors become con-taminated, sarin may produce an odor and a color. The CDC goes on to explain, "because it evaporates so quickly, Sarin presents an imme-diate but short-lived threat."[18]

Iraq deployed sarin as a chemical weapon during the 1980–1988 Iran-Iraq War. A right-wing Japanese religious cult used sarin in the infamous Tokyo subway attacks of 1994–1995.[19] Sarin is quite vola-tile and can't be stored for very long because it can corrode storage containers and warheads. So, sarin precursor chemicals are stored separately and then mixed prior to use. They can be mixed in a lab by trained technicians. Mixing in the battlefield can be very dangerous to both the technician and anyone nearby.[20] The Syrian army has admitted having sarin precursors in large quantities. Some extremist rebel groups may have had some as well.

I spent some time in Damascus interviewing government officials and experts about the chemical-weapons issue. The Syrians presented a version of events sharply at odds with the US government narrative. On March 19, 2013, rebels used sarin against a progovernment neighborhood in the village of Khan Al Asal near Aleppo, according to Dr. Bassam Barakat, a medical doctor and progovernment political consultant. He told me that blood samples and other physical evidence were sent to Russia for analysis. Officials there wrote a one-hundred-page report indicating rebel use of sarin and delivered it to the United Nations, but neither party ever made it public. According to Barakat, the Russians confirmed that the sarin had originally come from the chemical stockpiles of Libyan dictator Muammar Kaddafi, who had been supplied by the old Soviet Union. Extremists in Libya shipped the sarin chemical precursors to Turkey, where they were then smuggled across the border into Syria, according to Barakat.[21] Assad officials were so confident that they could prove the rebels had used the poison gas, they allowed UN chemical-weapons inspectors into Syria to investigate, but only after months of delay.

The final UN chemical-weapons report confirmed a number of points in the Syrian government version. Rebels were shelling Khan Al Asal prior to the chemical attack. At about 7:00 a.m., a munition hit the area some three hundred meters from a government checkpoint. The UN report indicated, "The air stood still and witnesses described a yellowish-green mist in the air and a pungent and strong sulfur-like smell. . . . The witnesses reported seeing people scratching their faces and bodies. They also observed people lying in the streets, some unconscious, some having convulsions and foaming from the mouth."[22]

The UN inspectors concluded that Khan Al Asal had been attacked with sarin. The UN inspection team was unable to visit the town due to security concerns but was able to interview eyewitnesses and take medical samples of residents who had come to Damascus. A Syrian government report indicated that twenty people died from the sarin attack and 124 were injured. The UN report noted that some witnesses said the gas was from a helicopter while others said it was a munition explosion. The UN report did not indicate who was responsible for this or any other chemical attack.

Sergey Batsanov, a former Russian ambassador and director of special projects at the Organization for the Prohibition of Chemical Weapons in Geneva, said delivery by helicopter seemed unlikely. The Syrian army would have had to install special spray tanks and put pilots in protective clothing. "I very much doubt it was delivered by helicopter," he told me. "It makes no sense."[23]

Those are the facts. Now the interpretation. It's been my experience that if something doesn't make sense politically, it doesn't make sense militarily. In this case, why would the Syrian army attack its own village? If it was seeking to discredit the rebels, why kill and injure so many of its own soldiers and civilians? On the other hand, the rebels—particularly extremists of al-Nusra and ISIS—would gain a lot from the use of chemical weapons. They would both kill the enemy, which included pro-Assad civilians, and discredit the Assad regime by blaming it for the attack.

One high UN official admitted that the government was not responsible for Khan Al Asal. Carla del Ponte told a Swiss TV interviewer, referring to the Asal incident, "This was use on the part of the opposition, the rebels, not by the government authorities."[24] Del Ponte was a member of the UN Independent Commission of Inquiry on Syria and a former war-crimes prosecutor for the International Criminal Tribunal for the former Yugoslavia. After her initial statement, she and other members of the commission of inquiry stopped commenting.

Then, in late May, Turkish newspapers reported that suspected members of al-Nusra were arrested carrying two kilograms of sarin with plans to attack the US Air Force base at Adana, Turkey.[25] By the time the case came to trial, however, the Turkish government did not prosecute the men for possessing sarin. There's no public record on why prosecutors didn't pursue the chemical-weapons issue.

In another incident in late May, Iraqi authorities arrested five alleged members of ISI, also known as al-Qaeda in Iraq, for building two labs to manufacture sarin and mustard gas. At a press conference, the police displayed lab equipment and weapons.[26] ISI had close ties with al-Nusra at the time and was also carrying out its own activities inside Syria.

US intelligence likely knew about the al-Nusra/ISI chemical-weapons capability. F. Michael Maloof wrote that he was given a classified document from the army's National Ground Intelligence Center. "The document says sarin from al-Qaeda in Iraq made its way into Turkey and that while some was seized, more could have been used in an attack last March on civilians and Syrian military soldiers in Aleppo [Khan Al Asal]."[27] Maloof is a former security-policy analyst in the office of the secretary of defense and a writer for the right-wing website *World-NetDaily*. He's a controversial character, having been associated with the Bush-era neocons and stripped of his security clearance.[28] But his right-wing contacts may well have supplied highly pertinent information.

Maloof wrote that the ISI had made a "bench-scale" form of sarin, that is, a small, homemade batch. He wrote, "Turkish security forces discovered a two-kilogram cylinder with sarin gas while searching homes of Syrian militants from the al-Qaeda-linked Jabhat al-Nusra Front following their initial detention."[29] Seymour Hersh also reported that US intelligence agencies knew of the rebels' chemical-weapons capabilities.[30]

Already by late May 2013, the CIA had briefed the Obama administration on al-Nusra and its work with sarin and had sent alarming reports that another Sunni fundamentalist group active in Syria, al-Qaeda in Iraq (ISI), also understood the science of producing sarin. At the time, al-Nusra was operating in areas close to Damascus, including eastern Ghouta. An intelligence document issued in midsummer dealt extensively with Ziyaad Tariq Ahmed, a chemical-weapons expert formerly of the Iraqi military who was said to have moved into Syria and to be operating in eastern Ghouta. The consultant (Hersh's unnamed source) told me that Tariq had been identified "as an al-Nusra guy with a track record of making mustard gas in Iraq and someone who is implicated in making and using sarin." He is regarded as a high-profile target by the American military.[31]

Weapons expert Eliot Higgins believed the Syrian army was responsible for the Al Ghouta attack, but the rebels may have used limited amounts of sarin in Khan Al Asal. The opposition "could have acquired small amounts of sarin," he wrote. "The regime recently stated that they had lost some [sarin] from Aleppo Airport. . . . The Khan Al Asal attack is different to the others, as it could be concluded that the opposition is responsible." He concluded with a warning. "If the opposition is responsible for Khan Al Asal, then we all need to be on our guard, because if the opposition has sarin, so does AQ [al-Qaeda] and ISIS, and this would now be a global threat which we all need to be resilient against."[32]

So it appears that al-Qaeda-affiliated rebels had the expertise and capability to carry out small-scale chemical attacks. In Khan Al Asal they may well have deployed sarin against the Syrian army and its supporters. The Syrians charge there was another, virtually unknown chemical-weapons attack in May 2013. Dr. Bassam Barakat described a sarin attack on an army checkpoint near the Scientific Studies and Research Center in Damascus, an area near Hamish Hospital. Barakat said a rebel mortar shell packed with sarin hit dozens of Syrian soldiers. Twenty died and one hundred were injured, according to Barakat.[33]

Syrian minister of justice Najm al-Ahmad confirmed the attack. "The soldiers died of suffocation," he told me.[34] He and Barakat argued that the Syrian army wouldn't use chemical gas against its own soldiers, and therefore the rebels had to be responsible. The incident was briefly reported on Syrian TV at the time but not mentioned further. I asked both men why such a horrific attack was not more widely publicized by the Syrian government. After all, an attack of such magnitude against government soldiers would point suspicion directly at the rebels. As far as I can tell, the incident was never reported to the United Nations and certainly wasn't included in the inspector's reports.

I became curious about one detail. The dead and injured soldiers were found at a checkpoint near the Scientific and Research Center, reportedly one of the top labs for creating sarin and other chemical weapons. Could an accident have happened at the center, causing the death and injuries? Of course, Syrian authorities deny it.

The United Nations reported on another sarin incident in Jobar, a town outside Damascus, on August 24, 2013, three days after the Al Ghouta attack. Because the UN inspectors were already in Damascus, they were able to conduct a firsthand investigation. According to the final UN report, ten soldiers were clearing an area when an improvised explosive device detonated, "releasing a very badly smelling gas." The United Nations took blood samples, and one of the soldiers tested positive for sarin.

The United Nations reported a total of seven alleged chemical-weapons incidents. Inspectors were unable to collect enough data in some cases. Incidents included attacks on both rebel and progovernment areas. In one incident, a fifty-two-year-old woman living in a rebel area was taken to Turkey and later died. An autopsy by UN and Turkish doctors indicated she had been exposed to sarin. So what does this mixed record of likely responsibility mean for the massive attack on Al Ghouta?

The Al Ghouta victims lived in rebel-controlled areas in towns to the southeast of Damascus. Virtually all the victims were treated in rebel-controlled medical facilities, not government hospitals. The UN inspectors were able to examine the Al Ghouta area in a timely manner. They collected contaminated soil, took medical samples from victims, and located at least some of the munitions used. The United Nations concluded that without doubt victims had been exposed to sarin. The gas was delivered by guided rockets and artillery-fired rockets. The guided rockets, a modified version of an old Soviet Grad, were launched independently. The other munitions, which have tail fins, are fired from artillery but have no independent guidance system.

UN inspectors found five munitions carrying sarin that hit the Al Ghouta area. Each of the two Grads were capable of carrying thirteen gallons of sarin, and three artillery-launched rockets could carry eleven to sixteen gallons each.[35] If those figures are correct, and the munitions were filled to capacity, whomever fired the rockets had to either transport the sarin from a sophisticated lab or mix and load fifty-seven to seventy gallons of liquid sarin in battlefield conditions, which is no small task. London-based chemical-weapons expert Dan Kaszeta told me that such a batch of sarin would require a huge amount of "precursor chemicals and produce a significant waste stream."[36] An organized army with proper facilities and trained technicians seemed to be the likely culprit. On the other hand, if UN inspector Sellstrom, as well as professors from MIT and Tesla Labs, are correct on the rocket trajectory, the rockets were fired from areas very near to or under rebel control.

And the political question remains: Why would Assad be stupid enough to launch a major chemical attack just days after UN inspectors entered Damascus? He may be evil, but he's not stupid. Justice Minister Ahmad told me, "When the Syrian army was making progress in Al Ghouta, the terrorists wanted the world to look at another issue, so they used chemicals again."[37]

Pro-Syrian government consultant Barakat claimed that rockets filled with sarin were shipped from Libya and that rebels were trained by special American and British units. He couldn't explain how such a large quantity of sarin precursors could have been prepared for battle. His story then became even more bizarre. He alleged that rebels had kidnapped hundreds of children from the progovernment city of Latakia, brought them to Al Ghouta, and then gassed them as part of a massive disinformation campaign.[38] Those were the children depicted in the videos.

Joshua Landis, director of the Center of Middle Eastern Studies at the University of Oklahoma, offered a possible answer as to why the Syrian army used weapons of mass destruction. He told me that the regime was fighting a desperate battle in the suburbs against rebels who had considerable popular support among Sunni residents. Assad didn't have the troops to retake all the towns, so the army used sarin. "It's like sending the US Marines into Japan in 1945. But the United States used atomic weapons."

He noted that "Syria doesn't operate its military efforts around weapons inspectors. As long as the United States wouldn't invade, he [Assad] could get away with anything." German intelligence intercepted Syrian radio communication indicating the army had been asking Assad to use chemical weapons for many months. Landis said sarin could have been used to "intimidate people: 'We're going to incinerate you.' The generals wanted to do that."[39]

Those German intercepts raised speculation in Europe that the military may have used sarin without Assad's knowledge. One German newspaper indicated that brigade and division commanders had been asking permission to use chemical weapons for four and a half months before the Ghouta incident.[40] No other sources confirmed this theory, however.

Investigative reporter Gareth Porter offered another explanation. He argued that much less sarin was used than commonly thought. The rebels could have diluted sarin with water. So they would only have had to manufacture as little as fifteen gallons of sarin. Some victims showed symptoms inconsistent with sarin poisoning, possibly caused by tear gas or smoke grenades. Under Porter's theory, extremist rebels didn't have to transport dozens of gallons of sarin from Turkey to Al Ghouta. "The new information suggests a much less lethal attack with munitions that were less effective and perhaps even using much less sarin than was initially assumed," he wrote.[41]

So what conclusions can we draw? Both sides quite possibly used sarin. Both sides lied and manipulated evidence. At a minimum, the Obama administration exaggerated its case to justify a military attack on Syria. At worst, the White House fabricated intelligence. Bottom line: no one has yet presented convincing evidence of who perpetrated the horrific Al Ghouta attack. But one thing remains clear: the Al Ghouta massacre changed US policy, and not in the way President Obama intended.

In early September 2013, the United States was preparing to wage war on Syria using public-relations techniques perfected in Iraq and

Libya. First, exaggerate the threat. The White House claimed the Syrian army had murdered over 1,400 civilians. Second, claim that secret US intelligence, which can't be made public, showed that the Syrian regime is responsible for monumental war crimes. Third, claim the US military action will be limited in scope while secretly hoping it will topple the regime.

In the days following Al Ghouta, the administration stepped up arms supplies to the rebels. Arms promised back in April suddenly began to arrive.[42] The aim was to give General Salim Idris more arms and supplies to coordinate attacks when the United States bombed. The White House started a campaign to rustle up international support. The United States sought support from the United Kingdom, a trusted ally in previous military adventures. Conservative Party prime minister David Cameron called members of Parliament back from vacation to vote on a possible Syria attack. Much to his surprise, Parliament voted against any military intervention, which reflected widespread British opposition to yet another Middle East war. The British people well remembered the lies spread by Labor Party prime minister Tony Blair in the run-up to the Iraq War.

The British parliamentary vote represented a huge setback for Obama, leaving France as his only major European backer. Only ten years before, the White House had attacked France for not supporting the Iraq invasion, calling their leaders "surrender monkeys." Now Secretary of State John Kerry proclaimed France as our oldest ally.[43] The Obama administration sought support from the Arab League, which had supported the Western attack on Libya. Not a single member of the league would openly support the United States.

The White House then tried to rally popular support at home. But a Reuters/IPSOS poll taken just a few days after the Al Ghouta massacre, when public opinion should have tilted in the president's favor, showed 60 percent of Americans opposing a UN-sanctioned attack on Syria and only 9 percent backing unilateral US action.[44] With mounting pressure at home, Obama agreed to allow Congress to vote on the issue. Strange political alliances developed. Centrist Democrats who had opposed the Iraq War joined mainstream Republicans in Obama's support. Progressive Democrats joined Libertarian and ultra-right-wing Republicans in opposition. Some of these same Republicans who had vocally supported President George W. Bush's wars suddenly became concerned about unnecessary foreign entanglements. Had Obama actually submitted a war resolution to the House of Representatives, he would likely have lost the vote.

Republican leaders promoted the narrative that Obama had been weak and indecisive. They argued that Obama had bumbled along from the beginning with no real Syria policy. He refused to adequately arm the rebels. He vacillated. He drew a red line at the use of chemical weapons but then wimped out when Assad used sarin in Khan Al Asal.

In reality, Obama had a Syria policy—it just didn't work. The CIA began working with Syria exiles very early but was unable to find or create credible, pro-US rebel groups despite strenuous efforts. The United States formed two different civilian coalitions, backed the Free Syrian Army, and then tried to broaden the FSA by creating a thirty-man directorate called the Supreme Military Council.

As for Obama's "red line," he faced a rather troublesome problem. A month after the Khan Al Asal attack, the White House announced that chemical weapons had been used. Intelligence agencies concluded that the Assad regime was responsible, but only "with varying degrees of confidence."[45] That's intel-speak for "We're not sure." We now know that at least some intelligence officers suspected that al-Nusra or ISIS used sarin in Khan Al Asal. The United States couldn't very well go to war based on a chemical attack perpetrated by the rebels. Neither could it reveal the rebel role, lest it weaken the entire anti-Assad campaign.

So Obama waited, which the Republicans interpreted as dithering. The White House insisted on more definitive proof and ultimately didn't attack that spring. When Obama did announce plans for war, he faced an unprecedented defeat, in part engineered by Republicans.

The administration did manage to make lemonade from a batch of very sour Syrian lemons. Secretary of State John Kerry made an offhanded remark at a press conference in London. When asked what

Assad could do to stop the looming US attack, Kerry replied, "He could turn over every single bit of his chemical weapons to the international community in the next week—turn it over, all of it, without delay, and allow the full and total accounting. . . . But he isn't about to do it, and it can't be done."[46]

The Russians, who had previously discussed that idea with the United States, seized the moment to propose a compromise. They pressured the Assad regime to give up its chemical weapons in return for the White House agreeing not to bomb. Until that moment, the Syrian regime had never officially acknowledged that it even had chemical weapons. Both sides quickly drew up protocols for destroying the chemicals, and the process began amid very difficult wartime conditions.

The United States insisted that all of Syria's chemical weapons be destroyed by mid-2014, an extremely short deadline, particularly since the United States had delayed the destruction of its own chemical stockpiles for years. Under terms of the Chemical Weapons Convention, the United States had agreed to destroy its Cold War–era stockpiles of deadly chemicals by 2012. But in 2013, the United States still had some three thousand tons of sarin, VX, and mustard gas in violation of the convention.[47] Washington unilaterally extended the deadline to destroy the chemicals, indicating it would cost some $35 billion and couldn't be completed until 2023 at the earliest.[48]

The Obama administration hailed Syria's agreement to destroy its chemical stocks as a major breakthrough. But the failure to bomb Syria was criticized by both conservative and ultraconservative rebels. In their view, Washington not only failed to provide adequate weapons, it now had a vested interest in keeping Assad in power, at least until he destroyed the chemical weapons.

In the months leading up to the Al Ghouta attack, the Syrian army had been on the offensive, seeking to turn the tide militarily. Nowhere was that more clear than in Qusayr, a small, dusty town located south of Homs and only a few miles from the Lebanese border. In antiquity, it was the site of the world's largest known chariot battle—between the

Egyptians and the Hittites. The town would soon become famous for yet another battle.

Qusayr had become important to both the rebels and the Syrian army because of its strategic location. Rebels smuggled men and arms into Syria from nearby Lebanon. Al-Nusra and other rebel groups had taken power in Qusayr and nearby towns. The army fought to take them back throughout the spring of 2013. Fighting continued for months with the rebels sandbagging apartments and digging deep tunnels under buildings. The Syrian government bolstered its forces with an estimated 1,200 elite troops from its Lebanese ally, Hezbollah.[49]

After weeks of house-to-house fighting, in June the Syrian army and Hezbollah retook Qusayr in what they described as a turning point in the war. A Hezbollah leader told me the fighting was intense. "The Qusayr battle was very difficult," Hezbollah spokesperson Haj Ghassan admitted during an interview in the eastern Lebanese city of Hermel, just a few miles from Qusayr. "The rebels had built many tunnels and had a lot of reinforcements."[50]

But Qusayr was a pyrrhic victory. Residents had fled. The fierce fighting had destroyed the entire downtown area. Interviewed just one day after the victory, Ghassan admitted the high cost of the win. "It's almost the complete destruction of Qusayr caused by both sides," said Ghassan. Whenever Syrian soldiers came under fire from rebels, he said, they retaliated with tanks and heavy weapons. "The Syrian army destroyed any place that shots came from. Now the Syrian government has to rebuild." The Assad regime boasted that the Qusayr victory would lead quickly to the retaking of Aleppo, Homs, and other important cities. Six months later, those cities remained partially under rebel control, as they had been in June. Qusayr turned out to be just one more battle in a very long war. Another battle turned out to be even more significant, but not for the reasons you might suspect.

With its concrete buildings and rutted streets, Raqqa was the somewhat threadbare capital of the Raqqa Governate in north-central Syria. Before the civil war, its population was about 240,000, but an estimated

800,000 refugees fled there from other areas of the country. In March 2013, a coalition of rebel groups from the Free Syrian Army, Ahrar al-Sham, al-Nusra, and ISIS took control of the city and created a rebel administration. It was the first time rebels had captured a regional capital—a huge defeat for the government. Raqqa residents strongly opposed the Assad regime. At first they welcomed the rebel coalition. One American reporter visited Raqqa in March and noted, "The city was ruled by a coalition of militias, and it was possible to move around as a woman without a headscarf. I met with an Alawite nurse who worked alongside Sunni peers."[51]

Conservative and ultraconservative Islamist groups predominated from the beginning. They had a reputation of incorruptibility and military prowess. Ahrar al-Sham, in particular, included many members from Idlib Governate just a few miles away. The rebels faced many difficult problems governing a large city devastated by civil war. The local economy was in shambles. Farmers were short of seed, and fertilizer from Turkey was very expensive. Some civil servants continued to receive their government salaries; others were not paid for months. The lack of government salaries remained an important issue because the government was a major employer. The government withdrew its troops but continued to bomb civilian areas with missiles and barrel bombs. Dropped from helicopters, those bombs—oil drums filled with shrapnel and explosives—were particularly devastating on civilians.

But the main threat to residents didn't come from the army. ISIS believed it was an Islamic state, not merely a powerful rebel group. In Raqqa and other northern cities, it proclaimed itself as the sole government, implementing a harsh version of Shariah law. It publicly beheaded three Alawites in the Raqqa central square. It forced women to wear the hijab, gender segregated the public schools, and banned smoking. Christians fled the city in fear, and churches were ransacked.[52]

Within two months, ISIS launched military assaults against fellow rebels for not following strict Islamic law. On August 14, ISIS blew up a car bomb in front of the headquarters of a rival rebel group, killing and wounding civilians. ISIS jailed and tortured rebels who disagreed with its policies. By monopolizing power, ISIS alienated Raqqa residents, who then held marches and rallies against them. A number of civil-society activists became ISIS victims.

Father Paolo Dall'Oglio is an Italian Jesuit priest who had lived in Syria for over thirty years. He was well known and respected for frequently participating in intrareligious events. He fasted during Ramadan out of respect for Islam. Unlike some other Christian leaders, Father Paolo opposed the Assad regime and supported the rebels. He spoke at a civil-society rally in Raqqa. On July 29, 2013, he entered ISIS headquarters in Raqqa in an effort to stop the internecine fighting and to find out the whereabouts of kidnapped activists and journalists. Father Paolo was not seen again after that meeting. Many months later, he remained missing, apparently one more ISIS victim.[53]

Anger at ISIS swelled so much that by the end of 2013 and the beginning of 2014, a new ad hoc alliance of Islamist groups fought back against ISIS. For a time they drove ISIS out of Raqqa, but ISIS eventually regained control. Meanwhile, civil-society activists attempted to maintain the gains made after the Assad troops fled. Raqqa was home to civil-society organizations providing emergency relief supplies and small economic programs. Other groups worked to organize teachers, students, and cultural workers.[54]

Rebels fought among themselves in other parts of the country as well. The Western-backed Supreme Military Council (SMC) didn't fare well. On December 6, 2013, the Islamic Front overran the SMC headquarters and warehouses, which were chock-full of US-provided armaments and supplies. SMC leader General Idris was reportedly forced to flee to Turkey from his headquarters in Atmeh, just a few miles inside Syria from the Turkish border. Stolen items included forty pickup trucks, buses, fifty thousand military rations, office and communications equipment, assault rifles, and even tanks. An SMC commander told the *New York Times* that the Islamic Front "stole everything in the headquarters."[55]

Later, Idris claimed it was all a big misunderstanding. He had asked for Islamic Front assistance because ISIS was going to overrun the headquarters. He also claimed to have been in Turkey the whole time.[56] It was never clear, however, if the depot was really threatened by ISIS or if that was an Islamic Front ruse. In any case, the front looted the buildings and never returned the supplies, causing a huge embarrassment for the United States and rebel ally Idris.

In response, the US State Department announced suspension of *nonlethal* aid to rebels operating near the Turkish border, but the aid resumed within a few months. There was no announcement of halting the CIA's *lethal* aid. On February 16, 2014, the SMC commanders held a secret meeting, sacked Idris without prior notice, then replaced him with Brigadier General Abdul-Ilah al-Bashir, considered by the United States to be a "moderate."[57] The SMC didn't even bother to notify General Bashir until after the fact. "I swear to God, no one was in touch with me," Bashir told the *New York Times*.[58]

The Obama administration once again began to revamp a failed policy. The White House was confronted with the waning power of its chosen military ally and the growing strength of ultra-right-wing Islamist groups—ISIS, al-Nusra, and the Islamic Front. One faction in the administration wanted to support the extremist Islamic Front by simply redefining it as "moderate." The United States opened up talks with the Islamic Front and pointedly did not declare it a terrorist organization, as it had with al-Nusra. The front leader has made numerous speeches calling for an Islamic state governed by Shariah and attacking Alawites (see chapter 5).

John Hudson wrote for the online magazine *Foreign Policy* that "US interest in the group [Islamic Front] reflects the bedraggled state of the Supreme Military Council and the desire to keep military pressure on President Bashar al-Assad." A senior congressional aide told him, "The SMC is being reduced to an exile group and the jihadists are taking over."[59]

The Obama administration considered another option. It could temporarily ally with Assad to defeat the extremist rebels and then return to the antiregime fight at a later time. Such a policy had been implicitly implemented when the administration and the Syrian regime agreed to dismantle the chemical weapons. It was in US interests to keep Assad in power at least until the process was completed. And in early February 2014, the opposition groups negotiating with the regime in Geneva quietly dropped their demand for Assad's resignation prior to forming a transitional government representing both sides.[60]

The Obama administration weighed yet another option. It could double down on its support for the SMC and provide pro-US rebels with advanced antiaircraft weaponry. Several media reported that the United States had agreed to spend millions of dollars to pay SMC salaries and had given Saudi Arabia permission to provide rebels with shoulder-fired missiles, which could seriously escalate the war.[61]

An important group was left out of these US machinations: the people of Syria, who want peace and a secular society. I had a chance to meet again in late 2013 with activists I had met two years earlier. Leen, who we met in chapters 1 and 5, still lives in Damascus. She spends much of her time dodging Syrian intelligence and local thugs. Two years ago she was a leading civil-society activist, fighting for a secular, parliamentary system in Syria. "Now the military checkpoints divide up the city, and repression is everywhere," she told me during a clandestine meeting in Damascus. "The civil-society movement doesn't exist here anymore."[62]

Ahmad Bakdouness, another activist I met in 2011, helped smuggle food and medicine to civilians under government attack in Homs. Then he was arrested and brutally tortured. Leen hoped that by making his name public, international pressure could force his release. Mahmoud, whom we met in chapter 5, once an avant-garde playwright and journalist, now fights with the Free Syrian Army in southern Syria. "We've all changed," Leen told me.

Civil-society activists continue to work in some of the rebel-controlled areas. They help provide food, medicine, and social services for the civilian population. And they maintain political ties with international groups that support neither Assad nor extremist rebels. At the end of 2013, one brave activist started a hunger strike in an effort to break the regime sieges imposed on rebel-controlled cities. The Syrian army refused to allow food, medicine, and other essentials into rebel areas.

Qusai Zakarya, a leader in the civilian local council of Moad-amiya, went on a hunger strike. The twenty-eight-year-old Palestinian, born in Damascus, had survived the chemical-weapons attack in the Al Ghouta area. He witnessed the even more devastating impact of conventional bombing, artillery fire, and the starvation siege of his town near Damascus. When Zakarya finished his protest, peace activists and prominent individuals took up the hunger strike in the United States, Europe, and the Middle East in order to help lift the siege on civilians.

The struggle for a peaceful, secular Syria has been diminished, but not crushed. And the civil-society activists had some potential allies in the pro-Assad camp, as we'll see in the next chapter.

CHAPTER 7

WHO SUPPORTS ASSAD?

The sound of artillery fire seemed to come from all directions. Machine-gun fire crackled until late at night. The Syrian army pounded towns held by the rebels on the outskirts of Damascus. The artillery rounds were so common that locals didn't even flinch when they exploded and the sound rumbled across the city. I definitely flinched.

Damascus had changed profoundly since my last reporting visit in 2011—and definitely not for the better. Back then, Damascus was home to frequent rallies and marches calling for freedom. Damascus of late 2013 was a city at war. Concrete barriers blocked formerly busy thoroughfares, and military checkpoints pockmarked the city. "We learned to ignore the sounds of war," said Dr. Bassam Barakat, a medical doctor and progovernment political consultant. He didn't mind the inconvenience of the checkpoints, he said, because they helped maintain security.[1]

Some Syrians agreed with Barakat and continued to support the Assad regime. After three years of civil war, the Syrian military and intelligence services remained loyal to the ruling regime, unlike their counterparts in Tunisia and Egypt. Sharmine Narwani, a senior associate at Saint Anthony's College, Oxford University, and regime supporter, argued that Assad had majority support. Key sectors included people in the major cities of Damascus and Aleppo; minorities such as Alawites, Druze, Christians, and Shiites; three million mostly Sunni Baath Party members; and the business elite. She argued that Assad had the support of "millions and millions of Syrians whose voices have been entirely ignored."[2]

Narwani and other Assad supporters argued that the government provided security and stability. Syrians saw the sectarian warfare in Iraq and Lebanon, and they quite understandably feared chaos. Assad cleverly played on the fears of minority groups that they would suffer under majority Sunni rule. David Lesch, a professor of Middle East studies at Trinity University in San Antonio, noted that the Assad family used sophisticated methods to silence critics. "Employing coercion, a pervasive spy apparatus, carefully constructed tribal and family alliances, bribery and the tactics of divide and rule, maintaining control over the remaining half of the population is not as difficult for a minority-ruled regime as would, on the surface, seem."[3]

Assad had some popular support, but he relied on the military to keep himself in power. And the military took on extraordinary powers. Take, for example, the drive from Beirut to Damascus, which I've made many times. It used to take about two and a half hours. At the end of 2013, it took me twice as long due to intensified border security and seven checkpoints along the highway. The traffic delays felt interminable.

Since 2012, when rebels bombed the Damascus military headquarters, the capital has been crisscrossed with checkpoints. Soldiers mostly waved cars through, occasionally stopping to inspect a back seat and trunk for smuggled weapons. But the resulting traffic jams caused havoc for emergency vehicles. I saw one maneuvering on a sidewalk and another driving the wrong way on a major street in order to get through. Most checkpoints had two lanes: civilian and military. The military lanes allowed soldiers, intelligence officials, and anyone with a special ID to pass quickly. The civilian lines, which included taxis, took far longer. Journalists usually traveled by taxi.

The national economy, which was never in great shape, had tanked. Inflation and unemployment were serious problems. In 2011, the US dollar bought fifty Syrian pounds. During my trip two years later, it bought 142. That was actually an improvement over earlier exchange rates, when the pound sank as low as 330 to the dollar. The few Syrians with access to foreign currency lived well, but most faced hardships from inflation-reduced salaries and shortages of goods. Western sanctions meant Syria could no longer export oil, a major source of hard currency. Domestic factories and infrastructure had been hit hard by the fighting.

In 2013, gasoline shortages meant long lines at gas stations. Taxi drivers had a hard time making a living because of high gas prices and longer times to reach destinations. Rebels blew up electrical stations and power lines, causing regular outages. One night during my stay, most of Damascus was blacked out for several hours. The city, once vibrant with night life, all but shut down after dark.

So why do people still support the government? Because they think the rebels are worse. The government played up extremist statements by right-wing rebel leaders; extremist groups that took over some cities killed Alawites and Christians. Rebels controlling the capital's outskirts regularly fired rockets and mortars into Damascus, seemingly aimed at civilian neighborhoods. Bishop Armash Nalbandian, a leader of the Armenian Orthodox Church in Damascus, told me, "When the crisis began in 2011, they [protestors] called for freedom." But opposition demonstrators "didn't bring stability," he said. "I want this government to be protected."[4]

The Assad regime claimed to uphold secularism in the face of Muslim extremism. But the regime has tried to drive a wedge between Sunni Muslims and Syria's minorities. Soldiers at checkpoints are automatically suspicious of Sunnis but not worried about Alawites and Christians. The various communities no longer trust one another. Alaa Ebrahim, a Damascus TV reporter, told me that before the civil war Sunnis and Alawites were friends and pretty much ignored their religious backgrounds. Now it's different. "As an Alawite government employee, if you're invited to dinner by a Sunni, you would be afraid of an ambush," Ebrahim told me. "You would refuse. Trust has broken down."[5]

For many years Syria survived as a secular dictatorship. How did the society come apart so quickly? I found out during a visit to Tartus, a coastal city in western Syria not far from Lebanon, where many Alawites live.

I stood in front of a large statue of Hafez al-Assad, Syria's former ruler and father of the current president. Traffic zoomed around the statue as dusk fell and people headed home from work. At the beginning of the uprising, something quite extraordinary happened here in Tartus. In March 2011, President Bashar al-Assad ordered the dismantling of his father's ubiquitous statues in order to take away flashpoints for demonstrators. But the people of Tartus objected and even set up a human barricade to prevent the statues' removal. Feras Dieb, a forty-two-year-old businessman, drove to Tartus from his hometown in order to participate in the protest. "The president asked the people to take down all the statutes around Syria," he said. "Here in Tartus everyone didn't want it. We stayed around the statute so no one could take it down. I stayed with the group for twenty-four hours."[6]

Alawites have a long history of going their own way. They split off from Shia Islam in the eighth century. Alawites lived mostly in what is modern-day Turkey, Lebanon, and Syria. During colonial times, the French favored Christians and suppressed Alawites, although they were encouraged to join the military. Before 1970, Alawites faced a lot of discrimination and lived in poor, rural areas. Today Alawites make up about 10 to 12 percent of Syria's population.

Life changed dramatically for Alawites after Hafez al-Assad came to power in a coup in 1970. Starting with his supporters in the Baathist military, the elder Assad created a power base among his fellow Alawites. Dieb said Assad helped Alawites and all Syrians. "When Mr. Hafez was president he did many good things for people, especially for the poor," said Dieb. "After 1972 there were no wars and no problems in Syria. We have almost free education and free medical. The total cost of a medical education is about two hundred dollars, maximum. In each village, he built a high school. So you don't have to go to another village for education."

I drove about thirty kilometers to a small town where Dieb's mother and father live. The rural community is surrounded by farms and bisected by a noisy, two-lane road. The Dieb family was retired and lived modestly. Feras's mother, seventy-five-year-old Shafika, said previous rulers in Syria didn't respect religious freedom. French colonialists, who occupied Syria between the world wars, favored the Christians. "When I was a child," said Shafika Dieb, "my mother told me that the French tried to make life difficult, especially for Muslim families. They gave Christian families a beautiful area for their farms and homes. They supported the Christian families, especially in the nearby town of Safita. After the liberation from France, all the religious groups lived together. For example, my husband's family lived next door to a Christian family. They never had fights. Christian and Alawite families lived in peace together."[7]

From 1970 onward, during the Assad family rule, many urban Syrians intermarried among different religious and ethnic groups. During all my previous journeys to Syria, I rarely heard references to someone's religious background in casual conversation. The Dieb family firmly believed that Western powers were once again seeking to divide and rule in Syria. They said the opposition wanted to impose an intolerant Sunni Muslim regime and that Assad was protecting religious minorities. Mahmood Dieb, Shafika's husband, was seventy-nine years old. "If something happens to Dr. Bashar, everyone here will fight. If he is overthrown, it will go back to the days of the French with people fighting each other."[8]

One night I went strolling through the city of Tartus. The government rebuilt the Corniche, or coastal road, and Syrians jammed onto the streets, chatted with friends, and sat in cafés. The night in October 2011 was calm and the air balmy. You wouldn't know that Syria was at war. My guide was another Dieb family member, a daughter named Wafaa. She was a medical doctor who studied and worked abroad. She said this whole discussion of religious and ethnic background was new to Syria. For her, Syria's secularism was a key component of what she called Syrian democracy. "Syria is one of the most democratic countries in the world, certainly more than any Arab country," she asserted. "We have democracy, which includes respect for my religion. I don't want to change. This is democracy for me."[9]

The United States had overthrown governments in Iraq and Afghanistan, she reasoned, and had then set its sights on Syria. "I think America wants to occupy many countries. Thank God we don't have very much petrol. If we had oil, the United States would occupy Syria like Iraq. The United States wants Syria to be like a slave. I don't want Syria to become like Afghanistan, either. I don't want to stay home; as a woman, I want to be able to work."

Dieb and other Alawite supporters of the government lived in a cocoon where government propaganda reinforced existing beliefs. They were never able to answer a simple question: If Assad enjoyed so much popular support and the rebels were all tools of foreign powers, why had the government lost control of so much of the country?

Tartus has changed a lot. During my 2011 trip, I was able to drive from Damascus to Tartus in a few hours, hitting only a few cursory military checkpoints. All the nearby cities were calm and under government control. By the end of 2013 I couldn't drive there from Damascus because the roads were closed to civilian traffic. Residents had to fly into nearby Latakia. The only safe area of Tartus extended to about ten square kilometers around the city center.[10] Going outside that zone became dangerous. That political and military instability hit not only Alawites, of course, but the country's business elite as well.

Dating back to the late 1950s and early '60s, Syria adopted a system of "Arab socialism." The government provided people with low-cost healthcare through public clinics. Education was free. The military, through its control of the government, nationalized important industries such as telecommunications. Military and government officials divvyed up the lucrative profits. Corruption ran rampant. Workers had even less control over the economy than they did over the government. It was socialism in name; kleptocracy in practice.

When Bashar al-Assad came to power in 2000, he faced a moribund economy and potential social unrest. Syria was the second-poorest country in the Middle East. Only Yemen had a lower per-capita income.[11] Under Assad's leadership, the government privatized some state-run industries and lowered tariffs on imported goods, following an economic model promoted by the International Monetary Fund and the World Bank. Baath Party cronies and Assad relatives bought the industries on the cheap or got licenses to open new ones, such as cell phone companies. The business elite benefited as the government allowed creation of private banks, insurance companies, and an airline. Government policies created economic growth and loyalty among business leaders. But the new liberalization policy also increased systematic and widespread corruption.

Early demonstrations in 2011, for example, singled out Rami Makhlouf, Assad's cousin and owner of the country's largest cell phone company. Critics said he'd made tens of millions of dollars due to family connections. Nabil Samman, director of the Center for Research and Documentation in Damascus, estimated that three hundred families controlled the vast majority Syria's economy. "An end of the regime means their demise, not only in terms of political power," said Samman. "People will ask, 'Where did he get this money from?'"[12] Bouthaina Shaban, a top adviser to the president, admitted to me that corruption remained a serious problem in Syria. "Rami Makhlouf isn't the only one who made money in the past period," she said in an interview at the presidential palace. "There are many people, big capitalists, who made a lot of money."[13] Syria had replaced Arab socialism with crony capitalism.

Those crony capitalists, along with the honest ones, continued to provide crucial support for Assad. Nabil Toumeh, CEO of the large conglomerate Toumeh Orient Group, supported Assad because he believed the opposition is controlled by extremists. "In Syria we are multicultured and multireligious," he told me.[14] He argued that extremists in the Muslim Brotherhood and other Islamist groups will impose an Islamic state on the country. "They will end the secular orientation in Syria and the whole Middle East. . . . The street must cool down in order to achieve the reforms. Otherwise they will never be implemented." Nabil Sukkar, a former World Bank economist who later headed an economic consulting firm in Damascus, said that big business remained a crucial pillar of support for the government. Business people are pragmatic, according to Sukkar. "They expect the unrest to end sooner or later," he said. "The regime is well-entrenched."[15]

The government's neoliberal policies benefitted a few progovernment big-business men but did irreparable damage to the economy. The
policies increased poverty in the mainly Sunni, rural areas, according
to progovernment analyst Barakat. "Textile and other factories were
no longer subsidized by the government," he told me. "They allowed
Turkish commodities to enter without taxes. The national industry was
completely damaged."[16] Unemployment grew as factories shut down
and farmers couldn't compete with cheap imports. "The Syrian regime
made a big mistake," Barakat said. "We had an army of unemployed
young people."

Syria's severe draught from 2006 to 2011 made bad economic policy
even worse. The country averaged less than eight centimeters of rain each
year, not enough to sustain farming. As much as 85 percent of Syria's
livestock died from thirst, and in some areas, crop failures hit 75 percent.
Hundreds of thousands of farmers fled from the countryside to the big
cities where they had difficulty finding work.[17] Some of the hardest-hit
regions, such as Al Hasakah, later became hotbeds of rebellion.

The civil war exacerbated the already-bad economic conditions.
International sanctions against Syria, the loss of most exports, and
the destruction of war sent the economy into a tailspin. Syria produced 425,000 barrels per day of crude oil in 2011, but that dropped
to zero by the end of 2013 as rebels seized control of the oil fields.[18]
The Syrian gross domestic product (GDP) grew by 3.2 percent in 2010
but dropped to −21.8 percent in 2012 and −22.5 percent in 2013.[19] The
economic crisis also hit the small-business people, many of whom had
supported Assad.

Rana Issa owned a successful marketing and advertising business
in Damascus focused, in part, on the construction industry. But the
industry had little to advertise. Construction had ground to a halt, along
with tourism and a host of other businesses. Issa laid off 25 percent
of her staff. "Businessmen are afraid of economic recession, and they
stopped their media buying," she told me in her Damascus office. "It
has a bad effect on the media agency. If the businessman doesn't buy

advertising, we don't have money, and we can't pay for anything. It's like a chain."[20]

She said that businesspeople generally supported Assad. "Big-business men trust the government," she said. Businesses of all sizes "just want to survive and work. We want the economy to recover." She blamed the rebels for Syria's economic problems, not the Assad government. "The opposition, what do they want? What are their ideas about government?" Issa is of Palestinian origin. She said the Syrian government had afforded more rights to Palestinian refugees and their children than either Israel or other Arab countries. "As a Palestinian living in Syria, I cannot imagine that the president will go because of the opposition. We didn't have restrictions; we live like Syrians. I love Syria. I love the president. I love everything he does. He gave us a lot of promises and achieved a lot of targets. The opposition, they didn't give him time to work on this."

I asked what she would do if the opposition took power. "I will leave," she said with finality. She didn't wait for Assad's downfall, however. Faced with mounting economic difficulties, by the end of 2013, Issa had moved to Erbil in the Kurdish region of Iraq.

But Issa's pro-Assad views weren't shared by all her peers. Some small-business people had switched sides. I have visited Damascus's main *souk*, or marketplace, many times since my first trip in 2002. Thousands of customers and merchants haggled over everything from food to rugs. But since the uprising began, business has been much slower. On the day of my visit, light flooded in from the windows above as I interviewed shopkeepers at random.

One clothing store owner, who asked me not to use his name, said the souk is "like a graveyard. Our whole business relies on the foreigners from the gulf, the tourists." He said tourism is not just down, "it's zero."[21] The clothing store owner lamented that he hadn't seen a foreign customer in months. And he can't export his clothing to Iraq or Jordan, previously major customers. His costs to import cloth have increased a lot because the value of Syrian currency had declined. "I can't compete. It's cheaper in their own countries."

The merchant was a longtime supporter of Assad. Now he blamed his president for the country's woes. He said the police began the crisis when they arrested and beat the teenagers for writing antigovernment graffiti on a wall in the southern city of Daraa. The government "should have tried the people responsible for the acts and tried the corrupt people," he said. "If the police who beat the children were put in jail, that would have stopped the demonstrations. We just want an end to corruption. Young people are fighting for their rights."

He leaned forward and, in a barely audible voice, said he supported the banned Muslim Brotherhood. He argued that the brotherhood is a moderate group, likening it to the Islamist party that ruled Turkey. "The Muslim Brotherhood wants an end to corruption," he said. The hatred of government corruption cuts across class and religious lines in Syria, even impacting Syria's Christians, who generally support Assad.

In late 2013, a twenty-year-old Christian student was kidnapped in broad daylight in front of his university in Damascus. His father received a call demanding a huge ransom in US dollars, said the student's uncle, Hagop, a university professor and regime supporter who asked that only his first name be used. "They think the Christians are all rich."[22] Dozens of Christians have been kidnapped for ransom in Damascus, according to Hagop and other Christian leaders. Christians are perceived to be more prosperous than the majority Sunni Muslims. They had felt relatively secure in the largely secular regimes of Hafez and Bashar al-Assad. The student's family was finally able to negotiate a deal, and the young man was released, according to Hagop. The family never discovered the identity of the kidnappers. Hagop said they could have been antigovernment rebels or common criminals. Rebels regularly kidnap civilians in areas under their control, according to human-rights organizations.[23]

"But most frighteningly, we suspect some kidnappings are carried out by the Popular Committees," Hagop said. The committees are a progovernment militia that was incorporated into the National Defense Force in late 2012. Militia members received a salary, uniforms, and arms from the government. "How could a rebel group infiltrate secure areas of Damascus, kidnap someone in front of the university, and then take him through all the checkpoints to an area they control?" asked Hagop. "No, it has to be someone on the inside."

Life became increasingly perilous for Syrian Christians. Some 10 percent of Syria's 22.5 million people are Christian, both Orthodox and Catholic. When the French occupied Syria and Lebanon after World War I, they implemented a divide-and-conquer strategy that favored some Christian sects. Many Syrian Christians achieved higher incomes and educational levels than their Muslim counterparts, differences that persist today. Christians also participated in the anticolonial struggle and helped found the nationalist Baath Party in the 1940s. Under the rule of Hafez al-Assad, some Christians rose to positions of power in business, government, and the military. Each Christian faith has its own story.

Armenian Christians fled to Syria after the Ottoman Turkish genocide of 1915.[24] For them, the current civil war is a double tragedy. About one-third of the prewar Armenian population of 120,000 had left Syria as refugees, according to Bishop Armash Nalbandian of the Armenian Orthodox Church.[25]

Christians also faced attack because of their politics, according to Father Simon Faddul, director of the Catholic charity Caritas in Lebanon. He explained that some of the Christian refugees in Lebanon are Syrian government employees. Others may be related to Syrian soldiers or members of the intelligence services. They face persecution because of their progovernment views. "They live in continuous fear," said Father Faddul. "Christians have paid in blood."[26]

While opinions vary within the diverse Christian communities, most have sided with Assad against the rebels. "The guarantee of security of minorities is to have good functional government, a strong government," Bishop Nalbandian told me. "This security we experienced and saw with the government of President Bashar al-Assad."[27]

When the Syrian uprising began in 2011, many Christians sympathized with the calls for democracy but worried about Islamic extremists who saw Christians as infidels. Bishop Nalbandian said that in the first few months Christians hoped the government would make significant reforms through meaningful dialogue with the opposition. "Unfortunately, the government lost this moment, or couldn't or didn't use this moment," he explained. "The government did some reforms according to the constitution, but actually it's not enough." For example, the government lifted its formal state of emergency first implemented in 1963, but then continued repressive policies. The government held parliamentary elections in 2012, but the new body has little power.

Meanwhile, over the past year, extremist rebel groups seized more territory. When the rebel group ISIS took over the northern city of Raqqa in 2014, for example, it closed the churches and forced most of the Christians to flee (see chapter 6).

The civil war has ripped apart relations between Christians and Sunni Muslims, even in Hagop's small hometown. As the crow flies, Hagop's town lies only twelve miles from central Damascus, but he must drive through half a dozen military checkpoints to get there. What used to be a thirty-minute commute now takes three hours. No one makes the drive at night because rebels sometimes hit the road with mortar fire and rockets.

"I drive into Damascus only a few times a week and otherwise stay home," Hagop said. "We don't mind the checkpoints. I said thanks to the soldiers because they are protecting us." Hagop's town is a mix of Christians, Sunnis, and Druze. Before the crisis, residents got along well. Friendships and business relations extended among all religious groups.

Officially, the Assad government is fighting to maintain this secularism. Officials claim that most Sunnis support the government, and the army fights only extremists, or *takfiris*. That epithet means "impure Muslims" and is used to describe all rebels. Hagop admitted, however, that the reality in his town has become far different. "The army blocked off the Sunni part of my town," he said. "Now we hardly see the Sunnis at all. Everyone is suspicious. Is he a terrorist?" Friendly relations with neighbors have broken down. "I tell my children not to talk politics with anyone outside our immediate family. You never know who might be a kidnapper." Soldiers are hostile to all Sunnis because they suspect them of supporting the rebels, Hagop said. "Because I have an Armenian name," he said, "I don't get hassled at the checkpoints. They are looking for Sunnis. One time a soldier asked if I was Kurdish because I was born in the north, in the Kurdish region. I said, 'No, I'm Armenian Christian.' 'OK—you're one of us,' the soldier said."[28]

Being "one of us" doesn't mean Christians are accepted as equals. Even progovernment Muslims see Christians as guests in a Muslim country. "We protect Christians and Jews," said Sheik Abdul Salaam al-Harash, a representative of the Muslim Scholarship Association. "That is our duty as good Muslims."[29] Hagop pointed out, however, that Syria was a Christian area for centuries before it became majority Muslim. Saint Paul traveled extensively in what is modern-day Syria, and Christianity spread rapidly during the era of the Roman Empire. "This was a Christian area before the Muslims came," said Hagop. "But they still see us as guests. We don't need protection. We need full rights as citizens."[30]

Christians can't hold the country's highest office. Syria's president must be a Muslim, according to the constitution, which was revised by Assad in 2012, carrying forward a provision in previous Syrian law. Christians wanted to see the constitution changed so that a person of any religion could be president, according to Bishop Nalbandian. That clause is "not democratic. But in this crisis we didn't raise our voice to change it."[31] That issue revealed the fragile relations between Christians and the majority Muslim community, one that is exacerbated by the militancy of the Islamists in the opposition. Hagop remembered that in 1973, Hafez al-Assad tried to change the old constitution to allow a president to be from any religion. Conservative Muslims protested, and dozens were killed in large demonstrations against the ruling Baath Party. "So I'm not sure if the provision that the president must be Muslim reflects Baath policy or popular will," Hagop said with a shrug. "The people want a Muslim president."[32] Bishop Nalbandian said making democratic changes in Syria will take time. "Democracy is not an item to be bought in a store," he said. "It is a process."[33]

But the larger question of Christian democratic rights was sidelined so long as the civil war raged. One day in late 2013, Armenian

Orthodox families gathered at a church in the old city of Damascus for the funeral of four children who died when a rebel mortar hit their school. Rebels on the outskirts of the capital regularly fire rockets and mortars into Damascus, sometimes aimed at military targets, sometimes not. A relative of one of the victims, Amira Hana, cried as she described the explosion. "We went running to the school to find out what took place," she told me. "All the buses were completely destroyed. Blood was all over the ground."[34] Bishop Nalbandian, who presided at the funeral, criticized the rebels who intentionally targeted civilian areas. "I can't understand what kind of vision, what kind of ideology they have," he said. "I do know that they don't pursue freedom or democracy as they said. They are actually criminals." He said indiscriminate attacks on civilians are a war crime. "What they are doing isn't against the government. It's against humanity. I'm speechless."[35]

For its part, the government indiscriminately shelled rebel-held neighborhoods, killing far more civilians than the rebels. At the end of 2013, a special UN human-rights commission accused the regime of systematic war crimes against civilians. The commission included Carla del Ponte, who had earlier declared that rebels had used sarin to attack regime soldiers and civilians. For the first time, a UN human-rights group held Assad personally responsible. "Evidence indicates responsibility at the highest level of government, including the head of state," according to Navi Pillay, the UN high commissioner for human rights.[36]

The civil war had taken its toll on the Christian community. Some left for neighboring Lebanon. Maryam, her husband, and two children fled the fighting in Syria and arrived in Lebanon with only one suitcase each. They left the war-torn city of Qusayr prior to its recapture by progovernment forces. "Bullets were flying everywhere," Maryam told me, asking that only her first name be used. "There were rockets. My children couldn't go to school."[37]

The family suffered months of hardships in Qusayr, in part because they were Christians, according to Maryam. "The mosques announced they wanted to round up all the Christian men. The families became scared." One night masked men came to their apartment intent on taking all the Christian men in the building. The masked antagonists weren't the infamous thugs of Assad. Nor were they fighters from other countries intent on waging jihad. They were local, anti-Assad rebels intent on purging Qusayr of pro-Assad Christians. The city had become a major battleground, with religion as a defining factor.

The family finally had to leave. "We either had to run for our lives or join the fight," said Maryam, who is Roman Catholic. The family fled to Zahle, a predominantly Christian city in the eastern mountains of Lebanon. Maryam is among the thousands of Syrian Christians who have fled the fighting but received little international attention. The Most Reverend Archbishop Issam Darwish, a Melkite Catholic whose archdiocese includes Zahle, said Syrians have lived in peace for generations. He preferred to blame the anti-Christian violence on extremist groups such as al-Nusra and other jihadists. "They believe Syria is a Muslim country, and the Christians must leave," he said. "But most Syrians are not like that."[38]

But some Muslim extremists are. Even in the early months of the uprising, some local Sunnis were chanting the slogan, "Christians to Beirut, Alawites to the *tabout* [coffin]."

"We heard that slogan," said Joseph, Maryam's husband. "The rebels said, 'We never said that.' But if you look, it's true. Where are the Christians? They are here in Lebanon."[39] Well, not exactly. According to UN statistics, some Christians have left but in far fewer numbers than their Sunni Muslim counterparts. Less than 1 percent of Lebanon's 900,000 Syrian refugees are Christians, according to Dana Sleiman, spokesperson for the Beirut office of the UN High Commissioner for Refugees (UNHCR).[40] Overall, over 2.5 million Syrians fled their country as of early 2014.[41]

Most Syrian Christians have hunkered down inside Syria, hoping for an Assad victory. Such views outrage other Christians. Basem Shabb, a Lebanese Protestant member of parliament for the Future Movement, said that supporting dictators has caused tremendous problems for

Christians in the region. The Future Movement, the party headed by Saad Hariri, has strongly opposed Assad and his Lebanese ally, Hezbollah. Shabb noted that Christians in Iraq largely sided with Saddam Hussein. "Now the Christians in Syria may be repeating the same mistake," he told me. "For the Catholics and Maronites in Aleppo [Syria] to openly support the regime is suicide."[42]

Elie El-Hindy, chair of the Political Science Department at Notre Dame University outside Beirut, agreed that Christians have been unwise to side with secular dictators against the Muslim majority. "The more they take sides or engage in alliances, the more they will be threatened," he said. "One party is going to win; another will lose."[43] Rather than lament the attacks on Christians around the region, he urged Christians to take a broader view about the rise of Muslim political parties and governments. "We should believe that democracy and human rights will adjust the situation in the long term," he said. He noted that Egypt's president Mohammad Morsi was overthrown, and non-Islamic movements have been attacking Turkey's president Recep Erdogan. Christians and their allies might lose elections initially, he said. "We should work on winning the next one."

Of course, that assumes that the winner in Syria allows free and fair elections. Catholic charity official Reverend Faddul said if the war goes on too much longer, Christian refugees "won't have a home to return to." He noted that Christians have confronted major crises many times before, including the fratricidal Lebanese Civil War of 1975–1990. Christians play a major political, social, and economic role, he said. "So many domains of life, like banks and tourism, are well maintained by Christians. We shouldn't squeeze ourselves in a corner and hide under the complex of persecution or inferiority."[44] El-Hindy agreed, expressing optimism about the continued Christian contributions to the region. "Christians are a factor for enlightenment and moderation," he said. "This is the way to fight the threat of extremism."[45]

Through the middle of 2014, Assad maintained the support of his repressive apparatus, a key factor to staying in power. He could also rely on Christian and Alawite supporters in the military and intelligence services. We first met a member of the Mukhabarat (Military Intelligence Directorate) in chapter 5. It was quite a shock for me to meet one of the feared secret police face-to-face. The only other time I had seen the Mukhabarat was from the other end of leather jackets and aviator glasses as they offered intimidating stares at airports or while rousting civilians. But here was a real human being, not a stereotype. And his perspective was fascinating.

He was stocky but solidly built, with a military-style buzz cut. He dressed in slacks and an open-necked shirt and drove an inexpensive car. In 2011 he and his wife, both Alawites, lived in a middle-income apartment complex built by the government. If people in the Mukhabarat were making big bucks from corruption, he was not among them. He told me that protesters may have had legitimate demands at the very beginning, but very quickly criminal elements and foreign powers hijacked the movement. During the first week of the uprising, he said, he was personally shot at by protestors carrying everything from AK-47s to hunting pistols. Such a claim couldn't be independently verified.

I asked if the Assad government had made any mistakes, thinking perhaps he would concede that the harsh measures only encouraged more anger at the government. "Yes, the government made mistakes," he told me gravely. "It should have cracked down harder from the very beginning. Officials initially took away our pistols so we wouldn't shoot demonstrators," he claimed. "We only got them back a few days ago."[46]

I asked that if that was true, why were so many civilians killed during demonstrations? He parroted the government position that over eight hundred members of the security forces had been killed and almost no protestors. At the time, the United Nations estimated that over three thousand civilians had been killed. The security forces saw themselves as victims of people in the pay of foreign powers. They claimed the United States, Great Britain, and Saudi Arabia smuggled arms into the country and paid people to come to demonstrations. Given the participation of millions of Syrians, the conspiracy must be vast indeed!

His arguments reminded me of how the US government twists the facts in describing the war on terrorism. Only the worst of the worst were locked up in Guantanamo. The drone attacks always kill evildoers, never civilians. The National Security Administration is protecting us from terrorism by having access to every phone call and e-mail sent in the United States. In Syria, it was the same Alice-in-Wonderland reasoning. The victims became criminals and the perpetrators became victims.

He took me on a tour of his town. People lined up at a government bakery where they paid half-price for bread. It was an everyday occurrence, but when I shot photos, he became worried. Although he was a member of the feared security forces, he was afraid to be seen with me. I got out to shoot photos, but he made sure I didn't speak so no one could figure out I was American. I look Middle Eastern enough to pass for Syrian if I don't open my mouth. We ran into a friend of his from the secret service. He didn't introduce me. He was worried that his friend would turn him in for some kind of unauthorized activity. Remember, I was traveling in Syria with a journalist visa and all the appropriate documents. But even a member of the Mukhabarat was scared of the Mukhabarat.

Even with the system of state-inspired fear, the secret police and regular army proved incapable of suppressing the uprising. Very early on, armed groups of regime supporters, known as *shabiha*, attacked demonstrators and tried to intimidate the opposition. The first shabiha, which means "ghosts," were smugglers in the western seaport of Latakia in the 1970s. During the Lebanese Civil War, the shabiha formed alliances with Syrian authorities who profited from smuggling consumer goods, drugs, and arms.[47] When the uprising began, the Mafia-like shabiha joined together with security forces to attack peaceful demonstrations. The opposition began to refer to similar groups around the country as shabiha, and the name stuck. The gangs managed to combine mindless loyalty to Assad with criminality. "We started by facing the protesters, but when the opposition became armed, we attacked them in their villages," shabiha member Abu Jaafar told *Global Post*. "In addition to our salaries we take whatever we can get during the attacks: TVs, video players, electronics."[48]

In early 2012 the regime organized the disparate militias into a national group called the Popular Committees. A year later, the Popular Committees were incorporated into the National Defense Forces.

The Iranian Revolutionary Guards provided arms and training to the NDF, following the model of the *basiji*, armed thugs who became infamous for attacking the 2009 popular demonstrations in Iran (see chapter 8). By the end of 2013, the NDF had grown to an estimated 100,000 members.[49] The government wanted the NDF to act as a civilian backup to the army. Following classic counterinsurgency tactics, it was supposed to take over and hold an area liberated from the rebels. But the NDF was unaccountable legally and militarily. TV reporter Alaa Ebrahim told me the "National Defense Forces don't have the ethics of the army, nor are they legally accountable."[50]

From the very beginning of the uprising, the shabiha were responsible for some of the regime's worst atrocities. On May 25, 2012, the Syrian army launched ferocious artillery and tank fire on Houla, a small village outside Homs. The shabiha waited on the outskirts of town and fired at civilians attempting to escape. When the bombardment stopped, the shabiha entered the village and massacred 108 people, including 34 women and 49 children, many with their hands tied behind their backs.[51] Nations around the world condemned the Houla massacre and withdrew their ambassadors in protest. The regime blamed the deaths on foreign terrorists.

On May 2, 2013, regular army soldiers and NDF militia entered the town of Bayda in the Tartus Governate in western Syria. They came under fire from armed rebels, and a dozen soldiers were killed. The government called for backup and launched artillery barrages at other nearby villages in and around Baniyas. They later entered the village and went door to door, stabbing and bludgeoning entire families. One video showed eight children dead on a bed.[52] A UN report later estimated that between 300 and 450 deaths had occurred from the massacre, most at the hands of government forces.[53] Syrian government TV reported that the army had defeated a band of "terrorists" and blamed them for the atrocities.

Government supporters argue that accounts of regime massacres are exaggerated by the opposition. Others say any civilians still living in rebel-controlled areas are prorebel. Ebrahim, who regularly interviewed NDF militiamen, said some government supporters justify the killings because civilians provide a "nurturing environment" for the rebels. Ebrahim strongly disagreed with this view but said some government supporters are convinced "if the civilians don't leave rebel areas, they must support the rebels."[54]

Ebrahim brings an interesting perspective to the civil war. Sitting down for coffee one evening in Damascus, he pulled out an iPhone to display idyllic photos of family and friends in his home village near Syria's Mediterranean coast. In happier times, they enjoyed the area's beautiful waterfalls and picturesque mountains. He also described the good relations among the village's diverse religious groups. Sunni Muslims, Christians, and Alawites got along well, he said, despite the increase in religious tensions elsewhere in Syria. Ebrahim said Sunnis in his village supported the government of Assad, so they didn't come under suspicion.

In the cities where rebels are fighting for control, however, entire Sunni neighborhoods are cordoned off with army checkpoints and became no-go zones at night. The army also laid siege to the mostly Sunni, rebel-controlled towns, frequently preventing entry of food, medicine, and other essentials. Ebrahim initially felt some sympathy for the peaceful protestors demonstrating in the early months of the uprising. But he said religious extremists came to dominate, leaving little room for civilian opposition.

And then earlier this year he faced a personal tragedy. His mother, a Syrian army officer, was assassinated by a rebel sniper, who killed her with a single shot at a distance of 1,300 yards while she was driving home. Firing a sniper rifle at a moving car at that distance is quite extraordinary. How could the sniper have known her route unless helped by someone in the army? An army investigation revealed the rebels had inside help. His mother's assassination was just one more indication of a technically proficient enemy with intelligence capability even within the military.

Ebrahim said outsiders are responsible for much of the violence. He predicted the conflict will continue as long as the United States and Saudi Arabia fund the rebels. Civilian opponents and rebels made the same argument, only in reverse. "Assad would fall quickly if he didn't receive support from Russia, Iran, and Hezbollah," said activist Leen.[55]

And that's precisely what we'll explore next: Iran and Hezbollah's role in the Syrian Civil War.

Lieutenant Colonel Thomas Edward Lawrence, known as Lawrence of Arabia, was a British liaison officer who helped the Arab revolt against the Ottoman Empire during World War I. He was a leading advocate for Arab independence under British neocolonial control. *Photo by Lowell Thomas, 1919.*

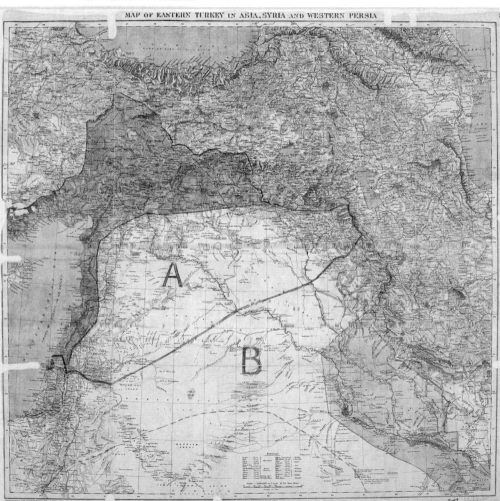

This map shows how the Sykes-Picot Agreement proposed to divide up the Middle East between the French (area A) and the British (area B). The agreement was signed in secret in 1916 without any concern for local peoples. This map is signed by Sykes and Picot. *Map from the National Archives, MPK 1/426, 1916.*

British diplomat Sir Mark Sykes negotiated the Sykes-Picot Agreement with France. The agreement split territory between imperialist powers and helped cause decades of turmoil in the Middle East. *Litho-graph by Leopold Pilichowski, 1918.*

French diplomat François Georges-Picot signed the Skyes-Picot Agreement in 1916. *Photo from Wikimedia Commons, 1918.*

Sultan Pasha al-Atrash led the 1925–1927 nationalist revolt against French occupation of Syria. That revolt helps inspire today's rebels fighting Bashar al-Assad. *Photo by American Colony (Jerusalem) Photo Department, 1926. From Library of Congress, Prints and Photographs Division, LC-M32-3398-A [P&P].*

Bashar al-Assad, who began his rule with much-needed reforms, proved to be a brutal dictator when he repressed the 2011 uprising.

This revolutionary poster shows an image of Mohammad Bouazizi in his hometown of Sidi Bouzid, Tunisia.

This sculpture commemorates street vendor Mohammad Bouazizi in Tunisia, whose death sparked the Arab Spring.

Hundreds of thousands of Egyptians rally against the Mubarak dictatorship and the Egyptian military, Tahrir Rally, Cairo.

Shia Muslims pray at the holy Rukaya shrine in Damascus. Shia youth wave flags during a holiday celebration; outside, Hezbollah stands guard along with Syrian troops.

Muslims pray at the Omayyad Mosque in Damascus. While proclaiming support for religious freedom, the Syrian regime laid siege to Sunni neighborhoods suspected of supporting the rebels.

Sheik Abdul Salaam al-Harash, a progovernment cleric, echoes the widely held view that Muslims must "protect" Christians. Christians say that's a condescending view.

Minister of Justice Najm al-Ahmad denies that the Syrian government ever used chemical weapons, claiming they were used only by the rebels.

Dr. Wafaa Dieb stands in front of a statue of Hafez al-Assad in Tartus. At the beginning of the uprising, the mainly Alawite residents of Tartus rallied in favor of the government and against tearing down Hafez al-Assad's statue.

A *Mukhabarat* (secret police) member worried that photographing this breadline in western Syria would show the regime in a negative light. The government provided subsidized bread, and sometimes the lines got long.

Rana Isa, owner of a public-relations company in Damascus, says big-business men strongly supported the government because Bashar al-Assad had adopted probusiness policies since the early 2000s.

During a 2011 visit to Damascus's famous *souk*, or marketplace, business had dried up.

In the Damascus souk, this shopkeeper displays his inlaid boxes but says foreign customers, his usual clients, have stopped coming.

Bishop Armash Nalbandian of the Armenian Orthodox Church says protestors originally had legitimate democratic demands but extremist rebels have taken over. He supports the Assad government.

Clerics attend the funeral of Armenian children killed by a rebel mortar that hit a Christian school in Damascus.

Iranians gather for Friday prayers in Tehran. Iran strongly supports Assad because of his opposition to the United States and Israel.

A young girl in Moqebleh, a Kurdish refugee camp in northern Iraq. Kurds have long opposed the Assad regime but are also wary of the Islamist opposition.

Author Reese Erlich interviews Syrian Kurdish refugee Barkhodan Balo in the Moqebleh camp in northern Iraq. Balo and most Kurds want greater rights for Kurds within the Syrian state.

A watchtower overlooks the Golan. Arabs living in the occupied Golan overwhelmingly support its return to Syria, although the civil war has put any future settlement on the back burner.

Mustafa Barghouti, Palestinian political leader, says the Israel lobby had a significant defeat in 2013 when it couldn't pressure Congress to support bombing Syria.

CHAPTER 8

WHY IRAN BACKS SYRIA

O n June 12, 2009, I went to sleep in Tehran fully expecting that the Iranian presidential elections had been resolved. I woke up the next morning to a country in turmoil. Spontaneous marches and rallies were starting. Rumors flew and facts simmered. Text messages burned up the lines. Within days, millions of ordinary Iranians were demonstrating in the largest protests in Iran since the 1979 revolution. Iranians asked, "Where is my vote?" and quickly concluded the election had been stolen.

Reformist candidate Mir Hussain Mousavi had campaigned promising greater civil liberties and an improved economy. He mobilized sentiment for reform that had been building against the regime for the previous thirty years. His supporters held huge rallies in Tehran and around the country. Iranians expected Mousavi to win outright or at least qualify for a run-off election. Instead, the official election results showed incumbent president Mahmoud Ahmadinejad winning with 62 percent of the vote.

Wealthy businessmen joined clerics and working-class women in chadors not only to protest vote fraud, but they also challenged the fundamentals of clerical rule. The Green Movement, as it became known, spread throughout the country.[1] Some protestors wanted to reform the Iranian Constitution, which puts ultimate power in the hands of Shia Muslim clerics. Others wanted to overthrow the constitution entirely and return to the parliamentary system Iran had before 1953. That year, the CIA instigated a coup against the democratic government of Prime Minister Mohammad Mosaddegh and installed the pro-US dictator Shah Mohammad Reza Pahlavi. The Green Movement protest lasted about eighteen months but was eventually crushed by the government.

145

The massive upheaval of 2009 presaged Bashar al-Assad's reaction to the Arab Spring of 2011. Millions of people protested peacefully only to be brutally attacked by the authorities. The rulers accused demonstrators of being tools of Western powers and Israel. The regime tried to crush all opposition. In 2011, the Iranian government sent riot-control equipment to the Syrian authorities, trained their police, and helped establish local militias based on Iran's infamous *basiji*, thugs who beat and killed regime opponents. The Iranian authorities learned their lessons well and passed them along to the Syrian ruling elite: try to crush the movement early by striking hard.

Iran's support for Syria's dictatorship is nothing new. The two countries had built a geopolitical alliance dating back to Iran's 1979 revolution. The alliance of a secular dictatorship with a clerical regime might seem to be a strange partnership. However, while they differed ideologically, they united around opposition to Israel, the United States, and its Arab allies such as Saudi Arabia. Assad sought to play a leading role among Arabs, while Iran wanted the leadership mantle for the entire Muslim world. The two goals overlapped but didn't directly conflict.

Over the years, Iran developed strategic interests in Syria. Iran's Revolutionary Guard helped create the Lebanese Shia group Hezbollah. Iran remained a key source of military and economic aid to Hezbollah, much of it transshipped through Syria. Assad remained Iran's only Arab ally, and Syria formed a crucial part of an Iranian-influenced region that stretches from eastern Lebanon through Iraq, Iran, and western Afghanistan.

Iran also felt threatened by pro-US regimes in the Sunni Arab world extending from Turkey to Jordan, to Saudi Arabia and the United Arab Emirates. If a regime hostile to Iran came to power in Syria, it would radically shift the geopolitics of the region. "If Syria cannot continue to be an absolute ally of Iran, Tehran will not allow it to become an enemy," wrote Jubin Goodarzi, an assistant professor at Webster University in Saint Louis. "Iran therefore has the capacity to act as a long-term spoiler in Syria if Assad does eventually fall."[2]

Iran's reputation in the region has suffered immensely as many

Arabs came to resent its Syrian intervention. In 2006 Iran enjoyed overwhelming popular support in the Middle East because of its support for Hezbollah in its short war with Israel. By 2013, majorities in almost every country questioned by a Zogby Poll said Iran was playing a negative role. Zogby is a major US polling company that surveys public opinion in the United States and the Middle East. Even Palestinians gave Iran a 70 percent negative rating.[3] To understand this reversal of fortune, we need to explore some recent Iranian-Syrian history.

The grim visage of Ayatollah Ruhollah Khomeini is deeply imprinted in the American psyche. His long gray beard, tightly wrapped black turban, hawkish nose, and harsh expression came to personify evil. Khomeini and his clerics took power in Iran after a popular revolution overthrew the Shah in 1979. Student demonstrators seized the American embassy and held fifty-five staff members hostage for 444 days. The new regime broke from the US economic orbit, diversified its oil sales, and made alliances with nationalist and religious movements in the Muslim world. Khomeini became the symbol for Muslim opposition to the United States.

Khomeini and the Iranian leaders had little in common ideologically with Syria's Hafez al-Assad. Khomeini believed that Iran, indeed the entire Muslim world, should be governed by trusted religious figures. Assad was a canny military man who held no truck for religious government and sought to unite the Arab world based on pan-Arabism (see chapter 4). But the two leaders did have common enemies. Both opposed the policies of the United States and Israel. And both hated Saddam Hussein's Iraq. Assad's Baath Party had been mortal rivals with Iraqi Baathists dating back to a 1966 split in their once-unified party. Assad saw the 1979 Iranian revolution as potentially creating a new ally in the region. He sent Khomeini a gold-illuminated Koran in recognition of the revolution's victory.

In September 1980, Hussein launched a surprise attack on Iran. The brutal and costly war was to last eight years. While the Arab world sided with Iraq, Syria threw its support behind Iran. During the war, Syria closed an oil pipeline coming from Iraq, causing serious financial losses to Hussein. For its part, Iran sent one million barrels of free oil to Syria each year and eight million barrels at below-market price, a huge boost to the Syrian economy.[4]

The Iran-Syria alliance became solidly cemented in the early 1980s with the formation of Hezbollah. Before then, Lebanon's Shias supported the Amal Movement. But Amal's spiritual leader didn't agree with Ayatollah Khomeini that clerics should play a leading role in politics, and he refused to subsume Lebanon's Shias to Khomeini's authority. So Iranian leaders set out to undermine Amal, build a new party, and expand their revolutionary presence in all countries with large Shia populations. In 1981, a very young Hassan Nasrallah visited Iran along with other Lebanese Shia. Iran sent Revolutionary Guard officers to Lebanon's Beka Valley to help form Hezbollah. Khomeini appointed Sayed Ali Khamenei to supervise the creation and development of this new group, a fateful decision. Khamenei was to become Iran's Supreme Leader after the death of Khomeini. Nasrallah later said Iran "offered Lebanon everything in its power: money, training, and advice."[5]

In 1982, Israel invaded Lebanon with the intention of destroying the Palestine Liberation Organization (see chapter 4). It quickly defeated both the PLO and Syrian troops. Israel sought to use right-wing Lebanese Christian parties as their proxies but couldn't consolidate power. Hezbollah gained its reputation as fierce fighters during this period. Washington accused Hezbollah of bombing of the US Marine barracks in 1983, forcing Western troops out of Lebanon. Hezbollah, which didn't officially form until 1985, always denied the accusation. Over the next few years, with the support of Iran, Hezbollah replaced Amal as the dominant Shia organization in Lebanon, a situation that persists to this day. Amal eventually reconciled with Hezbollah, and the two forged an electoral and political alliance with Amal as the junior partner.

In 2002, President George W. Bush declared Iran to be part of the "axis of evil," a triumvirate of countries supposedly threatening US vital interests. The other two countries were North Korea and Saddam Hussein's Iraq. The United States occupied Afghanistan in 2001 and Iraq in 2003, coincidentally also getting rid of regimes hostile to Iran. Not surprisingly, Iran and Syria drew closer together with each successive US intervention in the region. During the past thirty-five years, Iran and Syria also consolidated economic ties. Iran opened an automobile assembly plant, a cement plant, and a power generating station, and it made other investments in Syria. Iran's exports to Syria increased from $35.7 million in 2000 to $387.4 million in 2010. Syrian exports to Iran increased by twenty times during those same years.[6] While the economic ties were mutually beneficial, they were not essential to the alliance.

The Iranian-Syrian marriage of convenience always had marital spats. During the mid-1980s Syria backed Amal in Lebanon while Iran favored Hezbollah. Syria sent troops to support the US-led Gulf War while Iran remained neutral. Ideologically the leaders of both countries remained far apart. Ayatollah Khomeini never invited Hafez al-Assad to Tehran because he was suspicious of the secular leader. Only in 2008, years after the deaths of both Khomeini and Assad, did Bashar al-Assad visit Tehran. Despite these differences, the two countries found unity in opposing the United States and its allies.

Syria, Iran, Hezbollah, and the Palestinian group Hamas developed what they called a "resistance front" to oppose US and Israeli policies, and they claimed some successes. It forced the withdrawal of Israeli troops from Lebanon in 2000 and repelled Israel's invasion of that country in 2006, according to Hossein Ruyvaran, a leader of the Society for Defense of the Palestinian Nation, an Iranian advocacy group based in Tehran. Today Iran is a key ally of Syria, he noted. "Iran is the pivot of this coalition," he told me.[7]

US policymakers worried about Iran's leading role in the resistance front. Under Secretary of State for Political Affairs Wendy Sherman told the US Senate, "Today, Iran is training, arming, funding, aiding, and abetting the Assad regime and its atrocious crackdown on its own people. Iran has made it clear that it fears losing its closest ally and will stop at no cost, borne by both the Syrian and Iranian people, to prop up the Assad regime."[8]

At least US and Iranian leaders agree on something: Assad's downfall would tremendously weaken Iran's regional influence. From the beginning of the Syrian uprising, Iran worried that "if the Assad government fell, the replacement would have much stronger ties with the US government and Israeli government," according to Professor Foad Izadi, an assistant professor at the University of Tehran's Faculty of World Studies. He told me, "that was the dilemma that Iran had."[9]

Tehran was generally pleased with the "resistance front" right up to the beginning of the Arab Spring. Iranian leaders don't talk a lot about it now, but they were pleased when the Arab Spring uprisings began. They called the Arab Spring an "Islamic Awakening" against corrupt, Western-backed, secular regimes. Iran hoped that conservative Islamist parties such as the Muslim Brotherhood would be more friendly to Iran than the old, pro-Western dictatorships. Tehran put out feelers to opposition groups in the Arab Spring countries. Professor Izadi told me that both Iran and Hezbollah understood that there were strong ideological differences between them and the Sunni opposition groups. Nevertheless, they hoped to establish friendly relations based on their common Islamic faith and opposition to the United States. "An ideal situation would be to have a [Sunni] religious government that is tolerant of Iran," he said.[10]

Izadi cited Hamas as an example of a Sunni group that cooperated with Iran, a relationship that cut across religious and ideological lines. "A group like Hamas, which is religious but friendly with Iran, is much better than a secular government," he said. He admitted that there was a rather large problem with the analogy, however. Hamas, which had been allied closely with Damascus for years, broke relations and supported the Syrian uprising in 2011. Hamas closed its Damascus headquarters and decamped to Qatar (see chapter 9).

So the Syrian uprising posed a major dilemma for Tehran from the very beginning. It couldn't abandon Assad, its closest Arab ally. But opposing the popular revolt against Assad would discredit Iran on the Arab street. "Iran was disinclined to be the benefactor of an Assad regime run amok in a time of democratic hope in the Middle East," according to Alex Vatanka of the Middle East Institute in Washington.[11]

During the initial months of the uprising, Iran met with Syrian opposition leaders and Assad to seek a political accord. Iranian government officials told Assad "it would be wise to hold free and fair elections," said Professor Izadi. If Assad won, he would be the legitimate ruler. If he lost, the Baathists would be "a major political player like Hezbollah in Lebanon. You win the elections or become a strong opposition." But, according to Izadi, Syrian leaders rejected that option. "They thought they could suppress the uprising."[12]

The Syrian opposition leaders also rejected the proposal for such elections because they trusted neither Assad nor Iran. Assad was never willing to share power, let alone resign, as demanded by the opposition. Efforts by Iranian leaders to mediate the dispute failed, and they threw their full support behind Assad. But it wasn't easy convincing the Arab street—even when the street came to Tehran.

In February 2012 Iranian authorities held an "Islamic Awakening" conference in Tehran, flying in hundreds of activists from around the Middle East. Event organizers cheered on those rebellions they liked, but the Iranian leaders wouldn't allow discussion of the Syrian uprising, claiming it was a Western conspiracy. "We must be vigilant: the West is trying to foment sectarian conflict in our societies, as part of their goal of keeping Israel alive," Iranian president Mahmoud Ahmadinejad told the conference. "Today Syria, tomorrow your country."[13]

But the efforts to isolate Syria's rebellion from the Arab Spring failed at the conference as it had on the ground. One young activist held up a sign reading "Syria?" and received enthusiastic applause, later followed by officially inspired boos.[14] That incident reflected a worldwide debate whether to support or oppose Assad. There is also a debate about the role of religion in the civil war. Some analysts say the war pits the Sunni majority against the Alawite and Shia minority, reflecting a centuries-old religious antagonism. Others say the civil war is political, not religious. As I discovered during a 2013 trip to Tehran, however, both sides use religion to rally their followers and vilify the enemy.

Sayed Mohammad Husseini sat behind the counter at a Tehran store selling religious CDs as he explained his support for Bashar al-Assad.

"I support Shias all over the world, including the Shia leader Assad," he told me with a smile.[15] When informed that Assad is Alawite, he looked confused. Most Iranians are unfamiliar with the Alawite branch of Islam, which has virtually no presence in Iran. Alawites are a small but powerful minority in Syria that began as a split-off from Shia Islam centuries ago and revere some of the early Shia leaders. Upon hearing that, Husseini nodded his head. "That's good enough," he said.

Iranian leaders said they support Assad as a bulwark against Israel, the United States, and Sunni extremist rebels. Inside Iran, however, they rallied supporters such as Husseini with appeals to defend Shia Islam against what they refer to as *takfiris*, or impure Muslims. Many Iranians saw Syria's civil war as part of an attack on Shia throughout the region, according to Professor Izadi. Some deeply religious people see that "there are Salafis [extremist Sunnis] threatening to blow up the shrines," he told me. "They don't know enough to realize that the Assad government is not a Shia government, and [is] actually secular."[16]

Other countries and political parties have lined up to support Assad or the rebels, reflecting the Sunni-Shia divide but also geopolitical interests. Shia leaders in Iraq, Hezbollah, and Iran support Assad, along with Orthodox Christian Russia. Sunnis in Turkey, Saudi Arabia, and Qatar back the rebels, along with the non-Muslim United States.

Iran and Hezbollah initially justified armed support for Assad by claiming to protect holy Shia shrines, an issue that resonates with Shia worldwide. For more than thirty years Iran had subsidized religious pilgrimages to the Sayyidah Zaynab shrine located just outside Damascus. The government provided pilgrims low-cost airfares and hotel accommodations.

I visited Sayyidah Zaynab prior to the 2011 uprising. Its beautiful gold dome rose in the distance. Handmade inlaid tiles created intricate designs on the walls. On the day of my visit, hundreds of Shia pilgrims arrived from Iran, Iraq, and Lebanon. The women had to wear *chadors*, the large, black cloth that covers everything but the face. Fascinatingly enough, just outside, a young Syrian man sold sexy lingerie to the chador-clad women who were exiting the shrine. The English language packaging read *Lady's Fashion Teddy*. While Shia Islam has strict prohibitions against nonmarital sex, married couples are allowed considerably more leeway. I asked the lingerie vendor why he sold his products outside a holy shrine. He looked at me incredulously. "To make money, of course."[17] And, of course, shopping for this and other more mundane items were only of minor concern compared to the religious importance of the shrine itself.

The Sayyidah Zaynab shrine is said to hold the remains of Zaynab, a granddaughter of the Prophet Mohammad. The shrine is holy for all Muslims but particularly revered by the Shia because Zaynab was the sister of Imam Hussein, one of the founders of their branch of Islam, and because she called for rebellion against an unjust ruler. The Shia make pilgrimages to the shrine much as Catholics visit Lourdes or the Old City of Jerusalem.

Sending troops to protect the Sayyidah Zaynab and other shrines rang true for many Shia. They well remember when, in 2006, Sunni extremists blew up the al-Askari mosque in Samarra, Iraq, located about eighty miles north of Baghdad. That bombing led to retaliatory attacks against Sunnis and initiated Iraq's sectarian strife. "From the beginning, we wanted to prevent another Samarra," said Palestinian activist Ruyvaran. "The [Zaynab] shrine is very inspirational. Any disrespect to the shrine would cause conflict between Shia and Sunni. So Hezbollah protected it."[18]

The shrine is just a half-hour drive from central Damascus along the airport road. But on a 2013 trip to Damascus, I learned that almost no one visits the shrine these days, according to Fadi Burhan, a spokesperson for the Khomeini Academy at Sayyidah Zaynab. His academy is named in honor of the late ayatollah. Foreigners long ago stopped making the pilgrimage, and the airport road is often closed due to fighting, making the journey impossible even for Syrians. "A few local people visit us," said Burhan somewhat sheepishly. Rebel mortar shells regularly hit the neighborhood near the shrine. Hezbollah and Syrian soldiers stand guard. "The rebels are shelling the Shia neighborhoods because they are loyal to the regime," he explained.[19]

Burhan represents a sector of Syrians who criticize the Assad government for being too soft on the rebels. He said Assad pursued a correct strategy fighting "terrorist" rebels but made tactical errors. "The government hasn't hit hard enough," he asserted. "It should have used an iron fist against the terrorists in the beginning."

In mid-2013, the government formed a committee to seek a negotiated settlement with select opposition groups. The rebels said the Committee of Reconciliation was useless, but Burhan claimed it was too conciliatory. "When the army besieges an area and wants to strike hard, some intermediaries from the Committee of Reconciliation intervene and prevent the attack on the terrorists," he said.

That's certainly not the view of tens of thousands of civilians trapped in major cities, cut off from food, water, and medical care by the Syrian army. And by 2013 it became clear that the army couldn't win the civil war without outside troops. Assad had a large army designed for conventional war, but it proved far less capable at the block-by-block fighting of counterinsurgency war. An estimated six thousand to eight thousand Hezbollah militants have fought in Syria as of mid-2013, according to Palestinian activist Ruyvaran, although exact figures are a closely guarded secret. Hezbollah played a crucial role in the Syrian army's victory in June 2013 in the western Syrian town of Qusayr, near the Lebanese border. The army's brutal tactics shocked even Hezbollah, as noted in chapter 6.

Hezbollah and Iran had stepped up their intervention because the Assad regime faced a series of military setbacks. By 2012 rebels had seized control of Syria's northern provinces. In July of that year, a Free Syrian Army bomb at an intelligence headquarters assassinated Defense Minister Dawoud Rajiha, former defense minister Hassan Turkmani, and Assef Shawkat, Assad's brother-in-law and a high-ranking security official. The Syrian army and security services set up checkpoints throughout Damascus.

Iran sent hundreds of specialists in urban warfare and intelligence gathering to Syria. Revolutionary Guard leaders openly boasted about training pro-Assad militias, also known as *shabiha*. Revolutionary Guard major general Mohammad Ali Jafari said, "It is an honor for the Islamic Republic of Iran to share its experience and provide any kind of consultation to help defend Syria."[20]

The Revolutionary Guard also set up a military camp outside Tehran that mainly trained pro-Assad Alawites but also Lebanese Shia from Hezbollah. Fighters were divided into groups of sixty to get training as snipers, heavy machine gun operators, and other specialties. The *Wall Street Journal* reported that fighters got much better training in Tehran than from the Syrians. "Before I could only hit targets 50 percent of the time, now I can hit a target around 90 percent of the time," said one trainee quoted by the *Journal*.[21]

But the effectiveness of the training came into doubt when the civilian militias returned to Syria. They were supposed to hold towns after the army recaptured them from the rebels. But numerous sources indicate that the militias are undisciplined, unaccountable, and engage in criminal activities such as kidnapping for ransom (see chapter 6). The Syrian government tried on several occasions to reorganize the militias but failed each time to make them an effective force.

While Tehran acknowledged sending military advisors to Syria, it denied providing combat troops. The military advisers were legal under terms of a long-standing treaty, according to Palestinian activist Ruyvaran, who lives in Tehran. "If we had combat troops, the dead would have come home. There have been no funerals." But Western sources argued that Iran had significantly boosted the Revolutionary Guard presence, including using some as combat troops. The *Wall Street Journal* reported that Free Syrian Army leaders had collected IDs of Iranian soldiers killed in combat.[22]

Tehran also stepped up economic ties with Syria in several strategic sectors. Even while smarting from US sanctions, the Iranian Central Bank offered Damascus a $3.6 billion line of credit to buy Iranian oil. And both countries agreed to build the Iran-Iraq-Syria Friendship natural-gas pipeline that may run 3,500 miles from Iran to the Mediterranean coast in Lebanon. Construction of the pipeline was disrupted by the civil war.[23]

This stepped-up military and economic assistance to Syria caused controversy inside Iran. Many of the activists of the Iranian Green Movement sympathized with Syria's opposition in the early days of the uprising. So they opposed Iran's strong support of Assad. But they soured on the armed rebellion as extremist Islamist groups gained power, according to journalist and political activist Abbas Abdi. He helped lead the 1979 student takeover of the US embassy in Tehran and later became a leader in Iran's reform movement. Abdi described himself as a reformer and not part of the banned Green Movement. Iran's opposition is "confused because the rebels have long beards and Assad's supporters wear fashionable clothes," said Abdi with a chuckle.[24]

But Iran's leaders also faced a dilemma. Assad failed to win a military victory and used increasingly brutal tactics. In June 2013, Iranians elected a relatively moderate president, Hassan Rouhani. Some thought he would shift Syria policy. The issue came to a head when some important Iranian leaders criticized the Syrian regime in late August and early September 2013, after the chemical-weapons incident created a major international crisis.

Iran's former president Ali Akbar Hashemi Rafsanjani gave a speech in which he admitted, "The Syrian people have suffered much during the past two years. More than 100,000 were killed and seven to eight million have become displaced. Prisons are overflowing with people, and they have turned stadiums into prisons." He became the first high-ranking Iranian to say Assad's government was responsible for that month's chemical-weapons attack that killed hundreds. "The people have suffered a chemical attack by their own government," he said.[25]

In September, Iran's new foreign minister Mohammad Javad Zarif also criticized Assad, a first for a sitting government official. "We believe that the government in Syria has made grave mistakes that have, unfortunately, paved the way for the situation in the country to be abused," Zarif told a Tehran publication.[26] But did Iranian policy on Syria actually change? First, we have to look at the wider context of Iran's relations with the United States and the West.

Successive US administrations have considered Iran a major threat to America's national interests. The pro-US government of the Shah had safeguarded US oil companies, allied with Israel, and acted as a local gendarme against regional anti-imperialist rebellions. The 1979 revolution brought to power religious autocrats opposed to US imperialism and to Communism, men who hoped to spread their version of radical Islam.

At first the US denounced Iran for fomenting "terrorism," referring to such groups as Hezbollah. But by the 1990s the United States and Israel came up with an even more frightening line of attack. They insisted that Iran was about to develop a nuclear bomb. In 1995 a "senior US official" said Iran was five years away from making a nuclear bomb. In 2006 Israeli intelligence agencies estimated Iran might be only one to three years away from having the bomb.[27] Iran did secretly develop nuclear enrichment for power generation, but neither the UN's International Atomic Energy Agency nor US intelligence agencies say Iran currently has a nuclear-weapons program. Nevertheless, the United States, Israel, and some European countries remain suspicious because Iran insists on maintaining its nuclear-enrichment program.

Both Washington and Tel Aviv insist that "all options," including intense aerial bombardment, remain on the table to stop Iran's nuclear program. In reality, Iran would never launch an offensive military attack on Israel. It could have attacked that country with conventional rockets and bombers years ago. But such an attack would invite devastating retaliation by both the United States and Israel. Iranian rulers may be evil, but they aren't crazy. Washington and Tel Aviv's real concern is that if Iran ever did develop a nuclear capability, it would make a US or Israeli attack far more risky (see chapter 10).

Beginning in late 2011, the West sharply escalated sanctions on Iran. Officially, sanctions targeted Iranian leaders and key industries, not ordinary people. Under Secretary of State for Political Affairs Wendy

Sherman told the US Senate, "US regulations contain an explicit exception from sanctions for transactions for the sale of agricultural commodities, food, medicine, or medical devices." She went on to say, "We have demonstrated that supporting the Iranian people and pressuring the policies of their government are not mutually exclusive."[28]

But US government officials admitted that the real purpose of sanctions was to worsen conditions on ordinary people so they will pressure their government to reform. In early 2012, the *Washington Post* quoted a "senior US intelligence official" as saying sanctions "will create hate and discontent at the street level so that the Iranian leaders realize that they need to change their ways."[29] The United States is also pressuring Iran to stop supporting Assad. Such geopolitical strategy talk sounds profound echoing in Washington's towers of power, but US tactics are devastating to the people of Iran, as I found out during a June 2013 visit to Tehran.

Every weekday many dozens of people wait in long lines at the Thirteenth of Aban, a government-run pharmacy that is their last stop to find drugs in short supply. One man unable to fill his prescription shouts angrily as he stomps out. "A lot of people are angry when they can't get their medicine," "Yusuf Abdi" told me.[30] He was waiting to get a chemotherapy drug and asked that his real name not be used.

Tahereh Karimi, a woman standing in the same line, knew that pharmaceuticals are supposedly excluded from the list of prohibited items under US sanctions. But in reality they are blocked by foreign suppliers afraid of angering the US government. "The United States knows what it is doing," Karimi said. "Tell Obama not to hurt ordinary people."[31]

Partly as a result of sanctions, the Iranian economy has been in free fall. Oil revenues dropped by 50 percent, the local currency lost as much as two-thirds of its value, and inflation hit 40 percent. The drop in the Iranian rial's purchasing power makes importing foreign drugs and medical devices particularly expensive. In addition, Washington has threatened international banks with severe penalties if they break the sanctions. So while banks are supposedly allowed fund transfers for medicine and medical devices, many find it easier to ban Iranian transactions altogether. "We can't get certain vitamin tablets because we can't send money abroad through the banks," said Khodadad Asnarshari, administrative director at the Sapir hospital in Tehran.[32]

"Bank hesitation is understandable given that a mistake could earn a bank the wrath of the US Treasury Department and fines that exceed $1 billion," according to an authoritative study of sanctions issued by the Woodrow Wilson Center.[33] Pharmacy owner Ghader Daemi Aghdam told me even affluent Iranians in north Tehran are struggling to pay the high cost of medicine. "I estimate 30 percent of my customers walk out when they see the cost of filling their prescriptions," he said.[34]

The impact of sanctions on poor Iranians is even more severe. Sapir, a Jewish charity hospital, serves all faiths but mostly working-class Muslims in south Tehran. Dr. Asnarshari said the cost of imported medical equipment, such as endoscopes, has increased five times since 2012. "We hear that the United States doesn't want people to suffer, but we are." For example, cancer patient Abadi was unable to find his chemotherapy drug Mabthera at any hospital or private pharmacy. In 2011 Mabthera cost the equivalent of $70 for a one-hundred-milliliter dose. Eight months' worth of treatments costs $840. Today the price has gone up 17 percent, but it's extremely hard to find, even at that price.[35]

So Abadi and other patients often take a walk down Nasser Khosro Street. The massive thoroughfare, not far from the city's famous bazaar, is crowded with midday shoppers. Traffic is clogged with cars, motorcycles, and pedestrians all trying hard not to collide with each other.

Within a few minutes of walking down the street, a young man approached me and whispered, "Medicine?" He and dozens of others operate like drug dealers, which they are. They just sell drugs for chemotherapy, diabetes, and hepatitis. The dealers weren't educated men and may not be familiar with the requested drug. The patient usually provided a prescription. Street dealers then made a quick mobile phone call to check availability and price. This day, Abadi's chemo drug was available, but at three times the official cost.

"Our drugs are of the finest quality," claimed one dealer with the polished confidence of a used-car salesman. "All the drugs are from Europe." He said the pharmaceuticals are smuggled from Iraq and Iraqi Kurdistan, usually in people's luggage. It's impossible to determine the age or quality of the drugs, and patients take real risks when making purchases. Black-market medicine existed for decades in Iran. It began during the horrific years of the Iran-Iraq War (1980–1988). Back then, Iran faced US sanctions as well as massive wartime shortages. Black-market medicine wasn't in high demand again until recently, according to the street dealer. After US and European sanctions were tightened in December 2011, business picked up. "With the new US sanctions, we see more demand," he said.

Analysts say that not all the medical shortages can be attributed to sanctions. Inflation was a serious problem in Iran long before the intensified US efforts. Iran has a system of subsidies that are popular among ordinary people. The government kept gasoline priced at only fifty cents per gallon. Each individual, including children, got a cash subsidy of thirty-six dollars per month at the official exchange rate. The government also provided subsidies for food, for education, and for young couples when they marry.[36]

Unlike government investment in job-producing enterprises or infrastructure, cash subsidies only drove up inflation, according to Mohammad Sadegh Janansefat, a prominent economist and editor of *Industry and Development* magazine in Tehran. Subsidies, without any productive work involved, are like printing extra money. Poor people got the government cash, but prices also went up. The government was always playing catch-up as inflation eroded real income. "The government can't raise its own employees' salaries enough, nor can the private sector," he told me. "So workers are caught in a squeeze."[37]

Government mismanagement became a big issue in the 2013 presidential elections. A number of candidates accused President Ahmadinejad of illegally funneling money into cash subsidies that were supposed to fund job-development programs. The cash subsidies had populist appeal until inflation sapped their value. Efforts to avoid sanctions also helped foster a climate of corruption. One businessman, who asked to use only the first name Abbas, said he deposited Iranian rials in an account with a money-changing store in Tehran. The store worked with a partner business in Dubai, which converted rials to dollars and then wired the money to foreign suppliers. The process was reversed when Abbas sold his products abroad. The currency shop made money converting currency and charging for the wire transfers. In turn, shop owners had to pay bribes to Iranian officials in order to stay in business. "Some people are getting very rich off the sanctions," said Abbas, "while most people are suffering."[38]

Whatever the role of mismanagement and corruption in causing shortages, in the view of most Iranians, the sanctions had made their lives much worse. Even during previous years of high inflation, prices for drugs and medical devices didn't skyrocket as they did in 2013.

Iranians suspect that the sanctions are aimed at changing their country's policies on Syria as well as the nuclear issue. So if the United States and Iran can negotiate a settlement on one, it might help with the other.

On January 20, 2014, the United States, Iran, and other countries began implementing a historic agreement: Iran agreed to freeze its nuclear enrichment program in return for limited sanctions relief. The interim agreement was slated to last six months and lead to a longer-term settlement that would allow Iran to develop nuclear power while blocking any future nuclear weapons program. In return, the West would gradually lift sanctions.

President Rouhani wrote an article clearly stating Iran's position about nuclear weapons:

> We are committed not to work toward developing and producing a nuclear bomb. As enunciated in the fatwa issued by Supreme Leader Ayatollah Ali Khamenei, we strongly believe that the development, production, stockpiling, and use of nuclear weapons are contrary to Islamic norms. We never even contemplated the option of acquiring nuclear weapons, because we believe that such weapons could undermine our national-security interests; as a result, they have no place in Iran's security doctrine. Even the perception that Iran may develop

nuclear weapons is detrimental to our security and overall national interest.[39]

But even such unequivocal statements weren't enough for American and Israeli right-wingers. Israeli prime minister Benjamin Netanyahu denounced the agreement, claiming Iran couldn't be trusted. The American Israel Public Affairs Committee (AIPAC), the main pro-Israel lobbying group in the United States, initially opposed the agreement and later sought to increase sanctions on Iran in an effort to scuttle a final settlement.[40] Israel continued to favor a military attack on Iran to overthrow the regime.

While basing their arguments on Iran's supposed nuclear threat, in reality the right wing feared that the agreement would undercut their ability to attack Iran for supporting Syria and Hezbollah and unravel their justification for regime change in Iran. In their view, the agreement signals US weakness in the face of an implacable enemy.

Weakening of US power in the region creates a "power vacuum," according to STRATFOR, a think tank located in Austin, Texas, that analyzes geopolitical issues. "The potential for Iran to control a sphere of influence from western Afghanistan to the Mediterranean is a prospect that not only frightens regional players such as Israel, Saudi Arabia, and Turkey, but also raises serious concerns in the United States."[41]

The hardliners in Iran make much the same argument—but in reverse. If Iran concedes on the nuclear issue, they argue, Iran will appear weak and lose its influence in the region. So the nuclear issue has taken on a political dimension in Iran well beyond the need for more electric power.

Initially, Iranian authorities argued that Iran needed to diversify its sources of electric power. Iran relies too much on oil-burning power plants, an inefficient method of electric power generation, given that Iran's oil reserves are in decline. That was the reason cited by the US government in the 1970s when it arranged for US nuclear energy companies to sell reactors to the Shah.[42] Iran's oil reserves have continued to decline since then.

But why is nuclear power a better solution? Particularly in the wake of the Fukushima disaster in Japan, nuclear power is known to be unsafe and extremely expensive. I put the question to Sayed Muhammad Marandi, associate professor, Faculty of World Studies, at the University of Tehran. Nuclear power is "an issue of sovereignty now," he told me. "When the United States says you can't do it, we will pursue it to the end." He echoed the arguments of hard-liners in Tehran who said Western sanctions spurred defiance during the eight years of Mahmoud Ahmadinejad's presidency. "If there were no sanctions, I don't think the Iranian nuclear program would be developed as much as it is today," said Marandi.[43]

Critics said the hard-line stand of Ahmadinejad on nuclear and other issues helped cause Iran's economic disaster long before the imposition of harsh sanctions. The 2013 presidential elections reflected an Iranian desire "to put an end to the mismanagement and failed policies that had endured under the Ahmadinejad government," according to Reza Marashi and Trita Parsi, leaders of the National Iranian American Council. "The Iranian people had pushed for the same shift in 2009, before the imposition of 'crippling sanctions,' but the hardliners resorted to fraud and repression to prevent their votes from being counted."[44]

The sharp differences between reformers and hard-liners in Iran also manifested itself in the debate about its Syria policy. Ahmadinejad, the Revolutionary Guard, and other hard-liners remained steadfast in their economic and military support for the Assad regime. They seemed to have the full support of Supreme Leader Khamenei. In December 2012, Iran put forward a peace plan that sought to maintain Iranian influence in Syria. It called for a cease-fire and the lifting of sanctions against Syria, the release of political prisoners, the formation of a transitional government, and then the holding of free elections under international supervision. The plan closely resembled one proposed by the United Nations with an important difference: Tehran wanted Assad to be part of the transitional government, a position immediately rejected by the opposition.

But a year later, after continued military stalemate and election of a new president, cracks began to show within the Iranian elite. President Rouhani made a surprising comment during a national TV appearance in September 2013. He contrasted Iran's sharp criticism of the dictatorship in Bahrain with its stand on Syria. "We should not describe as oppressive brutal actions in an enemy country while refraining from calling the same actions oppressive if they take place in a friendly country," he said, clearly referring to Syria. "Brutality must be called brutality."[45]

Tehran still preferred a political solution that protected Iranian interests, according to Professor Izadi of the University of Tehran. It all hinged on the fate of Assad. Tehran believes that without Assad, "it's very difficult to hold Syria together. . . . Having free and fair elections is very difficult now. It's very difficult for the Assad government to be an [opposition] political party with all the fighting."[46]

But Iranian leaders do see an exit strategy that might eventually ease Assad out of power. They know the Islamic extremist rebels won't participate in peace talks. But other rebels might be persuaded to join a power-sharing cabinet with Assad, "something like South Africa . . . where old wounds are healed," said Izadi. That could lead to elections that Assad might lose. Iranian leaders realize Syria can't go back to its old ruling system. "If Assad loses an election, and the country doesn't fall apart, that's the ideal situation for Iran." That assumes, of course, that Assad would allow free elections and then accept losing.

Iran argued that the civil war will continue so long as the United States and its allies provide funding and arms, so it was trying to convince the West that extremist Sunni rebels posed a bigger threat than Assad's regime. Foreign Minister Zarif told *Time* magazine that Iran is prepared to participate in international peace talks. He said Syria could have a huge international impact by pitting religious groups against one another and spreading terrorist attacks. "If the sectarian divide that some people are trying to fan in Syria becomes a major issue, it will not recognize any boundaries," he said. "You will find implications of this on the streets of Europe and America."[47]

Washington rejected the suggestion that Iran join peace talks unless it first agreed to Assad's ouster from power. Rouhani and other moderates might favor reducing support to Assad, but that decision will be made by Supreme Leader Khamenei. "Rouhani probably could not change Iran's approach to Syria even if he wanted to," noted Mehdi Khalaji, a senior research fellow at the Washington Institute for Near East Policy. "There are some indications that Tehran's Syria policy is designed and implemented by the Islamic Revolutionary Guard Corps, and therefore not fully under the president's control."[48]

Washington has always been reluctant to allow Iranian participation in a Syria peace process. In 2014, neither Assad nor the rebels appeared willing to reach a political settlement.

Each still hoped for decisive military success. Tehran will likely continue to back Assad until some other leader comes along who is willing to have friendly relations with Iran. Similarly, Washington will back the rebels, hoping to install a pro-US regime in Damascus. Eventually, the United States, Russia, and Iran will have to directly or indirectly agree on a political settlement if peace is to arrive in that troubled land.

CHAPTER 9

WILL THE KURDS HAVE THEIR WAY?

I met twenty-two-year-old Barkhodan Balo at a Syrian Kurdish refugee settlement in northern Iraq. Balo took me on a walking tour of the three-hundred-person Moqebleh Camp, which consisted of dirt roads and concrete-block houses with plastic roofs. When it rained, she told me, "you hear every drip. In the winter it's very, very cold. In the summer, it's very, very hot."[1] Balo taught herself to speak English by watching TV and movies. "I love English, and I love to speak." I asked her the name of her favorite movie star. "Jackie Chan!" she shouted with glee. Ah, the joys of globalization. A Syrian Kurdish refugee learns English from a native Chinese speaker more famous for his fighting skills than his diction.

Kurds make up an estimated 10 to 15 percent of Syria's 22.5 million people. The Kurdish language, culture, and historic territory make them a group distinct from Arabs, but they have become part of multinational Syrian society. Assad's government considers the Kurdish-dominated northeast of the country strategically important because it borders Turkey and Iraq. The Kurdish region is fertile, water is abundant, and it contains virtually all of the country's limited oil supplies. Government leaders feared Syrian Kurds secretly favored independence because Kurds in other countries have made that demand. All Syrian Kurdish parties currently reject separatism; however, they do demand greater rights as a distinct nationality within Syria.

To get more background on the Kurdish struggle, Balo and I walk over to her family's tent. She and her family migrated here after a Kurdish rebellion in 2004 in the city of Qamishli. Thousands of Kurds fled Syrian government repression after engaging in antigovernment protests.

167

Balo introduced me to her father, a political activist who was arrested in 2004, released, and then jailed again two years later. "He was tortured and brutally beaten," said Balo. "After he got out, he came home and took off his shirt and showed his wounds. He said, 'I want you never to forget the Syrian government deeds.' I was thirteen years old. But like any Kurdish girl, I joined the Kurds in the demonstrations. In our country, when children are six or seven, children learn about our society. When I saw the wound on my father's back, I cried. I was so angry. If I caught any policeman or even any Arab, I would have killed him and drank his blood."

Balo's animosity stemmed from government policy of bringing Syrian Arabs into the Kurdish region in an effort to dilute Kurdish influence. The government then incited those Arabs to attack Kurds. As she became older, Balo no longer blamed ordinary Arabs. "I know it's the government's fault," she said. "They brought Arabs from other cities and gave them land owned by Kurds." Kurds have long faced government discrimination in Syria. "After Syria had its independence from France," said Balo, "the Arab governments haven't given Kurds any rights. They worried about the Kurds separating. They didn't give them half the rights of Arabs."

At the time of the 2011 uprising, most Kurds opposed the Assad dictatorship but were also highly suspicious of the Arab rebels. Tens of thousands of Kurds fled Syria because of the fighting. By the middle of 2014, the Kurdish region had become a patchwork of areas controlled by the government, by extreme Islamists, and by Kurdish militias. To understand Kurdish attitudes toward the 2011 uprising, we must first understand some modern Kurdish history.

I met a Kurdish revolutionary for the first time at a Berkeley forum in the late 1970s. He wore traditional pantaloons, a loosely fitting jacket, a sash wrapped around his waist, and a twisted headscarf. He looked like a dashing rebel out of the previous century. Only later did I learn that Kurds proudly wear their traditional dress on special occasions, a practice that hasn't changed much over the years. I guess speaking to a bunch of Berkeley lefties constituted a "special occasion." At the time

I knew nothing about Kurds and sat in fascination as he described his people's long history.

Kurds trace their roots back nearly a thousand years as a nomadic people in the Middle East. Their language and customs are distinct from Arabs, although over time most adopted Islam. Today, by conservative estimate, 30 million Kurds live in Turkey, Syria, Iraq, Iran, and former Soviet republics. They constitute one of the world's largest nationalities without a homeland.

The famous twelfth-century leader Saladin, who drove the Crusaders out of the Middle East, was a Kurd from Tikrit in Iraq. Indeed, the famous Crusader fortress in Syria known today as Krak des Chevaliers, conquered by Saladin, was originally called Hisn al-Akrad (Castle of the Kurds). After the Crusaders' defeat, Kurdish military units settled in Damascus, creating what became known as the Kurdish Quarter of the city. Some Kurds maintained a strong warrior tradition, serving as loyal troops during Ottoman and French colonial rule. Others became anti-imperialist *peshmerga* fighters. *Peshmerga* is the general term for a fighting unit, which literally means "those who face death."

Historically, most Syrian Kurds lived in the northern provinces while some migrated to Damascus and Aleppo. During World War I, British officials promised independence to Kurds living under Ottoman rule. But as with similar promises made to Arabs and Jews, the British had no intention of giving up any of their colonial territory to fulfill the promise. In 1920 the Allies and the Ottoman Empire signed the Treaty of Sevres, which included maps of an autonomous Kurdish region of Turkey and called for a referendum on Kurdish independence within one year.[2] The treaty was rejected by Kemal Ataturk and the newly empowered Turkish nationalists, however, and was never implemented (see chapter 3). In 1923 the Treaty of Lausanne replaced the Treaty of Sevres, and it ignored the Kurdish issue entirely. As a result, the Ottoman-era Kurdish region was divided up between Turkey, Britain, and France. Nearly a century later, the unfulfilled promises of the Treaty of Sevres remain a Kurdish rallying cry for those who feel the old story is being played out again by regional and international powers.

Leftist and nationalist Kurds joined the anti-French-colonial movement in Syria during the 1930s. They founded a party called Xoybun, which, loosely translated from Kurdish, means "independence." In late 1931 and early 1932, Xoybun elected three parliamentary deputies in Syria's first election under a French-imposed constitution. The party eventually dissolved, and many members joined the Syrian Communist Party.

Political battles surged back and forth across the always-porous borders in the Kurdish regions. And, as the Berkeley Kurdish revolutionary reminded us, only one independent Kurdistan has ever existed. It was led by leftist revolutionaries at the end of World War II.

Reza Shah, Iran's dictator from 1925 to 1941, brutally suppressed the Kurds, who lived mostly in the far northwest of Iran. He had been brought to power by the British, but in 1941, he angered the allies by declaring Iran neutral during World War II. The allies labeled him pro-Nazi. In 1941 British troops entered Iran and occupied southern Iran while Soviet troops did the same in the north. Most Kurds welcomed the Soviet troops as liberators from the oppressive Shah.[3]

Local Kurds administered a quasi-independent government after the last of the Shah's officials left the Kurdish area in 1943. Kurds ruled the small city of Mahabad and surrounding areas. A judge named Qazi Muhammad allied with local merchants and tribal chiefs to set up a self-defense militia. With help from the Soviet soldiers, the area prospered economically—albeit under wartime conditions. In 1945, Kurds in the region formed the Kurdish Democratic Party (KDP), which was eventually headed by Qazi Muhammad. The KDP's main military leader was Mustafa Barzani, father of today's Kurdish Regional Government (KRG) president Masoud Barzani. The Soviet Union backed an independent Kurdistan as a check against British and American domination of Iran.

So with Soviet encouragement in 1945, Kurds declared the independent Kurdish People's Government, which became known as the Mahabad Republic. The new republic immediately set about making significant reforms without the repression associated with the Stalin-era Soviet Union. The new government opened a girls' high school and passed laws for compulsory education and free education for the poor. It introduced Kurdish-language instruction for the first time.[4]

But by the end of 1946, Soviet policy shifted as the Soviet Union sought an accommodation with the government in Tehran. It withdrew troops from the Mahabad Republic, and without Soviet support, economic conditions worsened. The KDP also lost support as some merchants and tribal chiefs switched sides to support the central government. On December 15, 1946, Iran's troops occupied Mahabad and quashed the independent republic. Under the rule of Mohammad Reza Shah, son of the previous Shah, Iran banned instruction in Kurdish and closed the Kurdish media. Qazi Muhammad was convicted of treason and hanged. Mustafa Barzani fled to northern Iraq and eventually to the Soviet Union to live in exile until his return to the region in the 1950s. Today both Barzani and Qazi Muhammad are regarded as heroes in the struggle for Kurdish rights.

Modern-day Kurdish political parties trace their history, in part, to the KDP of 1945. Syrian Kurds established the Kurdistan Democratic Party of Syria (KDPS) in 1957. The KDPS called for peaceful struggle to achieve Kurdish rights within the Syrian state, but it was banned nonetheless, and its members were forced to work underground.[5]

The Baathists came to power in a 1963 military coup and maintained the same antagonistic view of the Kurds. The new regime proceeded with plans to create an Arab cordon (*Hizam Arabi*) some three hundred kilometers long and fifteen kilometers wide along the Turkish and Iraqi borders. The Baathists didn't trust the Kurdish population and started to settle Bedouin tribes there beginning in 1973.

One Kurd told investigators for Human Rights Watch, "The government built them [Arabs] homes for free, gave them weapons, seeds, and fertilizer, and created agricultural banks that provided loans. From 1973 to 1975, forty-one villages were created in this strip. . . . The idea was to separate Turkish and Syrian Kurds, and to force Kurds in the area to move away to the cities."[6] Hafez al-Assad ended the resettlement program in 1975 but never returned Kurdish land or provided reimbursement for confiscated property. Over the next decades, he pursued an opportunistic policy toward the Kurds, continuing domestic suppression while supporting Kurds from other countries when it suited his foreign policy.

Over a period of thirty years Assad became a major player in the Arab fight against Israel, exerted control over Lebanon, and allied with Iran against Iraq. Even without a major army or economic clout, Assad created strategic alliances to promote Syrian power. He turned a lightweight country into a major contender for regional influence. Assad was a clever fighter, punching well above his weight. And his policy toward the Kurds was just one more jab.

The Syrian Baath Party was engaged in a vicious political fight with Iraqi Baathists, who had come to power in a 1968 coup. The main dispute centered on who would lead the Baathist movement: Iraq or Syria. Saddam Hussein helped engineer the Iraqi coup, and he became Iraq's president in 1979. So Assad decided to make an alliance of convenience with leftist and nationalist Kurdish groups to defeat the Iraqi Baathists.

By 1979, Assad formalized relations with the two main Iraqi Kurdish parties: the Patriotic Union of Kurdistan (PUK), led by Jalal Talabani (later president of Iraq), and the Kurdish Democratic Party (KDP), headed by Masoud Barzani (later president of Iraq's Kurdish Regional Government). The parties considered themselves on the left, with the KDP ideologically lining up with Moscow and the PUK aligning with Maoist China. They both opposed Saddam Hussein, and Assad allowed them to set up offices in Qamishli near the Iraqi border. Assad also allowed the Turkish-based Kurdistan Workers Party (Partiya Karkerên Kurdistan or PKK) to operate in Syria. The PKK has a long and controversial history.

Abdullah Ocalan and a group of student radicals founded the PKK on November 27, 1978, in the Kurdish region of eastern Turkey. Ocalan, a former political-science student, was a fiery leader who inspired complete obedience in his followers. Today PKK supporters hold high a poster showing a handsome Ocalan with slicked-back gray hair and a huge brush mustache. But few know what he really looks like since he's been held in a Turkish prison since 1999. The PKK began as a nationalist and revolutionary socialist group that believed in armed struggle. It was part of a 1970s surge of Middle Eastern nationalist groups adopting aspects of Marxism only to change their ideologies in later years.

In that era, the US-backed military regime in Turkey engaged in harsh repression against Kurds, refused to recognize them as a nationality, prohibited education in the Kurdish language, and banned Kurdish-language media. The Turkish military imposed martial law in Kurdish areas, which wasn't lifted until 2002. As of 2010 the army's counterinsurgency campaign killed some 35,000 civilians, imprisoned 119,000 Kurds, and disappeared another 17,000.[7] The PKK established a reputation for fighting military repression and gained some popular support.

The PKK originally called for the formation of an independent, socialist state to include the Kurdish regions of Turkey, Syria, Iraq, and Iran. It recruited large numbers of women and promoted some to leadership positions. In my almost-thirty years of reporting from the region, I have met few women leaders in any government or opposition party. So the active participation of women is no small accomplishment. I met some of the PKK women while reporting a story for *Mother Jones* in the Kurdish region of northern Iraq.[8]

The journey began at the seedy Ashti Hotel in Sulaymaniyah. The Ashti looked like something out of a Graham Greene novel. Its smoke-filled lobby served as a meeting place for obscure diplomats, businessmen, soldiers, and spies. Men sat around, staring at glasses of strong tea. Every now and again they'd pour a bit of tea into their saucers, let it cool, and slurp it down. From the Ashti we made arrangements to visit a PKK guerrilla camp in the nearby Qandil mountains. We rode in a four-wheel-drive vehicle as we climbed the mountainside. Green and brown scrub brush covered the land as a chilly wind caused me to button my coat. After one particular death-defying curve in the road, a large, fertile valley opened up. Herds of goats and an occasional gaggle of ducks crossed the road. I knew we had entered PKK-controlled area when I saw two young women wearing PKK uniforms of green pants and shirts with the traditional twisted Kurdish headscarf.

While waiting for an interview, I chatted with the PKK women as we huddled around a wood stove. They were confident and talkative, saying that almost 50 percent of PKK members are female.[9] Other sources report the number may be closer to 40 percent, but in either case, the numbers are impressive. The PKK claims there are no sexual relations among unmarried guerrillas, a fiction maintained to comfort the parents of girls going off to fight in the mountains.

The women boasted of attacking the Turkish military and police. But they said they didn't intentionally target civilians. The PKK does kill civilians working with the government, however, as well as Kurds they consider collaborators. Turkey, Britain, and the United States label the PKK as a terrorist organization. Other Kurdish parties have many criticisms of the PKK, but they make a distinction between terrorist groups such as al-Qaeda and nationalist groups engaged in armed struggle such as the PKK. In Syria the PKK-aligned party protected the local population from extremist rebels. "The majority [of Kurds] believe that despite the PKK's practices, they're a better option than Jihadists and al-Qaeda," said Hozan Ibrahim, a leader of the Local Coordinating Committees now living in exile.

During the 1990s, Syria allowed PKK militants to live in Damascus and receive military training in the mountains surrounding the Beka Valley of Lebanon, then controlled by Syria. The Syrian-PKK cooperation was a marriage of convenience. Assad wanted to pressure Turkey to negotiate the return of the Hatay region (see chapter 3). He also opposed Turkey's close alliance with Israel and the United States. The PKK used Syria to launch military attacks on Turkey.

By 1998, the Turkish government had become fed up with the cross-border raids and Syrian intransigence. The Turkish military massed troops along the border and threatened to attack Syria. One newspaper headline read, "We will soon say shalom to the Israelis in the Golan Heights," meaning Turkish troops would advance all the way to Syria's border with Israel.[10] So Hafez al-Assad, ever the strategic boxer, made one of his famous pivots. In October 1998 Syria signed the Adana Agreement with Turkey, declaring the PKK a terrorist organization and prohibiting its activities inside Syria.

Ocalan was forced to flee Damascus, and in 1999 he was captured in Kenya with help from the CIA. Taken to Turkey, he was convicted of treason and sentenced to life in prison. He's been serving time in isolation at the Imrali island prison ever since. Ocalan's arrest capped a series of major PKK defeats in the 1990s. In response, the PKK sought accommodation with the Turkish government and moved to the Right politically, abandoning Marxism and calling for Kurdish autonomy, not independence.[11]

In the early 2000s the PKK formed separate political parties for each of the countries where it operated. The Partiya Yekîtiya Demokrat (PYD), or Democratic Union Party, was formed in 2003 as the Syrian offshoot, led by Saleh Muslim, a chemical engineer. The PYD argued that it is an independent party with only ideological ties to the PKK; critics said the two parties are controlled by the same PKK leadership.

The PYD has developed a reputation for sectarianism, putting its own interests ahead of the broader Kurdish movement. The Kurdish National Council, the umbrella Kurdish opposition group, "has accused the PYD of attacking Kurdish demonstrators [and] kidnapping members of other Kurdish opposition parties," according to a report by the Carnegie Middle East Center.[12] The PYD has also been accused of assassinating leaders of other Kurdish parties.[13]

The PYD also shared the PKK's cult worship of Ocalan. Supporters kept his picture in their homes, chanted his name at demonstrations, and wore his image on T-shirts. A PYD leader calling himself "Can Med" told me, "The leader Abdullah Ocalan gave us a solution for all the issues. He defined the way to solve our issues."[14] However, the PYD and its armed militias presented a disciplined, secular force in a region beset with religious extremism and chaos. The party gained popular support in northern Syria as the best among the bad alternatives.

These days, the Turkish and Syrian governments condemn the

PKK and PYD as terrorists and blame them for lack of progress in achieving Kurdish rights. But long before the PKK was founded, the Syrian government oppressed its Kurdish population.

In the late 1950s and early 1960s, the Turkish government cracked down on Kurdish activists. The repression forced some Kurds from Turkey to flee to Syria. The military rulers of Syria, even before the Assad family came to power, didn't trust the Kurds. In 1962 the government conducted a special census in the predominantly Kurdish province of Jazira. The government denied citizenship to an estimated 120,000 Kurds, claiming they were born in Turkey or Iraq.[15] That constituted some 20 percent of Kurds living in Syria at the time. Successive generations born in Syria didn't receive citizenship either because their parents weren't listed as citizens.

Noncitizen Kurds remained in limbo. They couldn't obtain passports, be hired for government jobs, officially open businesses, or receive government-subsidized higher education and healthcare. The government confiscated the land of unregistered Kurds and gave it to Arabs. The problem festered for almost fifty years. Some 80 percent of Kurds lived below the Syrian poverty line as of 2007.[16]

I interviewed Bashar al-Assad before the uprising and asked why many Kurds still had no citizenship rights. He claimed it was simply a technical problem of sorting out who was Syrian and who was Turkish. I pressed him by pointing out that since many Kurds criticized his rule, wasn't the dispute political? "We don't have political problems," he claimed. "Who is Syrian is Syrian."[17]

In reality Assad didn't want to resolve the citizenship issue without exacting concessions from Kurdish leaders who periodically criticized his government. By 2011 the number of Syrian Kurds without citizenship grew to an estimated 300,000. Fearing Kurdish support for the uprising, Assad shifted course on April 7, 2011. He suddenly granted citizenship to about 250,000 Kurds. The exact numbers remain in dispute.[18] The reform was popular among Kurds, and Assad bought some much-needed time. But Kurds disliked his government, in no small part because of how he handled the 2004 Kurdish rebellion.

On March 8, 2004, Iraq adopted the Transitional Administrative Law, which formally recognized a semi-independent Kurdish region in northern Iraq. Syrian Kurds celebrated what they considered a tremendous victory for Kurds throughout the region. That national pride expressed itself at a local soccer match. On March 12 the mostly Kurdish hometown soccer team from Qamishli played a match against the mostly Arab team from the city of Deir Ezzor. Riding around in buses before the match, Deir Ezzor fans held up portraits of Saddam Hussein and chanted insults against Kurdish leaders. Kurdish fans shouted slogans supporting George W. Bush.[19] Fights broke out between the two camps, and the security forces sided with the Deir Ezzor fans.

The police killed six people on the first day. Refugee camp resident Balo said, "The next day when they went to bury them, there was conflict between the police and the people. The uprising started there."[20] Soon there were running battles in the streets. By the end of March, forty-three people were killed, hundreds wounded, and some 2,500 individuals arrested.[21] It was the worst anti-Kurd repression in modern Syrian history up to that time. Thousands fled across the border to Iraqi Kurdistan, where many still live today. Their children and grandchildren learn about the Kurdish struggle and the evil Bashar al-Assad. "We know after this regime in Syria falls," said Balo, "we are going to work for our rights, and we are going to free our Kurdistan."

Freeing Kurdistan—whatever form that might take—won't be easy. The Syrian government, ultraconservative Arab rebels, and Kurdish groups all want to control the oil fields in the Kurdish region. Before the civil war and 2011 Western economic embargo, Syria produced 370,000 barrels per day, accounting for only 0.4 percent of total world output.[22] The country is a small-time player internationally, but control of the fields is vital for any new Syrian government.

The Assads brought Syrian Arabs to live in the predominantly Kurdish area, so the population is now mixed. But the Syrian government and some rebels fear that an empowered Kurdish minority would seek control of oil production as happened in neighboring Iraq. The Iraqi Kurds have asserted the right to sign independent exploration, drilling, and distribution contracts with Western oil companies, despite strong objections from the central government in Baghdad.

Iraq, like Syria, has a state-owned oil company. The Baghdad government negotiated service contracts with foreign companies, who earn a fee for drilling and distributing the oil. That gives the foreign companies about one dollar per barrel. The Kurdish Regional Government (KRG), on the other hand, signed production contracts in which oil companies own a percentage of the production and earn three to five dollars per barrel.[23] Looking to the future, US and Western oil companies would be pleased if they could cut a similar deal with a Syrian Kurdistan.

That's a hypothetical dispute, however, because Western sanctions halted all Syrian-government oil production starting in late 2011. The Syrian army withdrew from much of the area. Local tribes, extreme Islamist groups, and the PYD competed for control of the unprotected oil wells. Locals set up open-air refineries by boiling the oil and then extracting diesel and heating oil. Explosions periodically rock the area, and huge plumes of toxic, black smoke pollute the air.[24] While control of oil sets the backdrop for the struggle, the issue of Kurdish separatism always comes to the forefront.

For the first three years of the uprising, Syrian Kurdish groups rejected separatism and called for greater rights within the Syrian state. By mid-2014, conditions were rapidly changing in the region. The extremist group ISIS captured swaths of territory in Iraq. The Kurdish Regional Government in Iraq sent peshmerga and intelligence agencies into the Iraqi city of Kirkuk and took control of the city away from Baghdad authorities. Iraqi Kurds had long claimed oil-rich Kirkuk as their capital, and they appeared to have finally achieved their goal. KRG officials planned to hold a referendum on complete independence for the Kurdish region of Iraq.

Syrian Kurdish groups were closely watching developments in Iraq. Should conditions further deteriorate in Iraq and Syria, Kurds might have the option of joining an independent Kurdish state on their northern border. But as of mid-2014 all the groups still formally called for greater rights within the Syrian state, not independence. The numerous Kurdish political parties disagreed on particulars but united on certain broad principles for greater political and culture rights:

- All Kurds born in Syria should have full rights as Syrian citizens, including the right to government jobs, passports, healthcare, and higher education.
- Kurds should have the right to be educated in Kurdish (as well as Arabic) and have Kurdish recognized as a legitimate language. They want the right to celebrate Kurdish holidays and learn Kurdish history.
- The new constitution should recognize Kurds as a distinct people.
- The name of the country should be changed from the Syrian Arab Republic to the Syrian Republic, reflecting the fact that Syria is a multinational country, not just Arab. It's similar to the debate in the United States whether America is a "Christian nation." Jews, Muslims, Hindus, and many others are deeply offended by that notion. They are people of the United States, but no one religion defines them. Similarly, Kurds consider themselves part of Syria but not Arab.
- Kurds should have some kind of local political control. Kurdish parties offer different solutions, including federalism, autonomy, and decentralization. The Kurdish movement is still fiercely debating the issue, and that struggle will certainly continue if a new government comes to power in Damascus.
- Kurdish parties have advanced these democratic demands for many years, but they gained momentum as the Syrian uprising began in March 2011.

In the opening months of 2011, popular uprisings overthrew the military dictatorships in Tunisia and Egypt. By March, Syrians in

Damascus and the southern city of Daraa held peaceful demonstrations demanding reforms, such as free elections and an end to police brutality. Similar spontaneous demonstrations broke out in the Kurdish region but on a smaller scale. I met a leader of those demonstrations after he fled Syria and was living in Erbil, Iraqi Kurdistan. "Ciwan Rashid" agreed to do the interview on a crowded Erbil street with a shopping mall and restaurants. "Rashid" was his activist name; he kept his real name secret for obvious reasons.[25]

Rashid had helped organize demonstrations in his hometown of Qamishli. Protestors quickly discovered that the government tapped phones operated by Syriatel, the country's dominant carrier owned by President Assad's cousin, Rami Makhlouf. So protestors came up with an ingenious method to outsmart the authorities. Rashid and others traveled across the border, bought a bunch of Turkish SIM cards, and then handed them out to protesters in Syria. SIM cards are the small circuit boards inserted in mobile phones to provide a local phone number and payment system. The Turkish mobile phone towers picked up signals in northern Syria, and demonstrators were able to communicate with less fear of eavesdropping.

Rashid told me, however, that the local security forces eventually caught on. "I was accused by the government of distributing the SIM cards, which is illegal," he said. "So I left the country." Demonstrators generally weren't using Facebook or other social media to mobilize people because the government closely monitored those sites. Syria was not experiencing a Facebook revolution. It was more of a mobile phone uprising. "I wasn't afraid," Rashid said. I asked why not. After all, people were being arrested and brutalized in jail. "There are two choices," he said. "One is to escape and survive. The second is to die. If I survive, I will have my freedom."

In 2011, young Kurds such as Rashid were the minority among the Kurdish population. Kurds remained critical of Assad but were also suspicious of the opposition. The traditional Kurdish parties didn't join the uprising, fearing government repression, and they were concerned that the Islamist opposition wouldn't respect Kurdish rights.

Mohammad Farho, a Syrian Kurdish commentator and activist living in Erbil told me, "Kurds are afraid of the Arab opposition parties because their agenda is not clear."[26] The Arab opposition groups were willing to recognize Kurds as equal Syrian citizens but not as a distinct nationality with legitimate language, cultural, and political rights.

During most of 2011, the Assad government took full advantage of the divisions between Arabs and Kurds. The Syrian military brutally attacked Arab cities such as Homs and Hama but shrewdly decided not to launch such devastation in majority Kurdish areas. "The regime tried to neutralize Kurds," Yekiti Party leader Hassan Saleh told me. Yekiti is a nationalist Kurdish party that supported Assad's overthrow very early in the uprising. "In the Kurdish areas, people are not being repressed like the Arab areas. But activists are being arrested," he said.[27]

While older leaders remained cautious, young Kurds seized the moment to organize antigovernment demonstrations in Qamishli. In other cities such as Aleppo, they joined Arab Syrians to hold protests. And their champion among the Kurdish leaders was Mashaal Tammo.

For his official appearances, Tammo dressed in a dapper suit, tie, and stylish glasses. At age fifty-four he still exuded youthful charm. Tammo formed the Future Movement in 2005 as a center-left group committed to Kurdish rights within the Syrian state. He was arrested and spent two years in an Assad jail, being released in 2011 under popular pressure from the uprising. The charismatic leader supported the uprising from the very beginning. Tammo became a hero to the young Kurds risking their lives in the streets. "There is a new generation of young people in Syrian society who do not share the same fears as the older generation," he said. "These young people will build the new Syria."[28]

Tammo called for the overthrow of the Baathist regime and establishment of a parliamentary system with civil liberties for all. He said any new "constitution should be a mirror of the cultural diversity of the Syrian people. Laws must be developed for parties, voting, the press, and so on. . . . Those groups who want a modern and civil democratic state will win out."[29] The Future Movement demanded full language, cultural, and political rights for Kurds within the Syrian state. "Syrian Kurds are not looking to separate from Syria," Tammo said, "though of course the idea of a Kurdistan is a dream."[30] In a July 2011 interview, he called on the West to impose an economic embargo on Syria but opposed foreign military attacks. "We do not want military intervention from abroad," he said. "We will solve the problem ourselves."[31]

Tammo reached out to Arab opposition forces and joined the executive committee of the Syrian National Council (SNC), the US-backed opposition coalition bringing together secular, Islamist, and some Kurdish groups. He attended an early meeting of the SNC in Istanbul but walked out in a dispute over Kurdish rights: the SNC wanted to keep the country's name as the "Syrian Arab Republic." Tammo and the Kurds wanted the name changed to "Syrian Republic."

Tammo's views were gaining popular support because he called for Kurdish rights and for overthrowing Assad without foreign military intervention. Then on October 7, 2011, masked men assassinated him outside a safe house where he was hiding. The Syrian government accused opposition "terrorists" of carrying out the murder. But many Kurds blamed the Syrian authorities, who benefitted from the death of a popular leader with a significant following among young people. On the day of Tammo's funeral, fifty thousand people marched in Qamishli to protest his assassination. Government security forces fired live ammunition into the crowd and killed at least five people in Qamishli and several in other cities.[32]

Tammo's murder was a turning point in the Kurdish struggle. Mass demonstrations got bigger, the traditional Kurdish parties lost influence, and the youth-driven opposition gained stature. The Kurdish movement became radicalized with more people calling for the overthrow of Assad by force of arms.

The Democratic Union Party (PYD) was the first of the Kurdish groups to take up armed struggle in *Rojava*, Kurdish for the northern region of Syria. It smuggled in weapons using networks established by its affiliate, the PKK. I interviewed a PYD leader who used the name

Can Med in Erbil in the fall of 2011. At that time, the PYD called for limited foreign military intervention to protect civilians and topple Assad. He also predicted that the PYD would soon launch armed attacks on the Syrian military. "If you want to get arms in the Middle East, it's easy," said Med. "We can do that."[33] The PYD clashed with government troops but also with the Free Syrian Army and extremist Islamists who tried to take over towns in the Kurdish region.

In July 2012, Assad began to withdraw his army from the smaller Kurdish towns to concentrate forces in Damascus. A garrison remained in Qamishli, the largest predominantly Kurdish city in Syria. The PYD stepped into the gap and sent its fighters into four towns close to the Syrian–Turkish border and into a Kurdish district of Aleppo. They raised the PYD flag, with the Kurdish flag flying below it.[34]

Iraqi Kurdish leader Masoud Barzani saw that the PYD was gaining ground. So he began to give military training to Syrian Kurds, many of whom lived in refugee camps in northern Iraq. Barzani formed the Special Coordination Committee (SCC) with its own militia. But as of late 2013, those militia had not taken up fighting inside Syria, partly fearing retaliation by Assad—but mostly due to opposition from the PYD. In July 2012 the PYD, SCC, and all the other Syrian Kurdish parties met in Erbil at the invitation of Barzani. They signed what became known as the Erbil Agreement, which formed a united political and military coalition against Assad. But very quickly, internal rivalries caused splits. The PYD formed its own coalition, the People's Defense of West Kurdistan. The two groupings met again in September and called for a united front against Assad and for Kurdish rights within Syria.

Although sharp differences remained among the sixteen Syrian Kurdish parties, both the Syrian and Turkish governments became very worried. The Turkish military feared that the Kurds could create a de facto independent state in northern Syria that would have close ties with the PKK. So early in 2012, Turkish authorities and their Syrian rebel allies sought to discredit the PYD. They argued that the PYD and PKK supported Assad and had cut a deal to seize Kurdish territory in order to attack Turkey.

The Turkish government cited the 1980s- and '90s-era alliance between the PKK and Assad to prove that they were cooperating once again. That conveniently fit with Ankara's policy of supporting the Muslim Brotherhood while opposing political gains by Kurds. Turkish authorities told their national media that the Syrian government had rewarded the PYD for its support by allowing it to take over the four Syrian towns. Numerous Western media took up the refrain. Dutch journalist and analyst Wladimir van Wilgenburg offered a more nuanced view, noting that at various times the PYD has had de facto détentes with almost all the major armed players. "The main goal of the PYD is to create autonomous areas," he told me.[35] "So, it doesn't matter to them if they need to cooperate with al-Qaeda, Assad, Free Syrian Army, or anyone, as long as it serves their goals. They are not a proxy of anyone; they follow their own strategy."

The PYD opposed both Assad and the Turkish-backed rebel groups. Saleh Muslim, head of PYD, gave an interview to *Al Jazeera* in which he said, referring to Syria, "We cannot defend tyranny, oppression, and we want to bring down the regime, and the difference is only in the mechanisms and means."[36]

Turkish authorities didn't want to admit that, broadly speaking, Syrian Kurds opposed both Assad and the Islamist opposition backed by Turkey. The PYD reflected that view as well. "The Kurds have established themselves as a third way in Syria," wrote Mustafa Karasu on the PKK's official website. "They did not side with either the current regime or an opposition completely lacking in democratic and liberationist characteristics."[37] Ironically, he went on to echo a position that the United States and Europeans could endorse: "Bashar Esad [al-Assad] will leave Syria and the Baas [Baathist] regime will cease to exist, but a Syria in which political Islam will be sovereign will not be acceptable. There will not be a single hegemony. . . . Political Islamists will not be side-lined as they were by the Baas regime, but they will also not be the primary power holders." He also criticized the Arab nationalist opposition for not recognizing Kurdish rights.

The PYD has gained credibility on the Kurdish street because of its seemingly reasonable demands and its ability to defend Kurdish towns from both the Assad military and extreme Islamists. Many Kurds sharply disagree with the PYD, seeing them as sectarian and authoritarian. But accusing the PYD of supporting Assad only served to discredit the Turkish authorities.

When that campaign didn't work, the Turks shifted course. The Turkish foreign minister said his country wouldn't oppose autonomy for Syrian Kurds, a major PYD demand.[38] Then in July 2013, Turkey invited PYD leader Saleh Muslim to meet with high intelligence officials. Turkish officials told Reuters that they wanted assurances that the PYD firmly opposed Assad and that it wouldn't create an autono mous region through violence.[39] For its part, the PYD was willing to make alliances with the Turks, local Syrian government officials, and the Arab opposition. So the possibility existed for a political reconciliation between Turkey and the PYD.

"The PYD is a pragmatic party that has its own project to administer Syria's Kurd-populated areas," according to Maria Fantappie, researcher for the International Crisis Group. "We can expect them to make all the alliances they need as a temporary compromise."[40]

On January 21, 2014, Kurds declared autonomy in three provinces of northern Syria. Spearheaded by the PYD, representatives of fifty parties signed the declaration. The newly autonomous authorities promised to work with other Kurdish political parties and to protect the rights of Assyrians and Arabs who live in the area. They promised free elections within a few months. The autonomy announcement, which had been planned for months, came just before the start of the Geneva II peace talks and was designed to highlight the Kurdish issue internationally.

The PYD, as the main driver of the autonomy plan, took the initiative because it saw Syria fracturing, with Alawites and Sunnis exercising de facto control of their areas. PYD leader Aldar Xelil told Reuters that Syria should remain one nation but with a federal system in which Kurds would have considerable local control as they do in Iraq. "A division from Syria itself, it won't happen," he said. "A federalized system though—that is possible."[41]

While autonomous in name, the newly minted authorities struggled to provide basic services in the small cities they controlled. They refined diesel pumped from government oil wells and distributed it at low cost to farmers for use in tractors and home generators. The PYD was providing basic security against attacks from the Syrian army and extremist rebels. Human Rights Watch of New York sent a delegation to the newly autonomous zone. Delegation member Floyd Abrahams said, "Compared to other parts of the country . . . the security situation is relatively stable.[42]

Abrahams went on to criticize the PYD, however, for not allowing free expression and media, and for police routinely beating criminal suspects. He said the authorities don't have a "high intolerance" for different political views. Leaders of the other major Kurdish trend, the Kurdish Democratic Party (KDP), also criticized the autonomy plan as mere rhetoric. The Assad government still controlled much of Qamishli, noted KDP member Mohammed Ismail. "Government ministers still come on visits here," he told Reuters. "State employees still get their salaries, the phones still work, the healthcare system is in place. Where is this local autonomy they speak of?"[43]

The PYD had emerged as the strongest Kurdish party in Syria, controlling a number of towns and border crossings into Turkey. After over forty years of covering insurgencies around the world, I've developed a rule of thumb. You can learn a lot about how a group will govern after the revolution by how they exercise power in areas they control *before* the revolution. Let's take a look at how the PYD stacks up.

I interviewed Christians who had fled Hasakah, a mainly Kurdish region in northern Syria. They were terrified of the al-Nusra Front militiamen who had set up roadblocks, robbing and raping Christians. By comparison, the PYD militia respected Christian rights, according to Saba, a Christian female refugee I interviewed in Lebanon. "They protect their areas but they don't interfere in ours," she said. "They are very well organized. We've never had any problems with them."[44]

But some Kurds living in the PYD-controlled town of Afrin told a different story. "Almost everyone in Afrin has been threatened by the PKK," resident Tourlin Bilal told *Global Post*. "They demand taxes from everyone. If you refuse they threaten, steal, or destroy your property . . ."[45]

In theory, the Democratic Union Party (PYD) and Kurdish National Council (KNC) were jointly ruling the towns. Another resident named Oum Beshank said, "On paper, there is a coalition rule, but in reality the PKK [PYD] are the only ones with the weapons to force the people."[46]

The PYD faces strong opposition from other, smaller armed groups, such as the Islamic Kurdish Front, the Peshmerga Falcons, and the Martyrs of Mecca, all located near Aleppo.[47] Such groups fight along-side Arabs of the FSA and denounce the PKK. They want to remain part of Syria and oppose separatism, claiming that the PYD favors independence. Serious fighting broke out when two extremist groups, al-Nusra and the Islamic State of Iraq and al-Sham (ISIS), kidnapped 250 Kurds in July 2013. Most of the hostages were Kurdish civilians taken when the groups seized control of two Kurdish villages. The groups clashed with the PYD, and dozens were killed on both sides.[48]

Some FSA militias and extremist groups issued a joint statement denouncing the PKK/PYD, indicating a new level of antagonism. They accused the PYD of dividing Arab and Kurd, thus helping the Assad government. The PYD, they wrote, created "a hostile relationship with hate and resentment that drains a lot of our time, effort, blood, and money."[49] The groups made no mention of Kurdish rights, instead characterizing the entire Syrian struggle as religious. "Our goal is to pleasure Allah and to ensure a safe life for our people in Syria and to maintain the unity of the Muslim Syrian people, and to maintain the progress of our blessed revolution until the fall of the criminal regime."[50]

Even the FSA and conservative Islamists believe that religion will solve problems between Kurds and Arabs. They fear that the call for Kurdish rights is just a prelude to the dismemberment of Syria. To find out more about the mainstream Arab opposition view, I went to Istanbul to interview Muslim Brotherhood leaders.

I met with Omar Mushaweh, a member of the Directorate of the Muslim Brotherhood. Asked about Kurdish rights, he immediately criticized the

PKK for divisiveness. He made no distinction between the PKK and PYD. The brotherhood received strong financial, political, and military support from Turkey, so it wasn't surprising that he echoed the Turkish government position that the PYD was supporting Assad. "There are some extremist Kurds who are actually supporting the regime," he told me. "At the beginning of the uprising, some of them created instability in southern Turkey.[51] He criticized the PYD for raising the PYD and Kurdish flags in the towns it controls, saying they should fly the Syrian opposition banner. Mushaweh expressed a willingness to talk with the Barzani-backed KNC, which he saw as more moderate. "The KNC has their own vision about the Kurdish state, which doesn't necessarily represent the vision of all the Kurds in Syria," he said. "We are negotiating with them to reach the best solution."

Neither the brotherhood nor other Arab opposition groups are willing to recognize the Kurdish region's autonomy. Mushaweh argued that autonomy only promoted separatism. "Many of the Kurdish leadership don't express their desire to separate from Syria, but they sometimes list some demands that will lead eventually to separation," he said.

For years, Kurds were among the strongest opponents of Assad. But Kurdish groups found themselves fighting both Assad's army and political Islamists who were unwilling to recognize Kurdish rights. Kurdish leaders, at latest count, had formed sixteen parties broken into two coalitions. Those reflect the wider conflict between the major trends in Kurdish politics: Barzani's forces in the KRG and the PKK in Turkey. They sometimes form tactical alliances, but their underlying political differences make future unity difficult.

Masoud Barzani sees himself as a leader of all Kurds. He has the financial and military resources of the KRG and can thus potentially train a powerful Syrian peshmerga. Significantly, he has the support of the United States and Turkey, who strongly oppose the PKK. The United States, which claimed to be a staunch defender of Kurdish rights when seeking to oust Saddam Hussein, did an about-face in Syria. Because it sees the PKK as the main enemy, the Obama administration came out against autonomy. Assistant Secretary of State for European and Eurasian Affairs Philip Gordon said, "We don't see for the future of Syria an autonomous Kurdish area or territory. We want to see a Syria that remains united." He also said the Syrian opposition should be more inclusive of Kurdish concerns but didn't provide specifics.[52]

The Kurds weren't following US advice. They continued to oppose the Assad regime while asserting their national rights. Both Arabs and Kurds have a common interest in creating a parliamentary system in which the majority rules but minorities retain their rights. The Arab opposition must accept Kurdish demands for local political control while the Kurdish groups should seek unity among themselves and reach out to the civil-society opposition.

As the Syrian uprising continues, both the government and rebel forces are paying closer attention to Kurdish demands. The Kurds have become the wildcard in the Syrian uprising, and they have no intention of leaving the game.

CHAPTER 10

ISRAEL, PALESTINE, AND SYRIA

I grew up a Zionist—not out of ideological conviction, but because I thought all Jews were Zionists. Living in west Los Angeles in the early 1960s, being Jewish meant telling Jewish jokes, attending temple three times a year, having a discriminating palate for chopped chicken liver, and donating dimes to plant trees in the Negev desert of Israel.

Being Jewish also meant unconditional support for Israel. When studying for my bar mitzvah and later for confirmation, I learned the Zionist version of history: Jews had faced genocide in the Holocaust, Israel provided the world's only safe haven for our people, and now the Arabs wanted to kill us all.

By 1965, I had joined the growing anti–Vietnam War movement while attending the University of California, Berkeley. That movement for the first time presented me with an alternative view. It shocked me to learn that Israel supported the Vietnam War, allied with the dictatorial Shah of Iran, and had close ties with the apartheid regime in South Africa. Israel later even helped South Africa develop atomic weapons.[1]

I learned that Israel supported US, British, and French military aggression while opposing groups fighting colonialism. While claiming to be the victim of a far superior Arab force, in fact, Israel had the strongest military in the region. Most importantly, every time Israel went to war claiming self-defense, it grabbed new territory. By the end of the June 1967 War, Israel had expanded more than three times the size of its original borders under the 1948 UN plan while refusing to recognize the legitimacy of a Palestinian state. At that time, Israeli officials argued that if Palestinians wanted a homeland, they should go to Jordan.[2]

For me, this all came to a head in June 1967, when Israel waged war against Syria, Egypt, and Jordan. After only six days, Israel won a decisive military victory and seized the West Bank, the Gaza Strip, and Syria's Golan.[3] I opposed the war. When I announced my newfound beliefs to my parents in Los Angeles, they freaked out. It was worse than marrying a Catholic. They flew me down from Berkeley to meet the rabbi.

Rabbi Isaiah Zeldin was an outspoken liberal, a supporter of civil rights, and an opponent of the Vietnam War. A few years earlier he had founded Stephen S. Weiss Temple, a bastion of liberal Jewry. But like most Jewish liberals, he believed that Israel was only acting in self-defense. For people of my parents' generation who lived through the virulent anti-Jewish bigotry of the 1930s and '40s, and the horrors of World War II, Israel could do no wrong. Or if it did, as American Jews, they couldn't say anything about it.

I spent the day with the rabbi, arguing Middle East history and Zionism. I learned a lot from the discussion. For example, that there were labor and conservative Zionists. The labor Zionists advocated social democracy and some set up egalitarian *kibbutzim* (communes). But neither Zionist trend recognized the rights of Palestinians. The rabbi argued that American Jews shouldn't criticize Israel unless they were willing to move there. Engaging in a little Talmudic debate, I asked, "So if a Vietnamese living in America wants to criticize the Vietnam War, he must first move to Saigon?" The rabbi was not amused.

Rabbi Zeldin lost the argument that day. I broke with Zionism and supported a two-state solution in which Israeli and Palestinian nations could live in peace. I also wanted Israel to return all of the Golan to Syria. Little did I know that I would someday see the Golan from both sides of the disputed border.

An Israeli friend and I got ready for the five-hour drive from Jerusalem to the Golan. I planned to interview Israelis and Arabs living there about the Syrian Civil War. My friend took us on the scenic route, past the Dead Sea area, east to the Jordanian border, and then north on a two-lane road that skirted the Sea of Galilee. Then I realized why we took this route. On the left was the sea, the region's largest source of fresh water. On the right were hills sloped upward at a sharp angle.

"Before the Six Day War," my friend said, "Syrian army snipers would shoot at us from those hills." Syrian troops would also lob artillery shells into Israel. Israel captured the Golan in 1967, lost some of it in the 1972 war, and then annexed the remainder in 1981. For years the Israeli government considered these hills critical for its self-defense. Whatever the accuracy of that claim before 1967, today it makes no sense because missiles need no commanding heights. Extremist rebels have lobbed mortars and fired rifles from Syria into the Israeli kibbutzim in the Golan. Annexing the Golan hasn't guaranteed Israel's security. Only a mutually beneficial political settlement can do that.

We continued our journey as the road wound through the mountains. My rented car ("May I please have your least expensive model?") slowed as we hit the steep grades. The Golan has become quite a tourist attraction. Israelis come here to ski, backpack, and taste wine. Kibbutzim raise grapes and other fruit. One even became famous for dubbing TV and films into Hebrew. Broadband may one day replace drip irrigation as a source of sustenance.

An estimated twenty thousand Arabs of Syrian origin live in the Golan—those who didn't flee after the 1967 war. Most, but not all, are Druze, and they live in their own towns. The Israelis live in kibbutzim but say they get along well with the Druze. Compared to relations with Palestinians, that's true. But most Druze resent the continued occupation of Syrian land and also support Palestinian self-determination. The citizenship statistics tell the story. The Arabs could become Israeli citizens, enjoying the same status as Israeli Arabs, but 90 percent refuse. Since those born after 1967 aren't Syrian citizens either; they became stateless.

By midafternoon, we entered Majdal Shams, the largest Arab town in Golan. Now the road got really steep, potholes multiply, and I was downshifting into first gear. I can only imagine what the roads were like during the time of colonial occupation, when donkeys and horses must have suffered multiple hernias.

At the center of one traffic circle sits a statue of men in traditional Druze dress. There stands Pasha Sultan al-Atrash and his fighters from the 1925 rebellion against the French. From these Jabal Druze hills, he gathered his fighters to attack the French railroads and military camps. The Arabs of Golan proudly remember that history.

In 2006, I visited the same area, but from the Syrian side. The government had constructed a small building near a UN observation tower to accommodate meetings along this international border. Below was a chain-link fence and a no-man's-land mined by the Israelis. Syrians used bullhorns to shout to relatives standing on the Israeli side. It became known as "the shouting fence." For years it was the only way families could communicate after being separated by the 1967 war.

Cell phones and e-mail had almost replaced the bullhorns. But as Syria's civil war destroyed cell phone towers and sometimes slowed Internet connections to a crawl, the shouting fence came back into fashion. Residents just don't use bullhorns anymore. "There are problems with communications now," said Maryam Ajami, whose apartment overlooks the fence from the Israeli side. "I used to contact my relatives by Skype, but now we go over there, to the roof of that restaurant, and talk to each other over a public address system."[4]

The shouting fence was just one reminder of Israeli occupation. Akba Abu Shaheen, an elementary school teacher living in the occupied Golan, told me he wanted the area returned to Syria. He admitted that economic conditions are much better here in Israel than in Syria. But he quoted Jesus that "man does not live by bread alone." He added, "My history, culture, my family, and I belong to Syria."[5]

Given the civil war across the border, however, the question arises: To which Syria would Golan return? The civil war has split residents into pro- and antigovernment factions. Shaheen is Druze, an Islamic minority group. The war affects him personally because he said extremist rebels would persecute minorities if they came to power. "It's important for me not to live in a religious country, but in a secular country," said Shaheen. "It's important for Syria to remain a state for all its people."

Shaheen stridently supported President Bashar al-Assad, echoing the Syrian government argument that outside forces created the uprising. He argued that even before the Tunisian uprising that initiated the Arab Spring, imperialist powers were plotting against Syria. "I think it was an international conspiracy on Syria from the very beginning," said Shaheen. "Maybe the CIA or other agents took many young people from Arab countries to West Europe to train them."

But other Golan residents said the uprising reflected genuine popular discontent with the Syrian government. Dr. Ali Abu Awad favored the rebel Free Syrian Army and suffered the consequences. He said pro-Assad militants firebombed his car and attempted to burn down his house. He told me that in the long run, a rebel victory would improve the lives of ordinary Syrians. "Assad the dictator made Syria a desert politically," he said. "It will take time to make democracy in Syria. But we have a history. We have people who can do that."[6]

But how long will that take? I took a side trip in the Israeli-occupied Golan to try to find out. I was working with a local Arab journalist, Hamad Awidat, who had been recommended by a friend. But I hadn't known him previously. He was our fixer, the person who set up interviews, translated, and arranged transportation. After nightfall we drove down an isolated and pitch-dark dirt road outside Majdal Shams. He said our destination was a surprise. I wasn't sure if we were being set up for a scoop or a kidnapping. Even a flat tire would have stranded us for hours.

The Golan air was chilly and crisp. A kibbutz orchard stretched out on the right. Finally the driver stopped in front of a large rock and a concrete barrier. It was the end of Israel. Below were the fence, no-man's-land, and lights from Syrian towns. We could hear the distant pounding of Syrian army artillery. Awidat pointed out the areas controlled by the Syrian army, the Free Syrian Army, and al-Nusra. It was a minitableau of the civil war. It would take a long time before one side could prevail.

We saw a vehicle at the border flash its lights. Awidat explained that every night Israeli military ambulances went to the border to pick

up severely wounded people. Syrians living in the proregime areas generally had access to government hospitals. Rebels and their supporters
did not. The Israelis said they would treat severely wounded people as
long as they did not carry arms. The Israelis treated both civilians and
FSA soldiers. In order to make sure they don't allow al-Nusra extremists to enter, the Israeli military had to coordinate with the FSA.

Officially, Israel had proclaimed its neutrality in Syria's civil war.
But as indicated by its policies in the Golan, the reality was different.
To find out more, I had to visit Tel Aviv.

Israel's public-transport system is quite good. I arrived at Jerusalem's
central bus station one morning, stood in a short line, and paid the
equivalent of eleven dollars for a one-way ticket to Tel Aviv, which is
forty-two miles away. A bus left every twenty minutes. My bus quickly
filled with students, retirees, business people, and young soldiers clad
in olive-green uniforms and carrying Galil assault rifles. I was off to
interview experts at Tel Aviv University, one of the country's most
prestigious educational institutions.

While the transport system is cheap and efficient for Israeli Jews,
it's very different for Arabs. Palestinians from the West Bank can't
travel anywhere in Israel without special passes. Palestinian residents
of East Jerusalem are legally able to travel but are often afraid to ride
the bus. On a previous trip from Tel Aviv to Jerusalem, I sat next to a
young woman grading papers in English. She turned out to be a Palestinian resident of East Jerusalem who commuted to teach at an Arab
school near Tel Aviv. On the bus, she never wore a hijab nor spoke in
Arabic. She spoke only English, fearing the driver or a passenger would
throw her off. By being quiet, she hoped to pass as a foreigner.

I got off at the Tel Aviv station and took the short taxi ride to the
university. I walked into the sprawling campus to meet Eyal Zisser, a
history professor and dean of the Faculty of Humanities. Back in early
2011, when most of the world welcomed the democratic aspirations
of the Arab Spring, Israeli leaders were already wary, according to
Zisser. After all, demonstrations were targeting pro-US dictators who

had reached accommodations with Israel. Israel might have to pay the price for having cooperated with such repressive regimes.

So when Syrians rose up, Israeli leaders were wary once again. For all Syria's anti-Israel rhetoric and supposed support for Palestinians, the Assad family had kept the Israeli border quiet and secure. "He's the devil we know," Zisser told me. "We got used to Bashar al-Assad. This regime is evil . . . but at the same time, it kept the border quiet. Better to stay with Bashar al-Assad. Who knows what will happen if he falls?"[7]

Zisser explained that Israeli leaders held split opinions about Syria, much as in Washington. Some Israelis preferred to see the overthrow of Assad if a compliant Sunni regime came to power. Zisser summarized that view. "Any future Sunni regime will be better for Israel than Bashar . . . because this will be a blow against Hezbollah and Iran. Any Sunni government will be more moderate because it will be connected to the Saudis, Turks, and Americans." The flaw in that argument, he noted, is that a Sunni regime could also open the door for al-Qaeda.

Zisser said other government leaders believed Israel benefitted so long as the civil war continued. "Bashar will stay in power, strong enough to keep the border quiet but too weak to attack Israel. That's the ideal situation for Israel. Unfortunately, at one point or another, the war will end."

And I thought *American* leaders were callous about the impact of war on ordinary people.

I walked a few blocks over to the Institute for National Security Studies (INSS), a university-affiliated think tank. About half the analysts were former government officials. I figured this was as good a place as any to hear the divergent views within Israeli ruling circles.

"Assad is considered to be a serious enemy of Israel because he's firmly in the Iranian-led camp," said Mark Heller, an INSS analyst.[8] Israeli leaders initially thought Assad would be out of power quickly. In December 2011, Israeli defense minister Ehud Barak told the World Policy Conference in Vienna that Assad would be overthrown "within weeks."[9]

Israeli leaders considered various outcomes. One of the worst would be a new parliamentary government in Syria that respected minority rights, a result Heller thought highly unlikely. "If the dictatorship of Assad was replaced by a liberal democratic regime, then it might be a little harder for Israel to occupy the moral high ground and to resist demands for a peace agreement that included major territorial concessions."

Heller said the longer Assad stayed in power, however, the more Israeli leaders adjusted their policies. "People are in a watch-and-wait mode."

But critics said Israel was doing a lot more than watching and waiting. Israel was helping the FSA. It made use of close ties with the army and intelligence services of Jordan, where the CIA was training rebels. A commander who left the Free Syrian Army to join an extremist rebel group said Israeli intelligence helped train the FSA in Jordan.[10] Israeli leaders will never acknowledge such cooperation because they know full well that any public declaration of Israeli support would discredit the FSA.

In one of the great ironies of the war, both Assad and the rebels accuse Israel of helping the other side. And to some extent it's true. At one point Israel was happy to see a weakened Assad stay in power, although it soon sought his overthrow. Israel hoped all sides would exhaust themselves fighting, leading eventually to a new dictator willing to deal realistically with Israel.

In the fall of 2013, Israel acknowledged providing food and water to Syrian villages along the Golan border in addition to treating the wounded. Israel characterized this as "humanitarian assistance" and not taking sides in the war.[11] But Israeli officials certainly knew which villages were controlled by the FSA, the Syrian army, and al-Nusra. They made sure aid didn't go to al-Nusra or the army. But there were even more direct signs of Israel's opposition to Assad.

The Israel Defense Forces (IDF) attacked Syria on five occasions in 2013, each time claiming it wasn't taking sides in the civil war but only stopping arms shipments to Hezbollah. The IDF didn't publicly acknowledge any of the raids, but US intelligence confirmed them. In January Israeli planes fired missiles at a Syrian convoy carrying

Russian SA-17 antiaircraft missiles, allegedly being delivered to Hezbollah. Then twice in May, Israel launched missile strikes at a warehouse storing advanced surface-to-surface missiles and other arms.

US intelligence sources said the warehouses contained Iranian Fateh-110s, solid-fuel missiles with a capability of hitting Tel Aviv from Lebanon. Israel unilaterally asserted the right to deny Hezbollah such "game changing" weapons.[12] On those days, the IDF also attacked Syria's main military complex in Mount Qasioun and the Scientific Studies and Research Center, both in Damascus and well away from the missile warehouses. The attack killed over a hundred soldiers, with many dozens injured.[13]

It's difficult to verify claims that Israel attacked only weapons destined for Hezbollah. After all, the Syrian army also used Fateh-110 missiles. But even if true, why would "neutral" Israel attack a Syrian army headquarters? IDF officials knew Syrian soldiers would be killed. I think Israel hoped to weaken Assad at a time when his troops were winning some battles against the rebels.

Smaller-scale attacks continued. In July, the IDF attacked a missile depot in Latakia and then repeated the attack in November, having apparently missed some munitions in the original strike.[14] Israel launched yet another attack near the Syrian–Lebanese border in February 2014.[15]

Firing missiles at another country constitutes an act of war—unless you're Israel or the United States. Israel was just asserting its right to punish Syria for crossing a red line drawn unilaterally by Israel. As a practical matter, the Assad regime was too weak to respond. And Israel was getting ready to enforce a much bigger red line—this one drawn by the Obama administration.

In September 2013, Israel threw its full weight behind Obama's plans to bomb Syria in connection with the use of chemical weapons. Israeli officials argued that US credibility was on the line. Israel drew red lines and enforced them militarily. Now it was time for the United States to do the same.

A high-ranking Israeli official finally admitted that Israel favored Assad's overthrow. "We always wanted Bashar Assad to go," Israeli ambassador to Washington Michael Oren told the *Jerusalem Post*.[16] "We always preferred the bad guys who weren't backed by Iran to the bad guys who were backed by Iran." He continued, "The greatest danger to Israel is by the strategic arc that extends from Tehran, to Damascus to Beirut. And we saw the Assad regime as the keystone in that arc."

Around the same time, the *New York Times* wrote, "As the death toll has mounted, more Israelis joined a camp led by Amos Yadlin, a former head of Israeli military intelligence, who argues that the devil you know is, actually, a devil who should be ousted sooner rather than later."[17]

For Israeli leaders, the time had arrived to topple Assad. A US bombing campaign would provide cover for a rebel takeover. Israel mobilized its powerful lobbying apparatus in Washington to sway public opinion and pressure Congress. Such campaigns had always worked in the past, whether to increase US military aid to Israel or to tighten sanctions on Iran.

In August, the American Israel Public Affairs Committee (AIPAC) mobilized hundreds of followers to lobby Capitol Hill to back Obama's plans to bomb Syria. They spread out to meet with conservative Republicans and centrist Democrats, convinced they would prevail. But they lost, big time. Obama had so little popular support that he didn't dare risk a congressional vote authorizing war.

Abraham Foxman, national director of AIPAC, said rather defensively, "There's nothing sinister, nothing conspiratorial, nothing wrong with the lobbying arm relating to Israel and the Middle East supporting the president on this issue."[18] AIPAC was formed in 1951 to promote closer relations between the United States and Israel. In its mission statement, AIPAC carefully stresses the mutually beneficial nature of its work: "The mission of AIPAC is to strengthen, protect and promote the U.S.-Israel relationship in ways that enhance the security of Israel and the United States."[19]

But opponents said AIPAC uncritically accepted Israeli policies that made a peace settlement impossible. For example, AIPAC uncritically supported ultra-right-wing prime minister Benjamin Netanyahu's expansion of Jewish settlements in the West Bank and Jerusalem. AIPAC and other groups making up the Israel lobby had healthy war chests, strong support from key American politicians, and the reputation for defeating politicians at the polls who didn't support their pro-Israel positions.

That's why the Israel lobby's three defeats in 2013 were so surprising. The lobby failed to prevent the confirmation of Chuck Hagel as secretary of defense in February 2013, despite Hagel's alleged "anti-Israel" bias. In September it failed to mobilize public opinion to bomb Syria. And then in late 2013, the Obama administration began talks with Iran to prohibit development of nuclear weapons. The Israel lobby joined with right-wing and centrist senators in an effort to toughen sanctions against Iran, which would likely have ended the negotiations.[20] The Israel lobby lost and, as of mid-2014, new sanctions weren't imposed.

Mustafa Barghouti said AIPAC's defeats were quite significant. He leads the Palestinian National Initiative, a small socialist party in the Palestinian parliament. When Barghouti ran for president in 2005, he garnered 20 percent of the vote.

Referring to AIPAC's defeats, Barghouti told me in a West Bank interview, "For the first time, it became clear there is a huge divergence between the Israeli government policy and American policy. . . . Once AIPAC tried to get a resolution that hurts the interests of the American public, they couldn't pass it. This will go in history as a very important turning point."[21] He said American Jews didn't want war despite the heavy push from Israel and AIPAC. He praised the rise of liberal Jewish lobby groups.

An ad hoc coalition of liberal Jews, progressive Iranians, and peace groups helped defeat AIPAC. "This is the best we've ever been coordinated," Lara Friedman told the Jewish Telegraphic Agency. She's director of policy and government relations for Americans for Peace Now, a liberal Jewish peace group. "There's a whole bunch of groups, we're disparate, we have our own agendas, our own boards and positions, but we're sharing information the way an informal coalition should, and it's empowering people to be more effective. This is the most energizing and fun thing I've done in years. You feel you're not alone."[22]

A subheadline in the liberal Israeli daily *Haaretz* summed up the predicament of Israel and its lobby: "Israel finds itself isolated in the world arena, with only Saudi sheikhs and US lawmakers at its side; perhaps it's time to consider other diplomatic options besides perpetual petulance."[23]

AIPAC and the Israel lobby remained powerful, however. They had no intention of folding their tents anytime soon. So it remains to be seen if the 2013 defeats were temporary or a long-term trend.

Amid the upheaval of civil war, the future status of the Golan has gotten lost. It's worth reviewing recent history to see how it might be resolved.

When Israel captured Arab land in 1967, the United Nations passed Resolution 242, calling for the return of all occupied territory, among other provisions.[24] Israel promptly ignored 242. Through the 1970s, Israel sent settlers to build infrastructure and kibbutzim in the Golan. Israel ruled under military administration. Then in 1981, Israel decided to govern Golan with the same civilian laws used in other parts of Israel, effectively annexing the occupied territory. Neither Syria nor the United Nations recognized the annexation. In December 1981, the UN Security Council unanimously passed Resolution 497, declaring the annexation "null and void."[25] Even the United States—Israel's staunchest ally—rejected the annexation and continues to see the Golan as occupied territory.

Today the Golan includes some twenty thousand Israeli settlers living in more than thirty settlements.[26] An estimated twenty thousand Syrians and their descendants lived in their own towns, often getting jobs in the settlements. An uneasy peace prevailed as the vast majority of Arabs wanted to reunite with Syria while the settlers strongly opposed returning any of the land.

Israel and Syria periodically hold negotiations on the Golan issue. In 1999 and 2000, the two sides came close to a settlement. Israel proposed to return territory based on maps drawn by Britain and France in the 1920s. Israel would keep all of the Sea of Galilee and ten meters of its shoreline. Syria insisted on the 1967 border, which included all of the occupied land and a small northeast corner of the Sea of Galilee. The difference could be measured in yards, according to analyst Heller.

He said both sides descended into an argument that "only lawyers could appreciate." The dispute hinged on whether "the waterline as it existed in the early 1920s was the permanent feature or whether the border should move as the level of the lake fell or rose. The substantive point is that Israel doesn't want Syria touching the waterline."[27]

That difference is critical. The Sea of Galilee is an important source of fresh water for Israelis. They want complete control. Syria, on principle, wanted all of its territory back. It also wanted to have access to an important source of water. As Mark Twain reportedly said, "whiskey is for drinking, but water is for fighting."

In 2008 both sides tried again to reach a settlement, using Turkey as an intermediary. The conflicting sides never met face-to-face, instead passing messages along to Turkish leaders. Assad was reluctant to start one-on-one talks unless he could be assured of success.[28] Assad reportedly said that he and then Israeli prime minister Ehud Olmert came close to making a deal.[29]

As word leaked of a possible peace plan, settlers in the Golan strongly objected. They issued a statement that all settlement construction would continue unabated. Then, in December, Israel launched a three-week assault on Gaza in an effort to stop Palestinians firing homemade rockets into Israel. That eliminated the chance for any Golan settlement, and the Turkish dialogue ended.

In 2010 both sides tried yet again. Prime Minister Netanyahu's government held secret talks with Syria. Israel saw Syria as a potential weak link in a Syria-Iran-Hezbollah axis. It hoped to break off Syria and then move on to a settlement with Lebanon, excluding Hezbollah. Netanyahu offered to return all of the Golan if Assad would break with Iran, according to a report in the Israeli daily *Yedioth Ahronoth*. Netanyahu denied he made such an offer.[30] Talks ceased in 2011 with the beginning of the Arab Spring uprisings.

One reason talks never succeeded was that Israel kept shifting the goalposts. Israeli officials would launch Syrian talks when negotiations with the Palestinians weren't going well, hoping to reach a separate deal with Syria. Later, they added the new condition that Assad break with Iran in order to make progress on Golan. Then Israel argued that it couldn't return the Golan because there's no stable government in Syria. "As a general principal, Israel's permanent preference is to have authoritative decision making bodies on the other side so Israel can carry out a rational, strategic dialogue," analyst Heller said.[31]

As the civil war in Syria intensified, Israelis reached an informal consensus not to negotiate about the Golan. Zvi Hauser, Israel's cabinet secretary from 2009 to 2013, wrote an opinion article for *Haaretz*: "Israel will not be capable of dealing with a three-pronged front, consisting of Iran on a nuclear threshold, a failing Palestinian state . . . and a Syria dangling its feet in the Sea of Galilee."[32]

Instability in Syria certainly raised serious problems of how to return the Golan. But it could be resolved. Both sides could agree on borders in principle while postponing implementation until Syria became stable. That solution doesn't appear likely anytime soon.

I had learned the Israeli and Druze views about the civil war, but where did the Palestinians stand? For that I traveled to both the West Bank and the Gaza Strip.

Crossing from West Jerusalem to Ramallah was very easy when I first visited in 1986. I went to one of the main hotels in Arab East Jerusalem and found a collective taxi. They were old-school Mercedes limos with an added bench seat. The car for millionaires became transformed to a nine-seat taxi with several hundred thousand kilometers on the odometer. I'd pay a few shekels, grab an empty seat, and get dropped off anywhere in Ramallah.

The world changed in the 1990s. Under the guise of preparing for two states, Israel created militarized structures that functioned as border crossings between countries, except Israeli soldiers had total control of the border. Combined with the separation wall that cuts the West Bank off from Israel, Palestinians became trapped in an area designated by Israel, not the result of swapping land for peace. Israeli officials claimed these procedures protected the country from terrorism, but they served only to anger Palestinians and make reaching a peace agreement more difficult.

During a recent trip I drove on a modern four-lane highway from West Jerusalem, past Israeli housing in East Jerusalem, and then dropped off onto a side street that took me to the crossing point. It was traveling from the first to the third world. On the outskirts of the Kalandia checkpoint, dusty lots held a few cars, and there seemed to be no parking rules.

I didn't know where to cross, so I began walking toward some Israeli soldiers. One advanced menacingly toward me, motioning me away. I asked politely in English where I should enter. His mood suddenly brightened, and in excellent English, he pointed to a turnstile. As a foreigner I'm permitted to visit the West Bank. Israeli citizens are not allowed.

Once in the West Bank town of Kalandia, I was welcomed by a vibrant, third-world cacophony. Taxis gunned their engines and seemed to honk their horns in syncopation. The smell of hot olive oil and baking baklava filled the air. Pedestrians had no right of way in front of insistent drivers.

Taxi drivers quickly surrounded me, offering the best deal for the thirty-minute drive to Ramallah. At least, they assured me it was the best deal. I came to interview Hannan Ashrawi, a former spokesperson for the Palestinian peace negotiators, human-rights-group founder, and a member of the Palestine Liberation Organization executive committee.

I've interviewed Ashrawi numerous times because she's intelligent and capable of giving a straight answer in flawless English. She doesn't always *give* a straight answer, but at least I know it's not a communication problem. Ashrawi has aged, as have we all. She sat calmly behind her desk at the PLO headquarters and asked if the interview was for print or radio. For broadcast interviews, she would give short sound bites. For print, she would provide more elaboration. I was filing for both print and radio, I explained, causing momentary confusion. "Give me the long version," I said.

Ashrawi acknowledged that the Syrian uprising remained a controversial question. In general, Palestinians sympathized with people overthrowing dictators, she said, in part because the United States and Israel have a long history of allying with such men. "The United States has been dealing with dictators for years," she said. "Dealing with dictators is much easier. All you have to do is convince the big man, and generally, they are men."[33]

Ashrawi said Palestinian leaders in the West Bank are neutral. "We have Palestinians in every neighboring country that are vulnerable. Any side you take, the Palestinians will pay the price. We are in principle on the side of the people . . . and of course on the side of human rights, democracy, and rule of law. All we know is that violence won't solve anything."

Fatah is one of the two major parties in Palestine and the main force in the PLO. Fatah and the Palestinian movement had frequent conflicts with the Assads. In 1976, when Syria was backing the Christian right wing in Lebanon, Syrian troops helped lay siege to the Tel Al-Zaatar refugee camp, resulting in the death of an estimated three thousand Palestinians. Hafez al-Assad tried to take over the PLO and install his own man to replace Yasser Arafat in the 1980s (see chapter 4). "There's a long history of problems between Fatah and Assad," Ashrawi told me. "I remember when Fatah fighters and revolutionaries were in Syrian jails. But you're not supposed to hold a grudge."

Palestinians were extremely optimistic when the Arab Spring began, according to Ashrawi. "It was a transformational process. It was the will of the young, the reformers, the women, and civil society. We believed it was a defining moment in the history of the Arab world."

Mustafa Barghouti agreed. He told me Palestinians enthusiastically supported the Arab Spring for the same reason Israeli leaders opposed it. Genuinely popular Arab governments would support the Palestinians and refuse to make backroom deals with Israel. "We thought these movements will improve the Palestinian situation because the public in general is very supportive. If the public has the right to direct the policy, then this will be a stronger solidarity with Palestine."[34]

But Palestinians faced disappointments when the Arab Spring in Egypt and Libya turned to a frigid winter. Ashrawi said in some cases, the polarization between the old, corrupt regime and political Islam "led to the exclusion of the forces of reform and democratization that should have taken over. In other cases," she said, referring to Egypt, "the people who did rebel and bring down the regime mobilized in cyberspace but couldn't organize on the ground to bring out the vote."[35]

In the case of Syria, Palestinians thought Assad would be overthrown quickly, Ashrawi said. "People underestimated that the control of the Assad regime is powerful, not just the apparatus of government but also the private sector and others. . . . It's not just the Alawites." Ashrawi remained optimistic about the possibility of progressive change in the Arab world. "By definition transitions are painful, unpredictable, quite often destabilizing. We are still in this period of transition. The cost is exorbitant in human lives particularly in Syria. It's still in a state of flux."

Getting to Gaza wasn't easy. The Israelis strictly controlled their border, and for many years the Egyptian authorities made it impossible for journalists to enter from their side. That changed for a brief time in 2011. The people had overthrown the Mubarak regime and wanted greater support for the Palestinian cause. Border restrictions eased. That's when I entered Gaza.

I made arrangements through the Egyptian press office in Cairo. At that time no visa was required to enter Gaza. Anyone crazy enough to visit Gaza was apparently welcome. I hired a car and driver and we set out for the five-hour drive from Cairo to the Rafah border crossing. We jumped in the car, buckled our seatbelts, and couldn't leave the parking space for five minutes because the Cairo traffic was so thick.

We started late and got caught in Cairo's morning rush hour. Of course, it's always rush hour in Cairo. This was just worse. Once we got past the airport and onto a four-lane highway, the driver zoomed past cars at about eighty miles per hour. I liked the Cairo congestion better.

The Sinai is lots of desert—and flies. Moses and the Jews wandered here for forty years after outfoxing the pharaoh. I didn't fault them for getting lost. The Sinai stretches for arid miles, the sand only interrupted by an occasional lonely road.

An Egyptian press-office representative met me at the Rafah crossing point and escorted me through customs. I was pleased to have him there. The process of filling out forms and inspecting luggage was complicated, involving numerous lines. I would never have figured things out on my own. Finally, I paid a small fee and boarded a large bus. We drove about thirty yards to enter Gaza. There's no foot traffic or civilian cars, and certainly no commercial trucks. Requiring everyone to ride a bus gives authorities on both sides greater control.

The bus passengers included forty-nine Palestinians and me. When we arrived in Gaza, efficient guards with full beards took our passports: *Let's see: Ahmad, Deeb, Shafi, Erlich—Erlich?* The guard motioned me to wait at the side. Eventually a supervisor who spoke some English came to ask why I wanted to visit Gaza. I explained that I was a journalist, holding my hands in front of my head as if I was operating a movie camera. "CNN," I said, using the internationally recognized term for crazy American journalist. I explained that I wasn't *with* CNN but was a journalist like those *on* CNN. He smiled, perhaps thinking he would see himself on satellite TV that night.

I gave him the mobile number of a friend who was picking me up. He phoned, we all met, and then I went through an informal entry process. The supervisor asked my friend for the names of his father and brothers. Gaza had a population of about one million, so everyone knew everyone else, or at least someone in the family. My friend was warned that if I did something wrong, he would be held responsible. With that, we sped off as fast as the potholed roads would allow.

I interviewed a number of Hamas officials. They made clear that Hamas stood with the people of Syria against Assad. "We are with the people wherever they are fighting for their political and economic rights," said Ziad El-Zaza, Gaza's former deputy prime minister. "The blood of Arab martyrs is on the heads of the government leaders in

Syria."[36] That's a huge change for Hamas, which had been close allies of Syria. To understand why they split, let's look at some recent history.

Hamas had won the Palestinian parliamentary elections of 2006. International observers praised the elections as democratic.[37] But the United States, Israel, and Fatah wouldn't accept defeat. The long-simmering differences between Hamas and Fatah boiled over and fighting broke out. By 2007 Hamas seized control of Gaza, and Fatah took the West Bank.

The two parties, at that time, also differed in their attitude toward Syria. Fatah had an antagonistic relationship with the Assads dating back decades. The Syrian government prohibited Fatah from organizing among Palestinian refugees living in Syria or Lebanon. Hamas, on the other hand, had allied with Syria. Hamas moved its headquarters to Damascus in 2001. But it was always a marriage of convenience. Syria was a secular state that repressed its own Islamic movements. Hamas was a conservative Sunni organization that opposed secularism. As Khaled Meshal, chair of Hamas's Political Bureau, told me in a Damascus interview, "We and Syria have the Israel issue in common. So we have good relations."[38]

When the popular demonstrations began in Syria, however, Hamas criticized the Syrian regime's repression. When armed rebellion broke out, Hamas supported the rebels affiliated with Syria's Muslim Brotherhood. Meshal closed Hamas's Damascus office in January 2012 and moved to Doha, Qatar.

For a time, Hamas seemed to have come down on the right side of history. Conservative Islamists gained influence in Syria. The Egyptian Muslim Brotherhood, a close Hamas ally, won the parliamentary and presidential elections. The brotherhood expanded the Egyptian border crossings with Gaza, a policy begun under Mubarak. But Gaza residents still couldn't import goods on a commercial scale, so tunnel smuggling was allowed to increase.

The tide then turned against Hamas. When the Egyptian military overthrew the Muslim Brotherhood government in June 2013, Hamas lost an important ally. The military closed the smuggling tunnels and restricted border crossings through Rafah.

Hamas had also allied with Iran. They agreed on opposition to Israel but had many disagreements on other issues. When Hamas broke with Assad, Iran cut financial aid to Gaza. Iran had reportedly been paying $20 million per month to help provide basic services for Palestinians. But that ended in 2013.[39]

Hamas officials wouldn't discuss specific figures, but Ghazi Hamad, deputy foreign minister, said, "For supporting the Syrian revolution, we lost very much." He said military cooperation has stopped as well. Ahmed Yousef, an advisor to the Gaza prime minster, said "We never expected that a country like Iran, which talked about oppressed people and dictatorial regimes, would stand behind a dictator like Assad who is killing his own people."[40]

Hamas even broke with its old ally Hezbollah. On June 17, 2013, Hamas called on Hezbollah to withdraw its troops from Syria and concentrate on the fight against Israel.[41]

Hamas turned for support to Qatar, the United Arab Emirates, and Turkey. The emir of Qatar became the first head of state to visit Gaza and pledged $400 million in aid. Hamas's shift away from Syria and Iran could have long-term ramifications. Hamas leaders could remain independent, accepting money from diverse sources. Or their close reliance on money from US allies such as the gulf countries could open new possibilities for US and Israeli influence. If that seismic shift were to occur, at a minimum, Hamas would have to be included in the Palestinian-Israeli peace talks. That doesn't appear likely anytime soon.

Palestinian views on Syria are divided. In the beginning they welcomed an uprising that would replace Assad with a popular government more supportive of the Palestinian cause. As the civil war dragged on, however, they became concerned with external forces and extremist groups hijacking the uprising. Nevertheless, Palestinians overwhelmingly opposed Assad. A poll by the Palestine Center for Policy and Survey Research showed only 12.6 percent of Gaza and West Bank residents supported Assad's regime.[42] A University of Haifa opinion poll among Israeli Arabs, also known as 1948 Palestinians, indicated that 72 percent supported or strongly supported the end of Assad's regime.[43]

To be sure, some Palestinians in the West Bank and Gaza supported Assad. The Arab Socialist Baath Party in Palestine has held small rallies in the West Bank. Hamas prohibited pro-Assad demonstrations in Gaza, although some Assad supporters tried to organize rallies. A few prominent Palestinians supported the Syrian regime, most notably Bishop Atallah Hanna of the Greek Orthodox Church in Jerusalem.[44]

Political leader Barghouti, on the other hand, said the Arab Spring revolutions, including in Syria, would eventually triumph. "I believe this is just one stage, like has happened in many revolutions in the world. You have revolutions and counterrevolutions. People seek their way. I'm optimistic."[45]

Palestinians overwhelmingly rejected foreign interference in Syria's war. Sixty-three percent opposed US and European arms going to the rebels, according to a 2013 Pew research poll.[46]

A similar percentage opposed US military intervention in Syria, a view that united Hamas and Fatah as well. Both argued that any US attack would serve to put pro-US forces in power, not help the Syrian people. "The Americans do not want good [for] the Syrian people," said Hamas spokesman Salah Bardaweel. "The Americans only want to serve American and Israeli interests."[47] Fatah also strongly condemned US hypocrisy in criticizing Syria's use of chemical weapons. Fatah official Abbas Zaki said that the United States didn't act "when Israel used phosphorous weapons during its aggression against the Gaza Strip in 2008 and 2009."[48]

Palestinians don't want foreign domination of Syria, but neither do they want dictatorship—secular or religious. Assad used support for Palestine as a justification for staying in power. But it turns out that he had little justification to claim their popular support.

Israelis and Palestinians can't help but see Syrian developments through their own lenses. For Israeli leaders, the civil war gave them temporary respite from a devilish leader but presented the possibility of ultra-right-wing Islamists gaining influence. They continue to fear democratic reforms in the Middle East. "We are a minority in the region," explained history professor Zisser. "Minorities always prefer a strong authoritarian regime rather than a popular regime backed by an unreliable majority."[49]

Palestinians said such a view dooms Israel to isolation and paranoia. "The Israelis are afraid of Arab democracy," said political leader Barghouti. "Israel is shortsighted because democracy will come to the Arab world."[50]

This argument reminded me a lot of the discussion I had with Rabbi Zeldin in 1967. Back then, Israel had to ally with dictators such as the Shah of Iran and leaders of apartheid South Africa because if the masses took over in those countries, they would oppose Israeli policies. Memo to Israeli leaders: maybe Israeli policy is the problem, not the people of the world.

CHAPTER 11

UNITED STATES, RUSSIA, AND OUTSIDE POWERS

I got lost on my way to the State Department. I showed up at the main headquarters, a massive, fortresslike building taking up several city blocks in downtown Washington, DC. But guards at the building had never heard of who I was supposed to meet. Turns out I was at the wrong place. My meeting was in an annex across the street and down the block.

A young woman employee in this section had been after me for months to talk with her colleagues about what was wrong with US policy in Syria. I was openly skeptical about any impact my definitely outside-the-box views might have. But she was very insistent. I finally agreed but only if I could also get a State Department interview to use in my articles and in this book. We struck the deal. I put on my nicest sport coat and conservative tie, got on the metro, and headed to Foggy Bottom.

At the time of our interview, in April 2012, the State Department was officially supporting the nonviolent resistance in Syria led by the Syrian National Council (SNC). The State Department wanted the American people to believe that the SNC represented the major Syrian opposition groups. Its leader, Radwan Ziadeh, had lived in the United States, spoke fluent English, and promised democracy and pluralism for the new Syria.

I sat down with an official State Department spokesperson, who, under Washington rules, wouldn't allow his name to be used. When asked which group in the SNC actually provided a democratic alternative to Assad, he paused for a full fifteen seconds. "We continue to encourage and cajole them to lay out a vision. It's a work in progress."[1]

So even after working with internal and external opposition groups for over a year, US plans weren't going so well.

Another State Department source, we'll call her "Kathy," explained the US conundrum. She didn't want her name used, fearing retaliation for her critical views. She said the Obama administration had provided $100 million for salaries and equipment to the SNC as of April 2012. "But the SNC is faction-ridden," she told me. We're trying to find a horse we can ride but we're not having much luck."[2]

The official spokesperson admitted that Syria provided unique problems for the United States. Syria has a Sunni majority but also many minority groups. He insisted that the SNC was inclusive of all of these groups. He admitted, however, that they had little in common beyond favoring the downfall of Assad. "Once the common enemy is removed, that's when the divisions occur." He added, "We do understand this is a long haul."[3] However, the Obama administration had no idea how long the "long haul" would be.

In practice, the SNC was never able to gather broad support within Syria. By October 2012, Secretary of State Hillary Clinton declared the SNC a failure. The United States finally acknowledged that the SNC didn't represent the struggle inside Syria and lacked participation by minority groups.[4] In November, the SNC was replaced by a new coalition, the National Coalition for Syrian Revolutionary and Opposition Forces. That coalition also failed to develop significant support inside Syria, while conservative and ultraconservative Islamists continued to grow (see chapters 5–6).

Meanwhile, the Obama administration was pursuing a secret, military track. The CIA began overseeing arms shipments to the Free Syrian Army no later than June 2012 when it leaked the story to the *New York Times*. The CIA began directly arming and training rebels in early 2013 (see chapter 5).

Proclaiming support for nonviolent resistance while arming rebels was not seen as a contradiction, according to State Department critic Kathy. She said State was populated with "humanitarian interventionists," people who favor one or another form of military intervention by claiming it will, in the end, protect civilians. "But we never discuss the legality of such attacks, let alone the morality," she told me. Controversial policies are sent to the legal department for review. "They'll always find a way to justify whatever policy is decided."[5]

State Department officials insisted that Syrians would benefit from US policy in the long run. The spokesperson acknowledged that ordinary Syrians were hurt by American economic sanctions, which had caused a massive drop in their standard of living. But, as if admonishing naughty children, the spokesperson told me Uncle Sam would make it up to them. "Once the behavior changes, once we have the Assad regime step down, we will make good on making sure this is an environment where Americans can do business."[6] There's an interesting logic here. He assumed that the solution for economic collapse is American business investment. What's good for American business, apparently, is good for the Syrian people.

Similarly, the State Department saw no contradiction between criticizing Assad's human-rights record and supporting pro-US regimes elsewhere in the region also committing abuse, such as Saudi Arabia and Bahrain. The State Department simply assumed that US allies can and will change while enemies will not. The spokesperson explained that allies may abuse human rights, "but we work with them."

Peter van Buren, a twenty-four-year veteran foreign-service officer said the State Department excelled at such "clever use of words." Van Buren wrote a blog critical of US foreign policy that brought down the wrath of State Department officials. He retired in 2012. Word games about human rights "only carry weight here in the United States," he told me. "In the real world, none of these words mean anything. If you're in Saudi Arabia and you speak out against the government, you're going down. You'll not be found again. If you're in Syria and do the same thing, you'll be a freedom fighter as you go down."[7]

I hopped in a taxi to visit a former diplomat now living in Bethesda, Maryland, an upper-middle-class enclave bordering DC. Henry Precht was a career foreign-service officer, deputy ambassador to Egypt, and officer in charge of the Iran desk in Washington in the 1970s. The desk officer is the main State Department official following day-to-day activities in any given country.

Precht helped deflate a few popular myths about how US foreign policy is made. He told me that the much-ballyhooed secret intelligence that the public is not allowed to see was, in fact, not terribly insightful or useful. "If you read the *New York Times* and had some familiarity with how the government works, you'd be as well-informed as if you sat on the desk and read the classified cables," he told me.[8] In general the country desks, including the Syria desk, don't have better sources than those of a good journalist. On occasion, he said, "there were CIA reports that did an outstanding job," providing unique sources and analysis.

I asked Precht a question frequently asked of me in my Mideast travels: What would Americans think if Syria was training and arming dissident groups in the US? Does the State Department ever hold itself to the same standards demanded of others? "Certainly not," replied Precht. "We set the standards for the [people of the] world, and they better get in step," he said with an ironic smile. "If they don't, they'll be damned in our human-rights report." The State Department issues an annual human-rights report that inevitably finds the most severe abuse is perpetrated by countries considered hostile to the United States.

Precht did have some positive comments about Foggy Bottom. He said there are many dedicated foreign-service officers. Policy makers listen to advice from these professionals, he said. They don't just cherry-pick intelligence to bolster a preconceived policy. "If you have a good case, it's welcome." That doesn't apply during crises, however. Voicing contrary views during a run-up to war, for example, "might mean the end of your tenure. I had two kids to educate; I wasn't going to take that risk."

When I first became a student activist in the 1960s I discussed a similar issue with my dad. He urged me to get an education, join the government, and make changes from within. I argued that only massive pressure from the streets would change US foreign policy; individuals only get swallowed in the morass. My meanderings around Washington over the years confirmed my view from the 1960s. Very intelligent people wrote highly sophisticated analyses that often got ignored at the highest levels when pertaining to critical issues such as war and peace. US foreign policy is made by a political, military, and economic elite who care little about the grunts in a State Department annex, as my friend Kathy eventually found out. She quit the State Department and now resides in academia, where she can join those bringing pressure from the street.

The State Department, the CIA, and other government agencies claimed that the United States must be involved in Syria to protect American national interests. But what exactly are those interests, and do they benefit ordinary Americans? US Middle East policy relies on the bedrock principle that the United States is different from other powers. Russia and China are resource-greedy giants willing to support dictators when it's to their commercial advantage. Even close allies Britain and France have been known to advance their business interests at the expense of human rights. But the United States is exceptional because it operates out of concern for humanity and promotion of democracy. This notion of American exceptionalism was well-articulated by Obama in his 2013 speech to the United Nations. "Some may disagree, but I believe that America is exceptional—in part because we have shown a willingness through the sacrifice of blood and treasure to stand up not only for our own narrow self-interests, but for the interests of all."[9]

That would come as a great surprise to the people of Iraq, Afghanistan, Libya, Egypt, and Syria—to name a few recent examples. But by claiming that America protects the interests of all countries, American exceptionalism disguises the US ruling elite's real motives. The United States has considered the Middle East critical since the first oil fields began pumping in Iraq in 1927. US oil companies were given 23.75 percent ownership of the oil consortium that controlled the fields, part of the imperialist division of the region after World War I (see chapter 3). After World War II, the United States became the dominant power in the region. Its oil companies controlled vast wealth either directly or through joint agreements with local elites. The Persian Gulf region—which includes Saudi Arabia, Kuwait, Iraq, Iran, and the United Arab Emirates—is responsible for some 30 percent of the world's oil production and 55 percent of its reserves.[10] Protecting those oil supplies—and the profits they generate—has become a vital part of the American national interest.

Of course, US leaders don't mention the profit motive. They always argue that the United States is protecting the region from outsiders who are intent on disrupting the world's oil supplies. For example, Obama said, referring to the Middle East, "Although America is steadily reducing our own dependence on imported oil, the world still depends on the region's energy supply, and a severe disruption could destabilize the entire global economy."[11]

But who exactly can promote stability? Well, we certainly can't depend on oil companies owned by Russian, Chinese, or other suspicious countries. So we have to rely on companies owned by the United States and its close allies. Halliburton and Schlumberger must be able to drill for the oil and build the pipelines. Chevron/Texaco, Exxon/Mobil, BP, and other Western oil companies are the only reliable businesses to pump or distribute the oil. And while these patriotic companies are protecting the national interest, one cannot deny them a profit, can one?

Lest you think I'm just some incurable radical, an oil-industry-hating journalist, look at some of the US government documents leaked by Edward Snowden. The National Security Administration (NSA) spied on foreign leaders such as Brazil's president Dilma Rousseff and on the state-owned oil company Petrobras. Most of the NSA's spying on foreign leaders had nothing to do with suspected terrorism but focused on finding commercial advantage for US corporations. The NSA collected inside information about upcoming deals, trade negotiations, and new technologies.[12] Done by anyone else, it would be called industrial espionage.[13] Done by the NSA, it's protecting our national interests.

Syria has no strategic minerals and produces relatively little oil. It has no important seaports or military bases. But it has something any real-estate agent would envy: location. Syria borders Turkey, Iraq, Lebanon, Israel, and Jordan. Iran flies arms into Damascus, which are then transported over land to Hezbollah in Lebanon. So whoever holds power in Syria will have significant, long-term impact on the region.

Syria's location also puts it in jeopardy. Syria fought two wars with Israel and has continued a cold war with that country ever since. It became Iran's only Arab ally and a key supporter of Hezbollah. Israel and the United States had tried over the years to break Syria away from Iran. Had they been able to do so, Assad's other faults would have been forgiven. But Syria's continued alliance with Iran became one of the main justifications of Western attempts to overthrow Assad. Tom Donilon, President Obama's national-security adviser, said in 2011 that the "end of the Assad regime would constitute Iran's greatest setback in the region yet—a strategic blow that will further shift the balance of power in the region against Iran."[14]

Syria's location also came into play with plans to build a new natural-gas pipeline. Qatar wanted to construct a pipeline from its gas fields, through Saudi Arabia, Jordan, Syria, and ultimately to Turkey. It would have provided a new source of energy for Europe and potentially competed with Russia's gas exports. Assad refused to sign the deal in 2009, and instead in 2012, inked an agreement with Iran for a different pipeline.[15] It would cost $10 billion and carry Iranian gas through Iraq, Syria, and possibly Lebanon.[16] Although the civil war has made construction impossible, the Obama administration and its Middle Eastern allies were not pleased that Iran would have a potentially new and lucrative source of income.[17]

US leaders had plenty of reasons to get rid of Assad, given his alliance with Iran and hostility to US corporate interests. But when the uprising started, the Obama administration denounced Assad's repression but did little else. Like the Israelis, US leaders preferred the devil they knew. The United States feared militant Islamists would seize power and pose an even greater danger than Assad. After all, in the name of Islam, militants had tried to shoot up the US embassy in Damascus in September 2006.[18]

But as the uprising continued for months, the administration calculated that Assad would be overthrown soon or at least significantly weakened. As with Libya, the United States opportunistically shifted strategy and threw its support to the opposition. In August 2011 Obama made it official by famously declaring, "The time has come for President Assad to step aside."[19] The administration debated whether to create a no-fly zone in which the US Air Force would guarantee protection to civilians in an area near the Turkish border. Some exiled Syrians favored such outside military intervention. But most opposed it, according to the leaders I met. I interviewed Ahmad Bakdouness, the civil-society activist we met in chapter 1. Referring to exiled leaders, he told me, "He who has not suffered cannot speak. They can say whatever they want, but not many people agree with them. I oppose the Libyan model. Even with a no-fly zone, we would still be weak."[20]

Leen, another civil-society activist we met previously, admitted that some rebels were so desperate that they favored foreign military intervention. But she and her friends had closely watched Western interference in Libya and Iraq. "Libya will have a new dictator," she said. "We don't want another dictator with American backing."[21] But the opinions of civil-society activists mattered little in Washington's corridors of power.

The Washington debate on Syria revolved around tactics, not goals. Everyone agreed the United States should help overthrow Assad and install a pro-US regime in Damascus. They just couldn't agree on how to do it. Hawks argued that Obama was weak and indecisive. He should have armed moderate rebels sooner and set up a no-fly zone. Doves argued that Obama's policies made sense given difficult conditions on the ground. The administration was arming moderate rebels and had forced Assad to dismantle his chemical weapons.

Some Americans believe that the military industrial complex drags us into war. Under this theory, arms manufacturers consort with generals to start wars and make profits. The military are high-flying hawks advocating war while the State Department diplomats coo for peace like doves. In reality, the military is often the most cautious. The Pentagon flatly opposed establishing a no-fly zone or any other ongoing military presence in Syria. General Martin E. Dempsy, chair of the Joint Chiefs of Staff, said creating an effective no-fly zone would require as many as seventy thousand American troops because of Syria's "sophisticated anti-aircraft system." He argued that such massive deployment was needed to permanently ground Syria's air force and to prevent retaliatory attacks on US forces. The generals understood that bombing Syria, short of a full-scale invasion, would have limited impact without reliable US allies on the ground. Dempsy realized the United States had no such support. "The side we choose must be ready to promote their interest and ours when the balance shifts in their favor," he said. "Today they are not."[22]

The military's reluctance to bomb Syria stemmed from its experience during the Vietnam War. The United States had overwhelming military superiority in Indochina but lost the war because the US Army had no reliable allies on the ground and had lost support at home. The US Army had tried to create a South Vietnamese military force capable of fighting the enemy, but it quickly fell apart as US troops withdrew toward the end of the war. The United States managed to repeat the mistake in Afghanistan and Iraq. Of course the military is prepared to go to war; its leaders just want to make sure that strong Syrian allies "promote" American interests, as General Dempsy so aptly said.

The State Department and the CIA advocated a different set of tactics. They argued for "limited" military action very early in the war. In their view, arming rebels and/or creating a no-fly zone could win the war without significant US casualties or cost. The civilians at State are always enamored of quickie military solutions that never quite work out. CIA director David Patraeus and Secretary of State Hilary Clinton favored increased training of rebel militias. Clinton said the United States should get "skin in the game."[23]

Obama was cautious about the plan, given the disastrous Libyan intervention. He was well aware of "mission creep," whereby limited military action expands and the United States is drawn deeper into the struggle to avoid losing. But by the end of 2013 hawks and doves within the administration reached a consensus: they would step up arms and training of rebels while holding off on direct US intervention.

The administration debated whether to have the Defense Department openly do the arming and training. Some White House officials pointed out that publicly supporting Assad's overthrow violated international law. The United States could have simply canceled this illegal program. Instead the administration kept the CIA in charge of the covert program and could thus claim not to be officially involved in attacking a sovereign state.[24]

Some conservative Democrats and Republicans advocated for more-aggressive military intervention. Senator John McCain (R-AZ) called for creating a no-fly zone. Two right-wing analysts sketched out such a plan in a *Wall Street Journal* opinion essay. Jack Keane is a former vice chief of staff of the US Army, and Danielle Pletka is an analyst with the conservative American Enterprise Institute. They argued for limited attacks to ground Assad's air force, which might then expand to a no-fly zone. "Outfit moderate rebel units vetted by the CIA with man-portable [shoulder fired] antiaircraft missiles," they wrote. "If American forces use standoff cruise missiles and B-2 stealth bombers for these strikes, they will be out of the enemy's reach." They admit that airfields can be repaired. "These operations would need to be sustained for a period of time to preclude repairs."[25]

Such limited military engagements sound good in Washington because no Americans are likely to die and the bloated defense budget will hardly miss the billions it will cost to execute. Aside from the immorality of waging war in which civilians will inevitably die, the plan won't work. In Libya a similar scheme took seven months to depose Kaddafi, only to leave the country in the hands of warring militias.

The failure to develop a viable rebel coalition and general public opposition at home to another war bolstered factional splits in the Republican Party. Libertarians and isolationists criticized Obama and opposed his plans to bomb Syria after the chemical-weapons incident. They defied their own Republican House and Senate leadership.

Many Libertarians hold a consistent antiwar view when it comes to the Middle East. Doug Bandow is a senior fellow at the Libertarian Cato

Institute and a former special assistant to President Ronald Reagan. He wrote, "What if the United States helps blow up Syria? Washington will have no control over the outcome. But if the result is increased regional instability, terrorism, and civil conflict, highlighted by brutal revenge killings, murder, and ethnic cleansing of Alawites, and mistreatment of other minorities, the United States government will bear direct responsibility. If Washington intervenes, it will own the result."[26]

Right-wing isolationists, on the other hand, used anti-interventionist rhetoric to push a racist and xenophobic agenda. Isolationism has a long history in the United States (see chapter 3). Its advocates oppose America getting politically or militarily involved outside the Western Hemisphere. Conservative isolationists opposed US involvement in World War II, thus objectively helping Nazi aggression. Today political commentator Pat Buchanan carries the isolationist banner. He was a speechwriter and adviser to three American presidents, and he twice sought the Republican nomination for president himself.

Buchanan argued against bombing Syria in September 2013 by accusing the military of being in the pay of Arab sheiks. "The Saudis and Gulf Arabs, cash-fat on the $110-a-barrel oil they sell US consumers, will pick up the tab for the Tomahawk missiles," he wrote in a column. "Has it come to this—US soldiers, sailors, Marines, and airmen as the mercenaries of sheikhs, sultans, and emirs, Hessians of the New World Order, hired out to do the big-time killing for Saudi and Sunni royals?"[27]

Buchanan made both a populist and a racist argument. He blamed Arab rulers for what, in fact, is US corporate/military policy. He expressed no concern for the people of Syria who would become victims of US aggression, while fanning racist images of Arab plutocrats. It reminded me of how right-wing populists blamed Jewish bankers for starting World War II. The ultimate in right-wing isolationism sprang from the lips of former Republican vice presidential candidate Sarah Palin, who managed to combine populism, hatred of Obama, and Islamophobia. "Let these radical Islamic countries . . . where both sides are slaughtering each other as they scream over an arbitrary red line, 'Allah Akbar,' I say until we have someone who knows what they're doing, I say let Allah sort it out."[28]

Just as Syria has generated conservative anti-interventionists, so, too, has it produced liberal interventionists. Famed *New York Times* columnist Thomas Friedman, for example, is a master at finding liberal justifications for war. He was a leading apologist for the occupation of Iraq until the policy obviously failed.[29] And he did it again on Syria. It's worth quoting his views on Syria at length:

> I believe that if you want to end the Syrian civil war and tilt Syria onto a democratic path, you need an international force to occupy the entire country, secure the borders, disarm all the militias, and midwife a transition to democracy. It would be staggeringly costly and take a long time with the outcome still not guaranteed. . . . My view is that anything short of an external force that rebuilds Syria from the bottom up will fail. Since there are no countries volunteering for that role (and I am certainly not nominating the United States), my guess is that the fighting in Syria will continue until the parties get exhausted."[30]

Friedman managed to propose an outrageous plan for imperialist occupation and then slip out of it with a rhetorical flourish. Who could occupy Syria for a long time other than the United States or European powers? He made the racist assumption that Syrians and Arabs can develop a decent society only through occupation. Excuse me, Tom, but didn't that argument go out with the death of colonialism?

Some Syrian Americans and progressives made a more sophisticated argument for humanitarian intervention. They are justifiably outraged at the tactics used by the Assad regime. With the full backing of Russia, the Syrian army laid siege to rebel-controlled areas. Food and medicine were kept out. City services such as water and electricity were shut off. As a tactic to isolate the rebels, civilians were left to starve and die of disease. Some on the left have called for humanitarian military intervention. Danny Postel and Nader Hashemi, of the Center for Middle East Studies at the University of Denver, wrote in a *New York Times* opinion article that if the Assad regime didn't lift the sieges, "an external, international force must be introduced to guarantee the safe passage of food and medicine to starving Syrian civilians. . . . The sieges must be broken by any means necessary."[31]

Postel and Hashemi invoked the UN doctrine of Responsibility to Protect, which they define as "the principle that if a state fails to protect its populations from mass atrocities—or is in fact the perpetrator of such crimes—the international community must step in to protect the victims, with the collective use of force authorized by the [UN] Security Council." They recognize that Russia would likely veto any such authorization in the security council. Therefore "if a multinational force cannot be assembled, then at least some countries should step up and organize Syria's democratically oriented rebel groups to provide the necessary force on the ground, with air cover from participating nations." In another article, Postel made clear that he opposes US intervention. He wrote that some countries that might participate included France, Australia, Jordan, and Luxembourg. Without international action "hundreds of thousands of Syrians" will be consigned to starvation, he wrote.[32]

I have great respect for Postel and Hashemi, who have done important work in support of the Syrian people, and before that, in support of the 2009 popular demonstrations in Iran. But I profoundly disagree with the concept of humanitarian intervention. In the foreword to this book, Noam Chomsky discussed the origins and flaws in the Responsibility to Protect doctrine. What powers have the military capability and political will to spearhead an attack on Syria? We can safely eliminate Luxembourg and Jordan. Australia is too far away. That leaves France as the main protagonist, with possible token support from other countries. France had sent troops to fight in its former colonies in central Africa. France might be willing to attack Syria, also a former colony.

First France would have to disable the Syrian air force by bombing airfields and aircraft. Then it would have to land paratroopers into the city under siege and facilitate delivery of aid, presumably by the

United Nations or other international agencies. It would have to fight off attacks from the Syrian army in some areas and by extremist rebels in others. Even assuming this can be done with a minimum of civilian casualties, it's a difficult military operation. If significant numbers of French troops are killed or equipment destroyed, it would signal defeat. And, from the French perspective, defeat for intervention would be worse than no intervention at all. So the French military would have to mobilize a very large force. As noted earlier, the Pentagon said up to seventy thousand troops might be needed.

And if by some miracle all of this were accomplished with relatively little violence, would the French troops withdraw? If they did, then the Syrian regime would resume attacks on civilians with a vengeance. So the troops have to stay to prevent future civilian atrocities. You have the classic military mission creep with two stark choices: stay in Syria indefinitely or overthrow Assad and install pro-French rebels in Damascus. There is no humanitarian intervention without regime installation.

We don't have to speculate. What I describe for Syria actually happened in Libya. Civilians in Benghazi faced a vicious attack by Muammar Kaddafi's forces, although claims of impending massacres were intentionally exaggerated. The UN Security Council passed a resolution calling for limited intervention to protect the people of Benghazi.[33] France, Britain, and the United States then violated the resolution by waging a seven-month war, functioning as an air force for the rebels. When Kaddafi finally was murdered, a prime minster backed by the West was put in power. But he proved inept, and warring militias took over the country.[34]

Stephen Zunes, professor of politics and international studies at the University of San Francisco and coordinator of its Middle Eastern studies program, strongly opposed humanitarian intervention in Libya and Syria. He noted the Libyan intervention backfired, in part, because it empowered "al-Qaeda-aligned groups, like the one responsible for the deaths of four US officials, including the ambassador" in August 2012. Referring to Syria, he added, "Even large-scale direct foreign intervention will not lead to a quick collapse of the regime.[35]

You've heard my sharp-tongued critiques of various groups on the left and right. What, you may ask, should the United States do?

I oppose all outside interference in Syria, whether from the United States, Russia, Iran, Turkey, Saudi Arabia, or any other country. The United States, in particular, should stop all military support to the rebels. The United States should join with other nations to provide humanitarian aid to Syrian refugees inside and outside Syria, to be done peacefully, not by force of arms. Both the United States and Russia could play a positive role in reaching a diplomatic solution, possibly through the United Nations. But so far neither country has the credibility to act as an honest broker. Conflict over Ukraine will likely make diplomatic agreements on Syria even more difficult. Eventually, however, there will have to be a political settlement to the civil war.

I also support programs in which Americans directly help the people of Syria. Such people-to-people activities include political support to those Syrians seeking to establish an inclusive, parliamentary system. Groups such as the American Friends Service Committee[36] and the Friends for a NonViolent World[37] have publicized the work of Syrian activists fighting both Assad and extremist rebels. Other groups are providing food, medicine, and humanitarian aid to civilians in Syria. Sometimes the aid gets through to rebel areas because of local cease-fires with the regime, other times through neighboring Jordan or Turkey. These groups advocate for short-term, local cease-fires that would allow aid to reach civilians under siege.

But no solution will be forthcoming in Syria without Russian cooperation. And Russia's role is what we explore next.

From the opening months of the uprising, the Obama administration blamed Russia for supporting Assad, claiming Russian arms and intransigence at the United Nations have kept Assad in power. Secretary of State John Kerry, in a typical statement, blasted the Russians for continuing to arm Assad. "They are, in fact, enabling Assad to double down, which is creating an enormous problem."[38]

Without doubt, Russia has backed Assad, enabling the regime to brutally repress its own people while maintaining Russian influence in the region. And like the United States, Russia has its own perceived national interests at stake. The former Soviet Union allied with Syria back in the 1960s because of a common antipathy to Israeli and US policies in the Middle East. There was some ideological affinity between the nationalist and anti-imperialist Syrian Baathists and the Marxist-Leninist leadership of the Soviet Union. In 1971 the two countries signed a military pact, and the Soviet Union established a naval base in the port city of Tartus. It consisted of little more than a pier and ship-repair facilities, but it represented the Soviet Union's only Mediterranean naval base.

Over time, military and economic ties grew. The Soviet Union resupplied arms to Syria during the 1973 war with Israel. Soviet leadership regularly supported the Arab cause in the UN Security Council while criticizing Israel. Hafez al-Assad briefly broke out of the Moscow orbit in 1990 as the Soviet Union was collapsing. Syria sent troops to support the United States in the Gulf War. Assad had hoped that his new alliance with the United States would lead to the return of the Golan and resolution of the Palestinian issue. That never happened. So Syria stepped up its alliance with Iran and reestablished good ties with Russia.

By the 2000s Russia agreed to forgive three-quarters of Syria's Soviet-era debt, or $9.8 billion of the $13.4 billion total. By the time the Syrian uprising began, Russia had $20 billion in trade and investment with Syria, $8 billion of which was arms sales. "Russia is now a business-oriented country, and the Russian government obviously wants to protect the investments made by its businessmen in Syria," Yevgeny Satanovsky told the *Christian Science Monitor*. He was president of Moscow's Institute of Middle Eastern Studies.[39]

The *Moscow Times* reported that Russian companies had big investments in Syria infrastructure, tourism, and energy industries. Arms going to Syria accounted for about 10 percent of Russia's total arms sales. The Syrian regime bought MiG-29 fighters, Pantsir surface-to-air missiles, artillery systems, and antitank weaponry, much of which was later used to attack rebels and civilians.[40] "Syria has been a traditional ally and arms importer from Russia, and so Russia has a very different view from the West's hope of overthrowing the ruling regime there," Igor Korotchenko told the *Monitor*. He's director of the Center for Analysis of World Arms Trade in Moscow. "Therefore, Russia has put its stakes on providing political and military support for the Syrian regime, and Russian leaders believe this corresponds to the long-term national interests of Russia itself."[41]

Russian leaders, like their American counterparts, also saw Syria in a geopolitical context. After the devastating collapse of the Soviet Union and decade of turmoil in the 1990s, President Vladimir Putin had campaigned on promises to make Russia strong again. Russia had been steadily losing influence as some countries of Eastern Europe joined NATO and/or became part of the eurozone. Russian leaders were particularly wary of the rose revolution in Georgia and the orange revolution in Ukraine. While the West supported these color revolutions as struggles for democracy, Russian leaders said they were manipulated by the West to further weaken Russia.

Russians thought the Syrian uprising was cut from the same cloth. Alexander Golts, a military expert at *Yezhednevny Zhurnal*, an online newspaper, wrote, "Putin has a real paranoia about colored revolutions." Such uprisings are the "result of Western conspiracies. The attitude is, we're not going to be fooled anymore."[42]

Russian leaders also thought they had been suckered by the March 2011 UN vote on Libya. Both China and Russia abstained on the UN Security Council vote to establish a no-fly zone to protect civilians in Benghazi. Kaddafi had purchased billions in Soviet/Russian arms, and the two countries had close relations at one time. His overthrow resulted in huge Russian losses economically, politically, and militarily. "We made a big mistake on the Libya vote," one Russian diplomat told me. "We won't make it again on Syria."[43]

In the early days of the uprising, Russian leaders worried that Assad might not survive. But by 2013 they had poured in weapons to Syria and gave full political support to the Assad regime. Russia vetoed or threatened to veto every UN Security Council resolution critical of Syria. The Russians had firmly cast their lot with Assad. "We see serious reasons to believe the Assad regime can survive," said Georgi Mirsky of the Institute of World Economy and International Relations in Moscow. "Even if it's discredited, it could still hold on for a number of years. So there's no sense of urgency in Moscow to change policies."[44]

Following a circuitous route from Saudi Arabia up through Jordan or Turkey and then crossing a lawless border, thousands of young Saudis have secretly made their way into Syria to join extremist groups fighting against the Assad regime. With the tacit approval from the House of Saud, and financial support from wealthy Saudi elites, the young men took up arms in what Saudi clerics called a *jihad*, or holy war, against the Syrian regime.

The Saudis were part of an inflow of Sunni fighters from Libya, Tunisia, and Jordan that constituted a significant problem. Analysts in Damascus told me that over 100,000 foreigners were fighting in Syria. The Assad regime wildly inflated the numbers in an effort to discredit the rebellion. However, the thousands who did arrive were particularly dangerous because they joined extremist factions, according to Aaron Zelin, a senior fellow at the Washington Institute. "Most of the foreigners are fighting with al-Nusra or Ahrar al-Sham," Zelin told me[45] (see chapter 6). The Saudis hoped to weaken their regional competitor Iran, which is backing Assad. Saudi officials also hoped to divert demands for democracy at home by encouraging young protesters to instead fight in Syria, according to Saudi government critics.

The government sought to "diffuse domestic pressure by recruiting young kids to join in another proxy war in the region," said Mohammad Fahd al-Qahtani, a human-rights activist and economics professor at the Institute of Diplomatic Studies in Riyadh. He told me they are joining ultraconservative groups who "definitely are against democracy and human rights. The ramifications could be quite serious in the whole region."[46] Saudi authorities have a strategic goal in Syria, he said. "Their ultimate policy is to have a regime change similar to what happened in Yemen, where they lose the head of state and substitute it with one more friendly to the Saudis," Qahtani said. "But Syria is quite different. It will never happen that way" because the Syrian army has remained unified.

In March 2013 a Saudi court sentenced Qahtani to ten years in prison for sedition and providing false information to foreign media. Human-rights groups immediately defended Qahtani, saying he was being persecuted for his political views and human-rights work.[17]

For many months Saudi officials denied any knowledge of their citizens fighting in Syria. But then, at the end of 2013, they admitted that some 1,125 Saudi citizens went to Syria over the previous two years and about 180 had died.[48] Those numbers look suspiciously low to me, but at least the government admitted for the first time that significant numbers of their citizens were fighting with the rebels.

And sometimes, Saudi authorities were directly responsible for sending the young fighters to Syria. In one case I documented, a Saudi judge encouraged young antigovernment protesters to fight in Syria rather than face punishment at home. Twenty-two-year-old Mohammed al-Talq was arrested and found guilty of participating in an antigovernment demonstration in the north-central Saudi city of Buraidah. After giving nineteen young men suspended sentences, the judge called the defendants into his private chambers and gave them a long lecture about the need to fight Shia Muslims in Syria, according to Mohammed's father, Abdurrahman al-Talq.

"You should save all your energy and fight against the real enemy, the Shia, and not fight inside Saudi Arabia," said the father, quoting the judge. "The judge gave them a reason to go to Syria." Within weeks, eleven of the nineteen protesters left to join the rebels. In December 2012, Mohammed al-Talq was killed in Syria. His father filed a formal complaint against the judge late last year but received no response.[49]

Saudi officials deny that the government encouraged youth to fight in Syria. They point to a religious decree (*fatwa*) issued by Saudi Arabia's grand mufti, Abdul-Aziz ibn Abdullah Al ash-Sheikh. He urged youth not to fight in Syria, noting that aid to rebels should be sent through "regular channels." But Saudi authorities also admitted they have no control over people who legally leave the country and later join the rebels. Fighting with the rebels in Syria is illegal, declared Major General Mansour al-Turki, a spokesperson for the Saudi Ministry of Interior. "Anybody who wants to travel outside Saudi Arabia in order to get involved in such conflict will be arrested and prosecuted," he told me. "But only if we have the evidence before he leaves the country."[50] That position gave the Saudi government plausible deniability, according to Randa Slim, a scholar with the Middle East Institute in Washington. The Saudi government purged the country of young troublemakers while undermining a hostile neighbor, she said to me. "In the name of a good cause, they are getting rid of a problem."[51]

Qahtani argued that Saudi support for extremist rebels resembled their aid to the *mujahedeen* fighting the Soviet occupation of Afghanistan in the 1980s. Back then Osama bin Laden was a scion of a Saudi construction magnate who transferred his inherited wealth out of Saudi Arabia and into what came to be called "The Base," English for *al-Qaeda*. Both the United States and Saudi Arabia encouraged the flow of Arab fighters and arms to Afghanistan, part of a proxy war against the Soviet Union.

Saudi authorities set up networks to support the mujahedeen. "They recruited kids to fight there," Qahtani said. "They financed them and provided them with [airplane] tickets." When the Soviet-backed regime fell and the fighters returned to Saudi Arabia in the 1990s, some engaged in terrorist bombings and assassinations in an unsuccessful effort to overthrow the government. A nascent form of al-Qaeda began to take shape, metastasizing throughout the region and eventually lining up against the Saudi and US governments. Qahtani said he hoped history was not repeating itself in Syria.[52]

At the beginning of the uprising, Saudi Arabia, Qatar, and Turkey cooperated to fund and arm the rebels. For example, in May 2012, a Saudi- and Qatar-financed shipment of small arms landed in Turkey and was trucked to the Syrian border without interference from Turkish authorities. The shipment included AK-47 assault rifles, rocket-propelled grenade launchers, and small-caliber machine guns.[53]

Initially all three countries, along with the United States, helped supply militias led by the Muslim Brotherhood and similar conservative Islamist groups. But the funders complained that the brotherhood's leadership was out of touch with activists inside Syria. Its brand of populist Islam also conflicted with the austere, promonarchy views of the Saudi princes. They saw the brotherhood as a threat. Vali R. Nasr, dean of the John Hopkins School of Advanced International Studies, wrote: "Since Saudi identity is wrapped tightly around a puritanical interpretation of Islam, and Saudi nationalism draws on the centrality of Mecca and Medina to the Islamic faith, secular democracy has yet to find a large Saudi following. But the Brotherhood's populist Islamism, which promises justice and equity, and empowerment of the individual in religion and politics, does resonate with the many unemployed and restless young Saudis."[54]

So, for both ideological and practical reasons, Saudi Arabia shifted support from the brotherhood to ultraconservative groups such as Ahrar al-Sham. By the end of 2013, Saudi leaders threw their support behind the newly formed ultraconservative Islamic Front, led by Ahrar al-Sham. And by the spring of 2014, the government had officially declared the Islamic State of Iraq and al-Sham, al-Nusra, and the Muslim Brotherhood to be terrorist organizations.[55] The change would have a profound impact in both Syria and the entire region. The US and Saudi governments couldn't agree on which moderate groups to support, or, indeed, who the moderates *were*.

Qatar, on the other hand, continued to support the brotherhood. With only 200,000 citizens and some two million expatriate workers, Qatar is a small nation. It juts out on a peninsula bordering Saudi Arabia. The country's leaders had played no significant international role until recently. It was mainly known as a staunch US ally, home for an important US military base. Qatar is the world's third-largest producer of natural gas and perhaps most importantly, home to the *Al Jazeera* TV network. Since 2011 *Al Jazeera* Arabic became an unapologetic supporter of the Arab Spring uprisings and of the Muslim Brotherhood parties in Syria and Egypt. Qatar leaders combined the news outreach of *Al Jazeera* with fabulous wealth to become a significant regional player.

For a time, Turkey also supported the brotherhood, which had close ties to its ruling Justice and Development Party. Both groups shared common roots in political Islam and had a similar populist ideology that separated them from the Saudi sheiks. But Turkey eventually soured on the brotherhood's lack of success and shifted its support to more conservative rebels.

The regional divisions came to a head over developments in Egypt. In June 2012, the Muslim Brotherhood won presidential elections and also gained a plurality in parliament. Brotherhood leader Mohammad Morsi became president. When the West balked at continuing to finance the Egyptian government, Qatar pledged $8 billion. The brotherhood was unable to resolve the country's severe economic problems, however, and Morsi adopted authoritarian policies that angered ordinary Egyptians. Mass demonstrations broke out in June and July of 2013, which the military used as an excuse to seize power.

Qatar and Turkey denounced the coup. Saudi Arabia, the United States, and Bashar al-Assad all supported the military because it removed the brotherhood from power. In November 2013, Turkey and Egypt reduced their diplomatic relations. In March 2014, the regional divisions deepened as Saudi Arabia, Bahrain, and Egypt withdrew ambassadors from Qatar. The machinations and divisions among the various foreign powers have only made resolving the Syrian crisis more difficult.

In the course of writing this book, I reported from Washington, DC, and ten countries in the Middle East. I met with leaders, rebels, analysts, and ordinary people. Most agreed on the basic facts about the Syrian uprising. Spontaneous, popular demonstrations broke out against Assad as part of the wider Arab Spring. Harsh repression followed; Syrian opposition forces turned to armed rebellion. The longer the fighting continued, the more foreign powers interfered. Russia sent massive amounts of arms and provided diplomatic cover for Assad's repression. Iran sent arms and military advisors, and it facilitated the entry into Syria of Hezbollah and Iraqi militias. The United States, Saudi Arabia, Turkey, the United Arab Emirates, and Israel all backed the rebels. The CIA trained selected rebels in Jordan. Foreigners bolstered the ranks of al-Qaeda-affiliated and other extremist rebels, further complicating matters.

At the time of this writing, Syria remained in a military and political standoff, with neither side strong enough to prevail. Foreign powers seem determined to fight to the last Syrian. Israeli analysts were perhaps the most cynical, but by no means unique, when they hoped the war would go on indefinitely to take Arab minds off Israel.

But the Syrian war will end. Lebanon experienced a horrific civil war from 1976 to 1990. Despite the carnage, the Lebanese were able to resolve their civil war and rebuild their country. The Taif Accords, which ended that war, offer some interesting insights for a possible future settlement in Syria. The accords called for a cease-fire, disarming of all militias, withdrawal of all foreign troops, and establishment of a parliamentary system to include protections for minorities.[56] However, the accords were never fully implemented and Lebanon is certainly no model. Lebanon shows, however, that horrific civil wars can eventually end despite outside meddling.

Palestinian leader Hannan Ashrawi told me Palestinians stand in solidarity with the people of Syria. That makes sense to me. The people of Syria—with their tradition of tolerance—will ultimately prevail.

ACKNOWLEDGMENTS

While writing is a solitary task, producing a book is a collective effort. Numerous people helped me shape the original proposal, provided vital research, read over draft chapters, and offered moral encouragement as the deadline loomed.

Laura Gross, my book agent, offered invaluable suggestions on how to take a good idea and turn it into a book people might want to actually read. Steven L. Mitchell, editor in chief at Prometheus Books, offered a fresh perspective and made important suggestions for the manuscript. I offer special thanks to Noam Chomsky, who took time out of his busy schedule to write the foreword.

Charlie Sennott and Kevin Grant at *Global Post* published my writings from ten countries in the Middle East and helped deepen my understanding of the complex religious conflicts in the region. Tom Hundley and Nathalie Applewhite of the Pulitzer Center on Crisis Reporting were quite patient with my sometimes-last-minute phone calls asking for travel grants. The center enabled me to report from six countries in the Middle East, including two trips to Syria.

Numerous people were kind enough to read individual chapters and offer helpful suggestions. These include: Professor James Gelvin, UCLA; Professor Muhammad Sahimi, USC; Professor Soraya Fallah, California State University, Northridge; Professor Amir Sharifi, California State University, Long Beach; Kelly Niknejad, editor of Tehran Bureau; Meghan Sayres; and Bisher Alisa, Syrian Non Violent Movement.

Finally, I want to thank my wife, Liz Erlich, and son, Jason Erlich, for their moral support and encouragement during the researching and writing of this book. As for their concerns about my physical safety, I assured them that I travel only to the safest parts of dangerous countries.

APPENDIX 1

A QUICK GUIDE TO SYRIAN POLITICS AND TERMS

GROUPS OPPOSED TO ASSAD

Ahrar al-Sham (Islamic Movement of the Free Men of the Levant): One of the largest rebel militias. Founded in 2011 by ultraconservative, former political prisoners, it operated mainly in the Idlib Governate in northwestern Syria next to the Turkish border. It sought to establish an Islamic state without elections or a parliamentary system. It joined with other ultraconservative rebels to form the Islamic Front.

Al-Qaeda: The organization founded by Osama bin Laden has fractured into many local groups with no centralized control. In Syria, the Islamic State of Iraq and al-Sham (ISIS) was originally affiliated—as was Jabhat al-Nusra. Al-Qaeda groups commit suicide bombings against civilians, were intolerant of other religions, and killed rebels with whom they disagreed.

Free Syrian Army: Formed in July 2011 by defectors from the Syrian army. It called for a parliamentary system in which the rights of minorities would be protected. The FSA received money, supplies, and weapons from the United States, Saudi Arabia, Turkey, and Qatar. By the end of 2013, the FSA was losing ground to ultraright-wing rebels.

Islamic Front: Formed in September 2013 as a coalition of conservative and ultraconservative rebel groups, led by Ahrar al-Sham. The IF excluded al-Qaeda-affiliated groups and the FSA. Saudi Arabia became its main backer. The Islamic Front charter rejected a representative parliamentary system, saying only "God is sovereign." By early 2014 the front emerged as one of the strongest rebel alliances.

Islamic State of Iraq and al-Sham (ISIS): Sometimes called Islamic State of Iraq and Syria or Islamic State of Iraq and the Levant. Originally formed as the Islamic State of Iraq (ISI), or al-Qaeda in Iraq, during the sectarian fighting in Iraq in 2007–2008. Led by Abu Bakr al-Baghdadi, the ISI began secretly sending fighters to Syria, eventually announced its Syrian presence, and changed its name to ISIS. In early 2014 the leadership of al-Qaeda expelled the ISIS because of its extreme sectarianism and attacks on other rebel groups. In June 2014, the group changed its name to the Islamic State (IS) and declared the existence of an Islamic caliphate in northern Syria and Iraq.

Jabhat al-Nusra (The Support Front for the People of the Levant): Affiliated with al-Qaeda, although it operated independently. Al-Nusra is led by Abu Mohammad al-Jolani, who had fought against both the United States and the Nouri al-Maliki government in Iraq. Rather than support a parliamentary system, al-Nusra advocated a religious regime that would implement a harsh interpretation of Shariah. In December 2012, the US State Department put al-Nusra on its list of terrorist organizations because of its ties to al-Qaeda.

Jaysh al-Islam (Army of Islam): Formed from the September 2013 merger of dozens of smaller militias mostly in the Damascus area. It was led by Zahran Alloush. Jaysh al-Islam and the al-Nusra Front participated in a massacre of dozens of civilians just outside Damascus in December 2013.

Jihadists or Jihadis: Literally, "those who wage jihad or holy war." *Jihadist* is the generic term for ultra-right-wing rebels fighting Assad. In general they want to establish an Islamic state with a strict interpretation of Shariah law, led by themselves without elections or a parliamentary system.

Local Coordinating Committees (LCC): Civil-society and religious activists who came together to coordinate protests in the early days of the uprising. They developed considerable popular support and continued to do humanitarian work in some rebel-controlled areas.

Muslim Brotherhood: A political organization calling for an Islamic state with elections and a parliamentary system. The brotherhood is conservative on social issues, supports capitalism, and said it will respect minority rights. The brotherhood formed a militia in 2012 called the Shield. It has close ties with the Muslim Brotherhood in Egypt and Hamas in Gaza.

National Coalition for Revolutionary and Opposition Forces: Formed in November 2012 as the successor to the SNC. It was supposed to represent a wider coalition, including Syrian religious minorities and Kurds. Nonlethal US aid was channeled to this coalition, but it failed to attract significant support inside Syria as of mid-2014.

Supreme Military Council (SMC): Formed in December 2012, the SMC was an effort to expand the base of the Free Syrian Army. While it received arms from the United States and its allies, the SMC was unable to attract significant popular support as of mid-2014.

Syrian National Council (SNC): A civilian opposition coalition backed by the United States and its allies. It was supposed to represent the entire opposition and be the civilian leadership for the Free Syrian Army. The SNC never developed a base of support inside Syria and was dissolved in November 2012. It was replaced by the National Coalition for Revolutionary and Opposition Forces.

PRO-ASSAD GROUPS

Mukhabarat: Syrian government secret police, responsible for detention, torture, and murder of dissidents.

National Defense Force (NDF): Formed in late 2012, the NDF is a militia whose members received a salary, uniforms, and arms from the government. When the Syrian army defeated the rebels in an area, the NDF was supposed to take control. It has been accused of kidnapping for ransom and other criminal activity. By the end of 2013, it had an estimated 100,000 members.

Popular Committees: An effort to organize the Shabiha into a coherent pro-Assad militia. They were incorporated into the National Defense Force in late 2012.

Shabiha: The first shabiha, which means "ghosts" in Arabic, were smugglers in western Syria who cooperated with corrupt regime officials. When the uprising began, the Mafia-like shabiha worked with security forces to attack peaceful demonstrations. *Shabiha* became the generic terms for progovernment goons.

KURDS

Kurdish Democratic Party (KDP): The largest party in the Kurdish Regional Government in northern Iraq. Led by Masoud Barzani, the KDP has been training Syrian Kurdish fighters. But as of mid-2014 the fighters had not been deployed.

Kurdish National Council (KNC): Coalition of major Syrian Kurdish groups including the KDP but not the PYD.

Kurdistan Workers Party (Partiya Karkerên Kurdistan or PKK): Formed by Turkish revolutionary Abdullah Ocalan and a group of student radicals in 1978 in the Kurdish region of eastern Turkey. The PKK originally demanded an independent and socialist Kurdistan but later called for autonomy within a capitalist Turkey.

Partiya Yekîtiya Demokrat (PYD): The Democratic Union Party was formed in 2003 as the Syrian offshoot of the PKK. It was led by Saleh Muslim. The PYD argued that it is an independent party with only ideological ties to the PKK; critics said the two parties are controlled by the same PKK leadership. The PYD emerged as the strongest Kurdish rebel group and controlled a significant area in northern Syria as of early 2014.

FOREIGN ORGANIZATIONS

Al-Fatah: The Palestinian nationalist political party that controls the West Bank. Fatah was founded by the late Yasser Arafat. It remained officially neutral in Syria's civil war.

Hamas: Palestinian offshoot of the Egyptian Muslim Brotherhood that now controls Gaza. It once supported Assad but switched to the rebel side after the uprising began. Its headquarters in exile was in Doha, Qatar.

Hezbollah: Shia Muslim militia and political party in Lebanon. Hezbollah had close ties to Iran and supports the Assad regime. It had an estimated six thousand to eight thousand troops fighting in Syria.

Palestine Liberation Organization (PLO): Coalition of all the major Palestinian groups except Hamas. In practice, it's led by Fatah.

RELIGIOUS GROUPS AND TERMS

Alawite: A minority denomination that split off from Shia Islam in the eighth century. They comprised about 10–12 percent of Syria's 23 million people. The Assad family are Alawites. The Assads put Alawites in key business and military positions and continued to enjoy popular support from the Alawite community.

Christian: Syrian Christians trace their roots back to the time when Saint Paul preached in Damascus during the era of the Roman Empire. Christian denominations include Orthodox and Catholic. They make up a total of about 10 percent of the population. Many Christians support the Assad regime.

Druze: An ethnic group living in Syria and Lebanon that practice their own form of Islam, which dates back to the tenth century. Many Druze supported the Assad regime.

Salafist: A Sunni religious current that arose in the late 1800s as a reaction to Western philosophies and colonial expansion. Believers practice a strict interpretation of Islam but do not necessarily involve themselves in politics. Some Salafists have joined ultra-right-wing political groups.

Shia: A minority denomination in Islam that traces its roots to a schism with the Sunnis in the year 632. Shias in Syria tend to align politically with Shias in Iran. Several shrines holy to Shia are located in Syria. Most Shia support the Assad regime.

Sufi: An approach to Islam that can include worship through meditation, music, and dance. Extremist Sunni groups don't consider Sufis to be true Muslims and have attacked their communities in Egypt and other countries.

Sunni: The largest of the Muslim denominations. Sunnis comprise about 74 percent of Syria's population. The Assad regime called all rebels "takfiris," or impure Muslims, which critics said lead to discrimination against all Sunnis. Rebel groups drew their strongest support from Sunnis.

SYRIA TIMELINE: KEY DATES SINCE WORLD WAR I

WORLD WAR I: 1914–1918

July 1914: World War I begins, ultimately pitting Britain, France, Russia, and the United States against Germany, the Austro-Hungarian Empire, and the Ottoman Empire. Britain and France promise independence to Arabs if they revolt against the Ottoman Turks.

May 1916: British and French governments secretly sign the Sykes-Picot Agreement, which divides up the Ottoman-controlled Middle East into French and British mandates, a blatant violation of their promise of independence.

November 1917: British government issues the Balfour Declaration promising a Jewish homeland in Palestine.

October 1918: Arab insurgents capture Damascus, backed by British troops. Arabs elect the General Syrian Congress, which rules Syria for nearly two years.

November 1918: World War I ends.

FRENCH MANDATE: 1920–1946

July 1920: The French Army occupies Damascus with cooperation of the British, defeating the independent Arab government. France seizes control of what is today's Lebanon, Syria, and Hatay Province in southern Turkey.

1920–1921: France implements a divide-and-rule strategy by creating separate regions for Christians, Alawites, and Druze.

August 1925: Syrians rise in a two-year, nationalist revolt against French occupation. The French Army crushes the revolt using all the modern weapons available, including one of the first aerial bombardments of civilians.

September 1939: World War II begins.

June 1940: Germany occupies France during World War II and creates the Vichy government, which also controls France's colonial empire.

July 1941: Free French and British Army take control of Lebanon and Syria. The Free French promise Arab independence, but French leader General Charles de Gaulle quickly reneges.

August 1943: Nationalist parties win parliamentary elections in Syria, held under rule of the Free French. Syrians elect President Shukri al-Quwatli, a nationalist who opposes French occupation.

January 1944: Syria is declared an independent republic, but France remains the colonial power with the backing of French troops.

May 1945: Mass demonstrations against the French break out in Damascus. The French military launches a vicious air and artillery attack on the city, eventually killing over four hundred. But the nationalist movement forces the French to acknowledge Syrian independence.

May 1945: World War II ends.

INDEPENDENCE AND EARLY YEARS OF THE REPUBLIC: 1946–1966

April 1946: All French troops depart Syria; the country becomes fully independent.

April 1947: Michel Aflaq and Salah-al-Din al-Bitar cofound the Arab Baath Socialist Party, a leftist and nationalist party critical of imperialism and Syria's ruling elite.

May 1948: Israel declares independence from Britain and defeats Arab armed forces, including Syria's army. Israelis see a great victory for the Jewish people; Arabs call it the *Nakba* (catastrophe).

March 1949: Syria's defeat by Israel helps precipitate a coup against President Shukri al-Quwatli. Three military coups take place within one year.

August 1955: Shukri al-Quwatli reelected president.

October 1956: Britain, France, and Israel attack Egypt after its president, Gamal Abdel Nasser, nationalizes the Suez Canal. Syria sides with Egypt.

February 1958: Putting into practice their pan-Arabist ideology, Syria and Egypt merge to form the United Arab Republic (UAR). Nasser dissolves Syrian political parties, angering the Baathists and others.

September 1961: Syrian army officers, unhappy with Nasser's domination, seize power and withdraw from the UAR.

March 1963: After a military coup, a Baath Party cabinet comes to power and appoints Amin al-Hafez president.

ASSAD'S RISE TO POWER: 1966–2011

February 1966: A military faction within the Baath Party overthrows the civilian leadership and arrests the leftist leadership. Hafez al-Assad appointed defense minister.

June 1967: "Six Day War" pits Israel against Syria, Egypt, and Jordan. Israel seizes East Jerusalem and the West Bank of the Jordan River from Jordan, the Gaza Strip from Egypt, and the Golan from Syria.

November 1967: UN Security Council unanimously passes Resolution 242, which calls for return of all Arab land—including the Golan—in return for peace between Israel and Arab countries.

November 1970: Hafez al-Assad comes to power in Syria in a military coup.

March 1971: Assad holds a plebiscite that elects him president.

October 1973: "Yom Kippur War" pits Israel against Egypt and Syria.

Syria regains a small part of the Golan, but most remains under Israeli control.

June 1976: The Arab League sanctions Syrian intervention in Lebanon's civil war. Syria initially sides with the conservative, Maronite Christian leaders.

March 1978: Israel invades Lebanon and seizes control of southern Lebanon up to the Litani River in an effort to weaken Syria and the Palestine Liberation Organization (PLO).

June 1979: Islamist extremists attack the Syrian army's Aleppo Artillery School, killing eighty-three cadets and wounding scores.

June 1980: Assad escapes assassination by a Muslim Brotherhood member who attacks him with a hand grenade. The next day, Syrian forces murder over six hundred Muslim Brotherhood members and other political prisoners being held at Tadmur Prison.

September 1980: Iran-Iraq War begins. Syria sides with Iran because of long-standing opposition to Saddam Hussein's Iraq.

December 1981: Israel annexes the Golan by transferring governing authority from military to civilian rule.

February 1982: In the city of Hama, the Muslim Brotherhood calls for general strikes and an uprising against Assad. The Syrian military ruthlessly crushes the rebellion, killing over ten thousand people.

June 1982: Israel invades Lebanon again. The Syrian army faces major losses and withdraws from some areas. In September, under Israeli guidance, right-wing Lebanese massacre Palestinians in the Sabra and Shatila refugee camps. The PLO eventually agrees to withdraw from Lebanon.

May 1983: Syria and Libya sponsor a Palestinian defector from the PLO, Abu Musa, in a failed effort to split the PLO and remove Yasser Arafat from power. Lebanon and Israel officially end fighting, but both Israeli and Syrian troops remain in Lebanon.

August 1990: Iraq invades Kuwait. Syria joins the Gulf War coalition and sends 14,500 troops to participate in Operation Desert Storm against Iraq.

October 1991: Israeli-Palestinian peace talks begin in Madrid with Syrian participation. Syria and Israel discuss return of the Golan.

January 1994: Basil al-Assad, Hafez's son who is being groomed as successor, dies in a car crash. Bashar al-Assad later returns from studies in London to take Basil's place.

June 2000: Hafez Al-Assad dies of natural causes. Bashar becomes president.

November 2000: Bashar al-Assad releases over six hundred political prisoners, raising hopes of greater political tolerance.

September 2001: Government arrests opposition members of parliament and other political activists, indicating a return to authoritarian practices.

March 2003: United States government invades and occupies Iraq but is unable to find any weapons of mass destruction, the main justification for the war. Syria opposes the war.

March 2004: Kurds in the northern city of Qamishli rise up against the Syrian government. Security forces kill dozens of protestors and force hundreds to flee to nearby Iraqi Kurdistan.

May 2004: United States imposes sanctions on Syria, claiming Assad regime supports terrorists and insurgents in Iraq.

February 2005: Former Lebanese prime minister Rafic Hariri assassinated in a Beirut bomb explosion. Many believe Syria was responsible, leading to months of demonstrations calling for withdrawal of Syrian troops.

April 2005: Syria withdraws troops from Lebanon, but some secret police remain.

September 2006: Islamic extremists attack US embassy in Damascus.

September 2007: Israeli planes bomb northern Syria, claiming Syria is building a nuclear-weapons facility. Syrian government says it is a conventional military base.

October 2008: US helicopters attack a home under construction near Al Sukariya, Syria, claiming it killed a major terrorist from Iraq. The attack killed six construction workers.

May 2010: The United States tightens economic sanctions on Syria, arguing that Assad promotes terrorism in Iraq and Lebanon.

THE UPRISING: 2011–PRESENT

December 2010: Street vendor Mohammed Bouazizi immolates himself in Tunisia, setting off widespread demonstrations known as the Arab Spring.

January 2011: Popular demonstrations in Tunisia overthrow the dictator Zine el Abidine Ben Ali.

January 2011: Mass demonstrations and general strikes overthrow the Egyptian government of Hosni Mubarak, but the military remains in power.

February 2011: Facebook and YouTube are legalized in Syria in response to Arab Spring uprisings.

March 2011: Preteen children are detained, tortured, and killed for scrawling antiregime slogans on a school wall. Demonstrations against regime brutality break out in the southern city of Daraa and later in Damascus. Assad announces political concessions, including releasing some political prisoners, lifting the country's state of emergency, and granting citizenship to Kurds. Assad asserts that the protests are sponsored by Israel, the United States, and Saudi Arabia.

April 2011: Kurdish students demonstrate in the northern city of Qamishli. Kurds oppose Assad but are suspicious of the opposition led by conservative Islamists.

May 2011: Largely nonviolent protests meet with tanks and live ammunition in major cities, including the suburbs of Damascus. Assad grants amnesty to more political prisoners.

June 2011: Government mobilizes tens of thousands of supporters, who unfurl a giant Syrian flag. Assad retains support among religious minorities, some Sunnis, the business elite, and military.

July 2011: Some opposition leaders meet in Istanbul to form the Syrian National Council (SNC), a group that hopes to unite exiled and domestic opposition forces. The SNC is formally announced in August.

July 2011: US ambassador Robert Ford attends an opposition rally in Hama. Government instigates demonstrators to attack the US embassy in Damascus. The Obama administration calls for Assad to step down.

July 2011: Opposition conference in Damascus calls for multiple parties and other reforms. Broadcast live on state TV.

July 2011: Seven defecting Syrian soldiers announce formation of Free Syrian Army (FSA).

July 2011. Syrian parliament passes a new law allowing formation of other parties. But opposition criticizes the law because the Baath Party remains the leading party under the constitution. In practice, the loyal opposition has little power.

September 2011: Some rebels, including Muslim Brotherhood, call on the West to create a Syrian no-fly zone to help topple the regime. Others rebels oppose it.

October 2011: Russia and the People's Republic of China block a UN Security Council resolution condemning Syria, fearing it could be used to justify Western military intervention.

November 2011: The FSA attacks the Harasta Air Base near Damascus, a significant blow to the Assad regime.

November 2011: Arab League suspends Syria and imposes economic sanctions because Syria didn't abide by the league's peace plan. Assad says the Arab League is carrying out the needs of Western powers.

December 2011: Rebels bomb Baath Party offices and other targets in central Damascus. Bombings and attacks continue through the following summer.

December 2011: Syria agrees to allow a visit by an Arab League delegation, but many thousands of anti-Assad protesters demonstrate in Homs. The Arab League suspends its mission in January due to security concerns.

February 2012: Al-Nusra Front (The Support Front for the People of the Levant), affiliated with al-Qaeda, publicly announces its formation.

March 2012: UN Security Council enacts a proposed peace plan and appoints former UN secretary general Kofi Annan as negotiator. The Muslim Brotherhood publicly endorses armed struggle, although it had been quietly organizing armed groups earlier. It forms the Commission of the Revolution's Shields as a military coalition but fails to gain much support inside Syria.

May 2012: Pro-Assad militia massacres 108 people, including 34 women and 49 children, in the town of Houla, near Homs. Nations around the world withdraw their ambassadors in protest. Government holds parliamentary elections that include loyal opposition parties. Rebels argue that the elections merely legitimize the Assad dictatorship.

June 2012: CIA admits to vetting armed militias so they can be armed by Saudi Arabia and Qatar. Syrian military shoots down a Turkish plane that enters Syrian airspace. The incident heightens tensions between the two countries.

July 2012: FSA bombs Damascus intelligence headquarters, assassinating three major officials, including Assad's brother-in-law. Syrian army and security services set up checkpoints throughout Damascus.

August 2012: Kofi Annan resigns as UN negotiator in frustration with lack of progress in peace talks. The United Nations and Arab League appoint Algerian diplomat Lakhdar Brahimi as the new envoy.

September 2012: Most of the historic Aleppo *souk* (market) is gutted by fire.

November 2012: Unable to establish support inside Syria, the SNC dissolves and members form the National Coalition for Syrian Revolutionary and Opposition Forces. Al-Nusra and other ultra-conservative Islamists refuse to join.

December 2012: Free Syrian Army leaders create the Supreme Military Council in an effort to coordinate all the militias in Syria. But the SMC fail to become a broad-based coalition.

December 2012: The United States puts al-Nusra on its list of terrorist organizations, citing its affiliation with al-Qaeda.

December 2012: United States and some allies recognize the new National Coalition as the Syrian people's "legitimate representative."

January 2013: Israeli jets attack a Damascus military research center, claiming to stop shipments of Syrian arms to Hezbollah in Lebanon. Rebel groups regularly fire rockets and mortars into Damascus, often hitting civilian areas.

March 2013: A coalition of the FSA and Islamist rebels take Raqqa, capital of Idlib Governate. Syrian air force begins intensive bombing of rebel-controlled area. Khan Al Asal faces a small attack with chemical weapons. Rebels blame Assad. The Syrian government says it was rebels and presents evidence to UN inspectors months later.

April 2013: The Islamic State of Iraq (ISI), an al-Qaeda affiliate, changes its name to the Islamic State of Iraq and the al-Sham [the Levant] (ISIS), openly admitting its activities in Syria.

May 2013: A rebel commander, Abu Sakkar of the Farouq Brigades, eats the internal organs of a Syrian soldier to show his contempt for the government. The resulting video causes widespread revulsion. Government troops massacre Sunni civilians in the district of Baniyas. Pro-Assad militia kills over three hundred people. A bomb attack almost assassinates Syrian prime minister Wael Nader al-Halqi. Israel launched two different missile strikes at a warehouse allegedly storing advanced surface-to-surface missiles and other weapons.

June 2013: Syrian army and Hezbollah fighters take back control of Qusayr in northwest Syria. The government hails the victory as a turning point in the war, but the battle proves pyrrhic. At a Cairo conference of Sunni clerics, over one hundred prominent imams sign a declaration calling for jihad in Syria.

July 2013: ISIS engages in increasingly brutal actions in the parts of Idlib Governate it controls, including beheading of FSA commanders. Civilians in Raqqa complain about ISIS repression and imposition of a harsh version of Shariah law. Israel attacks a missile depot in Latakia.

August 2013: ISIS claim credit for capturing the Mennagh airbase, north of Aleppo, after a nine-month siege.

August 2013: Sarin gas attack kills hundreds of civilians living in rebel-controlled areas near Al Ghouta outside Damascus. Assad blamed the rebels. President Obama announces plans to bomb Syria, but popular opinion forces him to back down. Russia and the United States pressure Syria to eliminate its chemical weapons.

September 2013: UN weapons inspectors confirm use of chemical weapons in Al Ghouta but don't say who was responsible.

November 2013: Rebels attack the military vehicle depot in Harasta, just north of Damascus. Rebels dig a tunnel and plant bombs under the administrative building, killing over 150 soldiers and several generals. Israel again attacks a Latakia missile depot originally bombed in July.

November 2013: Major rebel groups form the Islamic Front with the aim of creating an "orthodox Islamic state." The front excludes al-Qaeda-affiliated rebels as well as the FSA.

December 2013: In a huge setback for the Western powers, the Islamic Front seizes US weapons and supplies in FSA warehouses in Atmeh, Syria, near the Turkish border. The United States and Britain temporarily suspend nonlethal aid to the rebels.

January 2014: Al-Nusra, al-Tawheed, and other rebel groups attack ISIS in Raqqa, freeing civilian and rebel prisoners. Fighting also breaks out among rebel groups in Aleppo. A Qatar-funded report from a Syrian defecting police photographer indicates the government killed and tortured over eleven thousand people in security forces' prisons. Geneva II peace talks begin in Switzerland. The West wants to discuss establishing a transitional government, but the Assad representatives insist on discussing only rebel terrorism. Nothing tangible emerges from the Swiss meetings.

February 2014: Ayman al-Zawahri, head of al-Qaeda internationally, formally expels ISIS from al-Qaeda and throws his support behind the al-Nusra Front, another al-Qaeda affiliate in Syria. The third round of peace talks end in Geneva without progress. Israel launches another missile attack near the Syrian–Lebanese border.

March 2014: After an offensive lasting months, Syria and Hezbollah forces take back Yabroud, a rebel town near Lebanon.

April 2014: Chlorine gas is used in the rebel-held village of Kafr Zeta, Hama Governate. Each side blames the other for use of chemical weapons. UN human rights commission issues a report detailing systematic torture by Syrian government. It also criticizes instances of torture used by extremist rebels.

May 2014: Through a negotiated settlement, rebels evacuate the old city area of Homs. The government claims a victory. Arab League and UN negotiator Lakhdar Brahimi resigns, telling the UN Security Council it must stop the flow of all outside arms to Syrian combatants. The United States, France, and other countries offer a UN Security Council resolution to allow the International Criminal Court to prosecute Syrian war crimes. The measure excludes any possible prosecution of the United States or Israel for its actions in the Golan. Russia and China veto the measure.

June 2014: Syria holds presidential elections and Assad wins 88.7 percent of the vote; critics say the poll is meaningless. ISIS seizes wide swath of territory in northern Iraq, giving it greater credibility in Syria as well. Kurdish forces take control of the Iraqi city of Kirkuk and assert the right to form an independent Kurdish state. Kurdish leaders continue negotiations continue with the Baghdad government.

To see an updated timeline, visit www.reeseerlich.com.

NOTES

CHAPTER 1. THE UPRISING THAT WASN'T SUPPOSED TO BE

1. Ahmad Bakdouness, interview with the author, Damascus, October 5, 2011.
2. "Leen," interview with the author, Damascus, October 2011.
3. Abdul Salman, interview with the author, Antakya, Turkey, August 10, 2012.
4. Ben Hubbard, "Islamist Rebels Create Dilemma on Syria Policy," *New York Times*, April 27, 2013, http://www.nytimes.com/2013/04/28/world/middle east/islamist-rebels-gains-in-syria-create-dilemma-for-us.html.
5. Omar Mushaweh, interview with the author, Istanbul, August 12, 2012.
6. Bashar al-Assad, interview with the author, Damascus, June 11, 2006.
7. Translator, interview with the author, Daraa, Syria, October 4, 2011.

CHAPTER 2. LAWRENCE OF SYRIA

1. R. Perceval Graves, *Lawrence of Arabia and His World* (London: Thames and Hudson, 1976), p. 21.
2. T. E. Lawrence, introduction to *Travels in Arabia Deserta*, by Charles Doughty, http://zineb-returns.blogspot.com/2012/05/te-lawrence-on-englishmen.html.
3. Lucy Ladikoff, "T. E. Lawrence: True and False (an Arab View)," http://.al-bushra.org/arabwrld/lawrance.htm.
4. James Barr, *Setting the Desert on Fire: T. E. Lawrence and Britain's Secret War in Arabia 1916–1918* (New York: W. W. Norton, 2008), p. 25.
5. Ibid., p. 13.
6. Ibid., p. 29.
7. T. E. Lawrence, *Seven Pillars of Wisdom* (London: Wordsworth Classics, 1997), p. 213.
8. James Barr, *A Line in the Sand: The Anglo-French Struggle for the Middle East, 1914–1948* (New York: W. W. Norton, 2012), p. 58.
9. Mudar Barakat, interview with the author, Damascus, November 15, 2013.

10. Barr, *Line in the Sand*, p. 7.

11. Sykes-Picot Agreement, http://wwi.lib.byu.edu/index.php/Sykes-Picot_Agreement.

12. Lawrence, *Seven Pillars of Wisdom*, p. 67.

13. Barr, *Line in the Sand*, p. 22.

14. Ibid., p. 24.

15. Josh Glancy, "Chaim Weizmann and How the Balfour Declaration Was Made in Manchester," *Jewish Chronicle Online,* November 1, 2012, http://thejc.com/lifestyle/lifestyle-features/89026/chaim-weizmann-and-how-balfour-declaration-was-made-manchester.

16. Barr, *Line in the Sand*, p. 27.

17. Ibid., p. 29.

18. The Balfour Declaration can be found at http://unispal.un.org/UNISPAL.NSF/0/E210CA73E38D9E1D052565FA00705C61.

19. Doreen Ingrams, *Palestine Papers 1917–1922: Seeds of Conflict* (London: John Murray, 1972), p. 73.

20. Neil Tweedie, "We Must Draw on Our Historians," *Telegraph*, August 1, 2012.

21. Lawrence, *Seven Pillars of Wisdom*, p. 647.

22. Elie El-Hindy, interview with the author, Lebanon, June 5, 2013.

CHAPTER 3.   TREATIES, REBELLIONS,
AND INDEPENDENCE: 1919–1946

1. Julian Gorbach, "The Making of a 'Matinee Idol': Representations of Islam in Lowell Thomas's Lawrence of Arabia," p. 25, http://citation.all academic.com//meta/p_mla_apa_research_citation/2/9/7/9/3/pages297935/p297935-1.php.

2. Clio Visualizing History, "The Show," http://www.cliohistory.org/thomas-lawrence/show/.

3. Richard Aldington, *Lawrence of Arabia: A Biographical Enquiry* (Westport, CT: Greenwood, 1976), pp. 287–88.

4. Lowell Thomas, *With Lawrence in Arabia*, 16th ed. (London: Hutchinson, n.d.), p. 46.

5. Ibid., p. 61.

6. Jeremy Wilson, "Lawrence of Arabia or T. E. Lawrence?" *Military Times*, http://telstudies.org/discussion/biography/wilson_lofa_or_tel.shtml.

7. Bill Swanson, ed., *Encarta Book of Quotes* (New York: St. Martin's Press, 2000), p. 550.

8. James Barr, *A Line in the Sand: The Anglo-French Struggle for the Middle East, 1914–1948* (New York: W. W. Norton, 2012), p. 62.

9. "Agreement between Emir Feisal and Dr. Chaim Weizmann, January 3, 1919," http://www.mideastweb.org/feisweiz.htm.

10. Robert D. Kaplan, *The Arabists: The Romance of an American Elite* (New York: Free Press, 1993), pp. 70–72.

11. "The King-Crane Commission Report, August 28, 1919," http://www.gwpda.org/1918p/kncr.htm. Pages 7–8 list the response from various religious and ethnic groups.

12. Ibid., p. 9.

13. Ibid., p. 80.

14. Barr, *Line in the Sand*, p. 94.

15. Elie El-Hindy, interview with the author, Lebanon, June 5, 2013.

16. Mudar Barakat, interview with the author, Damascus, November 15, 2013.

17. Barr, *Line in the Sand*, p. 120.

18. Michael Provence, *The Great Syrian Revolt and the Rise of Arab Nationalism* (Austin: University of Texas Press, 2005) p. 63.

19. Ibid., p. 58.

20. Ibid., pp. 81–83.

21. Ibid., p. 42.

22. Bisher Allisa, phone interview with the author, January 31, 2014.

23. El-Hindy, interview with the author.

24. Alison Pargeter, *The Muslim Brotherhood: From Opposition to Power* (London: Saqi Books, 2010), p. 21.

25. El-Hindy, interview with the author.

26. Eugene Rogan, *The Arabs: A History* (New York: Basic Books, 2011), p. 246.

27. Barr, *Line in the Sand*, p. 315.

CHAPTER 4. WARS AND COUPS—THEN THE ASSADS ARRIVE: 1947–2011

1. Joshua Landis, "Syria and the 1948 War in Palestine," in *Rewriting the Palestine War: 1948 and the History of the Arab-Israeli Conflict*, ed. Eugene Rogan and Avi Shlaim (Cambridge: Cambridge University Press, 2001), p. 178, http://faculty-staff.ou.edu/L/Joshua.M.Landis-1/Syria_1948.htm.

2. Michael Oren, *Power, Faith, and Fantasy: America in the Middle East, 1776 to the Present* (New York: W. W. Norton, 2007), p. 525.

3. Joel Perlmann, "The 1967 Census of the West Bank and Gaza Strip: A Digitized Version," Levy Institute, http://www.levyinstitute.org/pubs/1967 _census/vol_1_intro_tab_d.pdf. An Israeli census counted 954,378 Palestinians in the West Bank and Gaza in 1967. Palestinian sources estimate there were two million.

4. UN Security Council, "Text of UN Resolution 242, November 22, 1967," http://unispal.un.org/unispal.nsf/0/7D35E1F729DF491C85256EE700686136.

5. Taleb Ibrahim, interview with the author, Damascus, June 7, 2006.

6. Mohammad Ali, interview with the author, Quneitra, Syria, June 16, 2006.

7. CAMERA (Committee for Accuracy in Middle East Reporting in America), "Syria's Quneitra Hoax," May 10, 2001, http://www.camera.org/ index.asp?x_article=49&x_context=3.

8. UN General Assembly, *Report of the Special Committee to Investigate Israeli Practices Affecting the Human Rights of the Population of the Occupied Territories* (n.p.: UN General Assembly, November 29, 1974), http://www.refworld.org/cgi-bin/ texis/vtx/rwmain ?docid=3b00f1c74.

9. US senator James Abourezk, e-mail interview with the author, October 17, 2013.

10. Elie El-Hindy, interview with the author, Lebanon, June 5, 2013.

11. Hugh Eakin and Alisa Roth, "Syria's Refugees: The Catastrophe," *New York Review of Books*, October 10, 2013, http://www.nybooks.com/articles/ archives/2013/oct/10/syrias-refugees-catastrophe/.

12. Oren, *Power, Faith, and Fantasy*, p. 524.

13. Associated Press, "PLO Leader Who Opposed Arafat Dies in Damascus," *Times of Israel*, January 29, 2013, http://www.timesofisrael.com/plo -leader-who-opposed-arafat-dies-in-damascus.

14. Sean McBride et al., *Israel in Lebanon: Report of the International Commission to Enquire into Reported Violations of International Law by Israel during Its Invasion of Lebanon* (London: Ithaca Press, 1983).

15. Oren, *Power, Faith, and Fantasy*, p. 553.

16. Central Intelligence Agency, "Syria," in *CIA World Factbook*, https:// www.cia.gov/library/publications/the-world-factbook/geos/sy.html. The CIA writes that Kurds make up 10 percent of the Syrian population, but many Kurds argue that the figure is closer to 15 percent.

17. Alison Pargeter, *The Muslim Brotherhood: From Opposition to Power* (London: Saqi Books, 2010), p. 77.

18. Ibid., pp. 77–78.

19. Robert Fisk, *The Great War for Civilization: The Conquest of the Middle East*

(New York: Alfred Knopf, 2005), p. 814. See also Robert Fisk, *Pity the Nation: The Abduction of Lebanon* (New York: Nation Books, 2002), pp. 181–87.

20. Fisk, *Great War for Civilization*, p. 815.

21. "George Bush Sr. on War and Peace," On the Issues, http://www.onthe issues.org/celeb/George_Bush_Sr__War_+_Peace.htm (accessed March 10, 2014).

22. David W. Lesch, *Syria: The Fall of the House of Assad* (New Haven, CT: Yale University Press, 2012), p. 4.

23. Tim Lister and Jamie Crawford, "Meet Syria's Wealthiest and Most Elusive Man," CNN, March 7, 2012, http://security.blogs.cnn.com/2012/03/07/ meet-syrias-wealthiest-and-most-elusive-man/.

24. Shaam News Network, "Protesters Burn Syriatel SIM Cards Owned by Rami Makhlouf," May 21, 2011, http://www.youtube.com/watch?v=r9Y5 q?HnmaY

25. Hamad, interview with the author, Damascus, June 16, 2006.

26. Anne Barnard, "Syrian Officials Sound a Conciliatory Note toward the Opposition," *New York Times*, October 6, 2013, http://www.nytimes.com/ 2013/10/07/world/middleeast/syrian-officials-sound-a-conciliatory-note-toward -the-opposition.html.

27. Ayman Abdel Nour, interview with the author, Damascus, June 13, 2006.

28. Bashar al-Assad, interview with the author, Damascus, June 14, 2006.

29. Sheik Nawaf al-Basheer, interview with the author, Deir Ezzor, Syria, June 12, 2006.

30. Canadian Government Publishing, *Commission of Inquiry into the Actions of Canadian Officials in Relation to Maher Arar* [Arar Commission], http://www .sirc-csars.gc.ca/pdfs/cm_arar_rec-eng.pdf.

31. CBC News, "US Legislators Apologize to Maher Arar," October 18, 2007, http://www.cbc.ca/news/world/us-legislators-apologize-to-maher-arar-1.600301.

32. Bashar al-Assad, interview with the author, Damascus, June 11, 2006.

33. Marlise Simons, "Fifth Suspect Is Indicted in 2005 Killing of Ex-Lebanese Premier," *New York Times*, October 10, 2013, http://www.nytimes .com/2013/10/11/world/middleeast/fifth-suspect-is-indicted-in-2005-killing-of -ex-lebanese-premier.html.

34. Basheer, interview with the author.

35. "Damascus Declaration in English," Syria Comment, November 1, 2005, http://faculty-staff.ou.edu/L/Joshua.M.Landis-1/syriablog/2005/11/damascus -declaration-in-english.htm.

36. Basheer, interview with the author.

37. Assad, interview with the author, June 14, 2006.

38. Bobbi Nodell, "New Estimates Give Updated Count of Iraq War Deaths between 2003 and 2011," University of Washington Health Sciences, October 15, 2013, http://www.eurekalert.org/pub_releases/2013-10/uow--neg101113.php.

39. Gilbert Burnham, Riyadh Lafta, Shannon Doocy, and Les Roberts, "Mortality after the 2003 Invasion of Iraq: A Cross-Sectional Cluster Sample Survey," *Lancet* 368, no. 9545 (2006): 1421–28.

40. Paul Post, "Taking up 4,486 Flags for Slain Soldiers, but Holding on to Their Memory," *New York Times*, May 28, 2012, http://www.nytimes .com/2012/05/29/nyregion/removing-4486-flags-for-slain-soldiers-but-keeping -their-memory.html.

41. Reese Erlich and Peter Coyote, "The Murders at Al-Sukariya," *Vanity Fair Online*, October 22, 2009, http://www.vanityfair.com/politics/features/2009/10/ al-sukariya-200910.

42. Lesch, *Syria*, p. 15.

43. Ibrahim, interview with the author.

44. Dr. Mahmoud al-Agassi, interview with the author, Damascus, June 13, 2006.

45. Basheer, interview with the author.

46. Jay Solomon and Bill Spindle, "Syria Strongman: Time for Reform," *Wall Street Journal*, January 31, 2011, http://online.wsj.com/news/articles/SB1 0001424052748704832704576114340735033236.

CHAPTER 5.   THE UPRISING BEGINS

1. Reese Erlich, "For Most Tunisians, Little Has Changed," *Global Post*, April 29, 2012, http://www.globalpost.com/dispatch/news/regions/middle -east/120427/tunisia-economy-sidi-bouzid-arab-spring-protests.

2. "Death Toll Rises as Syria Crackdown Continues," *Al Jazeera*, May 1, 2011, http://www.aljazeera.com/news/middleeast/2011/04/20114301749598 35564.html.

3. Maciej Bartkowski and Mohja Kahf, "The Syrian Resistance: A Tale of Two Struggles," Open Democracy, September 23, 2013, http://open democracy.net/civilresistance/maciej-bartkowski-mohja-kahf/syrian-resistance -tale-of-two-struggles.

4. Nada Bakri, "Draft Reform Law in Syria Fails to Mollify Protesters," *New York Times*, July 25, 2011, http://www.nytimes.com/2011/07/26/world/ middleeast/26syria.html.

5. Governor Mohammed Khaled Hanos and Attorney General Tayseer al-Smadi, interview with the author, Daraa, Syria, October 4, 2011.

6. When the interviews took place in October 2011, the United Nations had estimated three thousand civilian deaths. The total number of civilian and military deaths reached over 140,000 by March 2014.

7. Mahmoud, interview with the author, Damascus, October 2011.

8. Ahmad Bakdouness, interview with the author, Damascus, October 5, 2011.

9. Mahmoud Hassino, interview with the author, Antakya, Turkey, August 11, 2012.

10. Roucida Mabardi, "Syrian Gays Edge Gingerly out of the Closet," Agence France Presse, June 2, 2009, http://www.google.com/hostednews/afp/article/ALeqM5g1exXPToXhY8l9aLmQTCTD-JPCPQ.

11. UN Office for Human Rights, "UN Issues First Report on Human Rights of Gay and Lesbian People," December 15, 2011, http://www.un.org/apps/news/story.asp?NewsID=40743#.UyCUyfrn_gg.

12. Miral Bioredda, interview with the author, Antakya, Turkey, August 8, 2012.

13. Nasradeen Ahme, interview with the author, Antakya, Turkey, August 8, 2012.

14. Mahmoud Hassino, e-mail interview with the author, January 28, 2014.

15. "Bashar," interview with the author, Damascus, October 2011.

16. Anonymous, interview with the author, Tartus, Syria, October 8, 2011.

17. The concept that all terrorists are Muslim is accepted as fact among some American conservatives. See, for example, Tanya Somanader, "Fox Host Brian Kilmeade Says 'All Terrorists Are Muslim' in Defense of O'Reilly's 'Muslims Killed Us' Remark," Think Progress, October 15, 2010, http://thinkprogress.org/media/2010/10/15/124417/kilmeade-muslim-terrorists/.

18. Reese Erlich, *Conversations with Terrorists: Middle East Leaders on Politics, Violence, and Empire* (Sausalito, CA: PoliPoint Press, 2010), p. 6.

19. Aron Lund, "Struggling to Adapt: The Muslim Brotherhood in a New Syria," Carnegie Endowment for International Peace, May 7, 2013, http://carnegie endowment.org/2013/05/07/struggling-to-adapt-muslim-brotherhood-in-new -syria/g2qm.

20. Ibid.

21. Alison Pargeter, *The Muslim Brotherhood: From Opposition to Power* (London: Saqi Books, 2010), p. 101.

22. Omar Mushaweh, interview with the author, Istanbul, August 12, 2012.

23. Miral Bioredda, interview with the author.

24. "Bashar," interview with the author.

25. Michael R. Gordon, Mark Landler, and Anne Barnard, "US Suspends

Nonlethal Aid to Syria Rebels," *New York Times*, December 11, 2013, http://www
.nytimes.com/2013/12/12/world/middleeast/us-suspends-nonlethal-aid-to
-syrian-rebels-in-north.html/.

26. Senator John McCain, "Statement by Sen. John McCain concerning the
Grave Situation in Syria," June 8, 2013, http://www.mccain.senate.gov/public/
index.cfm/press-releases?ID=259635e5-f898-046e-4c63-3cf88c4c523f.

27. Elizabeth O'Bagy, "The Free Syrian Army," *Middle East Security Report*
9, March 2013.

28. Ghaith Abdul-Ahad, "How to Start a Battalion (in Five Easy Lessons),"
London Review of Books, February 21, 2013.

29. Hassan Hassan, "The Army of Islam Is Winning in Syria and That's Not
Necessarily a Bad Thing," *Foreign Policy*, October 1, 2013, http://www.foreign
policy.com/articles/2013/10/01/the_army_of_islam_is_winning_in_syria.

30. "Syria: Jaysh Al-Islam Rejects Geneva II Conference," *Asharq Al-Awsat*,
November 12, 2013, http://www.aawsat.net/2013/11/article55322150.

31. John Hudson, "US Weighing Closer Ties with Hardline Islamists in
Syria," *Foreign Policy*, December 17, 2013, http://thecable.foreignpolicy.com/
posts/2013/12/16/us_weighing_closer_ties_with_hardline_islamists_in_syria
#sthash.b9QyA3KZ.dpuf.

32. Joshua Landis, "Who Are Syria's Big Five Insurgent Leaders?" Syria
Comment, October 1, 2013, http://www.joshualandis.com/blog/biggest
-powerful-militia-leaders-syria.

33. "Islamists Kill 15 Alawite and Druze Civilians in Syria—Activists,"
Reuters, December 12, 2013, http://www.reuters.com/article/2013/12/12/us
-syria-crisis-adra-idUSBRE9BB0PM20131212.

34. Lund, "Struggling to Adapt."

35. Hudson, "US Weighing Closer Ties with Hardline Islamists in Syria."

36. Anne Barnard, "Jihadist Leader Envisions an Islamic State in Syria,"
New York Times, December 19, 2013, http://www.nytimes.com/2013/12/20/
world/middleeast/jihadist-leader-envisions-an-islamic-state-in-syria.html.

37. "Syria's Rebels: 20 Things You Need to Know," CNN, September 7, 2013,
http://www.ozarksfirst.com/story/syrias-rebels-20-things-you-need-to-know/d/
story/zm3cWsQD3UC54FnSi8LOtQ.

38. Aron Lund, "Major Salafi Faction Criticizes Jabhat al-Nosra," Syria
Comment, May 4, 2013, http://www.joshualandis.com/blog/major-salafi
-faction-criticizes-jabhat-al-nosra/.

39. "Iraqi al-Qaeda and Syrian Group 'Merge,'" *Al Jazeera*, April 9, 2013, http://
www.aljazeera.com/news/middleeast/2013/04/201349194856244589.html.

40. Ben Hubbard, "Al Qaeda Cuts Ties with Jihadist Group in Syria Involved

in Rebel Infighting," *New York Times*, February 4, 2014, http://www.nytimes
.com/2014/02/04/world/middleeast/syria.html.

CHAPTER 6. CHEMICAL WEAPONS, MILITARY OFFENSIVES, AND STALEMATE

1. Liu Sly, "Syrian Rebel Leader Says Any American Strike on Regime
Targets Should Be 'Powerful,'" *Washington Post*, September 4, 2013, http://www
.washingtonpost.com/world/middle_east/syrian-rebels-say-any-american-strike
-on-regime-targets-should-be-powerful/2013/09/04/fa1784ea-15a2-11e3-961c
-f22d3aaf19ab_story.html.

2. "Government Assessment of the Syrian Government's Use of Chemical
Weapons on August 21, 2013," Office of the Press Secretary, the White House,
August 30, 2013, http://www.whitehouse.gov/the-press-office/2013/08/30/
government-assessment-syrian-government-s-use-chemical-weapons-august-21.

3. "Syria: John Kerry's Statement in Full," *Telegraph*, August 30, 2013,
http://www.telegraph.co.uk/news/worldnews/middleeast/syria/10277442/
Syria-John-Kerrys-statement-in-full.html.

4. Rick Gladstone and C. J. Chivers, "UN Implicates Syria in Using
Chemical Arms," *New York Times*, September 16, 2013, http://www.nytimes
.com/2013/09/17/world/europe/syria-united-nations.html.

5. C. J. Chivers, "Data in Gas Attack Points to Assad's Top Forces," *New
York Times*, September 17, 2013, http://www.nytimes.com/2013/09/18/world/
middleeast/un-data-on-gas-attack-points-to-assads-top-forces.html.

6. "Syria: Thousands Suffering Neurotoxic Symptoms Treated in Hospitals Supported by MSF," Doctors Without Borders, August 24, 2013, http://
www.doctorswithoutborders.org/article/syria-thousands-suffering-neurotoxic
-symptoms-treated-hospitals-supported-msf.

7. David E. Sanger and Eric Schmitt, "Allies' Intelligence Differs on Details,
but Still Points to Assad Forces," *New York Times*, September 3, 2013, http://www
.nytimes.com/2013/09/04/world/middleeast/allies-intelligence-on-syria-all
-points-to-assad-forces.html.

8. Zeina Karam and Kimberly Dozier, "Lingering Doubts over Syria Gas
Attack Evidence," Associated Press, September 9, 2013, http://news.yahoo.com/
lingering-doubts-over-syria-gas-attack-evidence-072755287.html.

9. Gwyn Winfield, "Modern Warfare," CBRNe World, February 2014,
http://www.cbrneworld.com/news/ake_sellstrom_interview_now_available#ax
zz30rhCd2Ky.

10. Adam Entous, Nour Malas, and Rima Abushakra, "As Syrian Chemical Attack Loomed, Missteps Doomed Civilians," *Wall Street Journal*, November 22, 2013, http://online.wsj.com/news/articles/SB10001424052702303914304579194203188283242.

11. Seymour M. Hersh, "Whose Sarin?" *London Review of Books*, December 19, 2013, http://www.lrb.co.uk/v35/n24/seymour-m-hersh/whose-sarin.

12. As seen in a YouTube video of the chemical-weapons inspectors' press conference. Sellstrom's comment begins at 15:55. http://www.youtube.com/watch?v=5CFn9pWNKeI.

13. Winfield, "Modern Warfare."

14. Richard Lloyd and Theodore A. Postol, "Possible Implications of Faulty US Technical Intelligence in the Damascus Nerve Agent Attack of August 21, 2013," Document Cloud, January 14, 2014, https://www.documentcloud.org/documents/1006045-possible-implications-of-bad-intelligence.html.

15. C. J. Chivers, "New Study Refines View of Sarin Attack in Syria," *New York Times*, December 28, 2013, http://www.nytimes.com/2013/12/29/world/middleeast/new-study-refines-view-of-sarin-attack-in-syria.html.

16. Robert Fisk, "Gas Missiles 'Were Not Sold to Syria,'" *Independent*, September 22, 2013, http://www.independent.co.uk/voices/comment/gas-missiles-were-not-sold-to-syria-8831792.html.

17. Eliot Higgins, "Sy Hersh's Chemical Misfire," *Foreign Policy*, December 9, 2013, http://www.foreignpolicy.com/articles/2013/12/09/sy_hershs_chemical_misfire.

18. Centers for Disease Control and Prevention, "Facts about Sarin," http://www.bt.cdc.gov/agent/sarin/basics/facts.asp.

19. Dr. Yasuo Seto, "The Sarin Gas Attack in Japan and the Related Forensic Investigation," Organization for the Prohibition of Chemical Weapons, June 1, 2001, http://www.opcw.org/news/article/the-sarin-gas-attack-in-japan-and-the-related-forensic-investigation/.

20. Dan Kaszeta, "Industrial and Economic Aspects of Sarin: Why Poor Quality Is Not an Indicator of Non-state Manufacture," *Brown Moses Blog*, November 6, 2013, http://brown-moses.blogspot.com/2013/11/industrial-and-economic-aspects-of.html.

21. Dr. Bassam Barakat, interview with the author, Damascus, November 15, 2013.

22. "United Nations Mission to Investigate Allegations of the Use of Chemical Weapons in the Syrian Arab Republic," December 12, 2013, https://unoda-web.s3.amazonaws.com/wp-content/uploads/2013/12/report.pdf.

23. Sergey Batsanov, phone interview with the author, Geneva, February 14, 2014.

24. Reuters, "Syrian Rebels May Have Used Sarin," *New York Times*, May 5, 2013, http://www.nytimes.com/2013/05/06/world/middleeast/syrian-rebels-may-have-used-sarin.html. A partial video of her interview can be viewed at http://www.youtube.com/watch?v=yQPMqsxpHSE.

25. Reuters, "Turkey Arrests 12 in Raids on 'Terrorist' Organization," May 30, 2013, http://www.reuters.com/article/2013/05/30/us-syria-crisis-turkey-idUSBRE94T0YO20130530.

26. "Iraq Claims Foiling al-Qaeda Nerve-Gas Plot," *Al Jazeera*, June 2, 2013, http://www.aljazeera.com/news/middleeast/2013/06/20136117362322130.html.

27. F. Michael Maloof, "Classified Document Shows Deadly Weapon Found in Home of Arrested Islamists," *WorldNetDaily*, September 11, 2013, http://www.wnd.com/2013/09/u-s-military-confirms-rebels-had-Sarin/.

28. See the Institute for Policy Studies profile of Maloof at http://rightweb.irc-online.org/profile/maloof_f_michael.

29. Maloof, "Classified Document Shows Deadly Weapon Found in Home of Arrested Islamists."

30. Hersh, "Whose Sarin?"

31. Ibid.

32. Eliot Higgins, "Responses to the Final UN Report into the Use of Chemical Weapons in Syria—Part 2," *Brown Moses Blog*, December 14, 2013, http://brown-moses.blogspot.com/2013/12/responses-to-final-un-report-into-use_14.html.

33. B. Barakat, interview with the author.

34. Syrian minister of justice Najm al-Ahmad, interview with the author, Damascus, November 16, 2013.

35. Higgins, "Responses to the Final UN Report into the Use of Chemical Weapons in Syria."

36. Dan Kaszeta, phone interview with the author, London, February 18, 2014.

37. Al-Ahmad, interview with the author.

38. B. Barakat, interview with the author.

39. Joshua Landis, phone interview with the author, December 11, 2013.

40. "Syrian Forces May Have Used Gas Without Assad's Permission," *Reuters*, September 13, 2013, http://www.reuters.com/article/2013/09/08/us-syria-crisis-germany-idUSBRE98707B20130908.

41. Gareth Porter, "New Data Raise Further Doubt on Official View of August 21 Gas Attack in Syria," Truthout, April 29, 2014, http://truth-out.org/news/item/23368-new-data-raise-further-doubt-on-official-view-of-aug-21-gas-attack-in-syria.

42. Ernesto Londoño and Greg Miller, "CIA Begins Delivering Weapons to Syrian Rebels," *Washington Post,* September 12, 2013, http://www.washington post.com/world/national-security/cia-begins-weapons-delivery-to-syrian-rebels/2013/09/11/9fcf2ed8-1b0c-11e3-a628-7e6dde8f889d_story.html.

43. Reese Erlich, "From Surrender Monkey to Closest Ally," Common Dreams, September 1, 2013, https://www.commondreams.org/view/2013/09/01-0.

44. Oliver Holmes, "Syria Lets UN Inspect Gas Attack Site, Washington Says Too Late," *Reuters*, August 25, 2013, http://in.reuters.com/article/2013/08/25/syria-crisis-idINDEE97M0C620130825.

45. Mark Landler and Eric Schmitt, "White House Says Syria Has Used Chemical Arms," *New York Times,* April 25, 2013, http://www.nytimes.com/2013/04/26/world/middleeast/us-says-it-suspects-assad-used-chemical-weapons.html?pagewanted=all.

46. Harriet Alexander, "Syria: If Bashar al-Assad Hands Over Chemical Weapons, We Will Not Attack, Says John Kerry," *Telegraph*, September 9, 2013, http://www.telegraph.co.uk/news/worldnews/middleeast/syria/10295638/Syria-If-Bashar-al-Assad-hands-over-chemical-weapons-we-will-not-attack-says-John-Kerry.html.

47. William R. Polk, "Reflections on the Syrian Chemical Weapons Issue and the Possibility of Ending the Civil War," Syria Comment, September 15, 2013, http://www.joshualandis.com/blog/syrian-chemical-weapons-possibility-ending-civil-war-william-r-polk/.

48. Bob Kesling, "Lessons from US Arms Destruction," *Wall Street Journal*, September 12, 2013, http://online.wsj.com/news/articles/SB20001424127887324549004579069561052663626.

49. Nicholas Blanford, "Hezbollah Marks Major Triumph as Qusayr Tips Back into Assad Camp," *Christian Science Monitor*, June 5, 2013, http://www.csmonitor.com/World/Middle-East/2013/0605/Hezbollah-marks-major-triumph-as-Qusayr-tips-back-into-Assad-camp.

50. Haj Ghassan, interview with the author, Hermel, Lebanon, June 7, 2013.

51. Sarah Birke, "How al-Qaeda Changed the Syrian War," *New York Review of Books*, December 27, 2013, http://www.nybooks.com/blogs/nyrblog/2013/dec/27/how-al-qaeda-changed-syrian-war/.

52. Chris Looney, "Al-Qaeda's Governance Strategy in Raqqa," Syria Comment, December 8, 2013, http://www.joshualandis.com/blog/al-qaedas-governance-strategy-raqqa-chris-looney/.

53. Mohammed al-Attar, "Al Raqqa: The Reality of the Military Brigades, the Administration of the Liberated City and the Revolutions to Come," Republic GS, September 16, 2013, http://therepublicgs.net/2013/09/16/al

-raqqa-the-reality-of-the-military-brigades-the-administration-of-the-liberated
-city-and-the-revolutions-to-come/.

54. Birke, "How al-Qaeda Changed the Syrian War."

55. Michael R. Gordon, Mark Landler, and Anne Barnard, "US Suspends Nonlethal Aid to Syria Rebels," *New York Times*, December 11, 2013, http://www.nytimes.com/2013/12/12/world/middleeast/us-suspends-nonlethal-aid-to-syrian-rebels-in-north.html.

56. Adam Entous and Rima Abushakra, "Moderate Syrian Rebels Try to Recover after Islamists Take Over Headquarters. US Changes Account of Commander Fleeing Syria to Turkey during Incursion," *Wall Street Journal*, December 12, 2013, http://online.wsj.com/news/articles/SB10001424052702303293604579254162228246876.

57. Associated Press, "Syrian Rebels Name New Military Commander," *Washington Post*, February 17, 2014, http://www.washingtonpost.com/world/middle east/syria-says-us-created-negative-climate-in-geneva/2014/02/16/d19b6128-977d-11e3-ae45-458927ccedb6_story.html.

58. Ben Hubbard and Karam Shoumali, "Top Military Body against Syria's Assad Is in Chaos, Undermining Fight," *New York Times*, February 23, 2014, http://www.nytimes.com/2014/02/24/world/middleeast/top-military-body-against-syrias-assad-is-in-chaos-undermining-fight.html.

59. John Hudson, "US Weighing Closer Ties with Hardline Islamists in Syria," *Foreign Policy*, December 17, 2013, http://thecable.foreignpolicy.com/posts/2013/12/16/us_weighing_closer_ties_with_hardline_islamists_in_syria#sthash.b9QyA3KZ.dpuf.

60. Anne Barnard and Nick Cumming-Bruce, "Syrian Rebels Sketch Peace Plan That Omits Demand for Assad's Ouster," *New York Times*, February 12, 2014, http://www.nytimes.com/2014/02/13/world/middleeast/syria.html.

61. Maria Abi-Habib and Stacy Meichtry, "Saudis Agree to Provide Syrian Rebels with Mobile Antiaircraft Missiles," *Wall Street Journal*, February 14, 2014, http://online.wsj.com/news/articles/SB1000142405270230470380457938297419684 0680.

62. "Leen," interview with the author, Damascus, November 2013.

CHAPTER 7. WHO SUPPORTS ASSAD?

1. Dr. Bassam Barakat, interview with the author, Damascus, November 14, 2013.

2. Kourosh Ziabari, "Sharmine Narwani: Syrian Opposition Is Not United

and Cohesive," *Fars News*, December 9, 2013, http://english.farsnews.com/newstext.aspx?nn=13920916001486.

3. David W. Lesch, *Syria: The Fall of the House of Assad* (New Haven, CT: Yale University Press, 2012), p. 52.

4. Bishop Armash Nalbandian, interview with the author, Damascus, November 14, 2013.

5. Alaa Ebrahim, interview with the author, Damascus, November 17, 2013.

6. Feras Dieb, interview with the author, Tartus, Syria, October 8, 2011.

7. Shafika Dieb, interview with the author, Tartus, Syria, October 9, 2011.

8. Mahmood Dieb, interview with author, Tartus, Syria, October 9, 2011.

9. Wafaa Dieb, interview with the author, Tartus, Syria, October 8, 2011.

10. Aboud Dandachi, "Observations of a Homsi Living in Tartous," *Syria Comment*, January 21, 2014, http://www.joshualandis.com/blog/observations-homsi-living-tartous/.

11. "Poorest Countries in the Middle East," Aneki, http://www.aneki.com/poorest_middle_east.htm.

12. Nabil Samman, interview with the author, Damascus, October 5, 2011.

13. Bouthaina Shaban, interview with the author, Damascus, October 5, 2011.

14. Nabil Toumeh, interview with the author, Damascus, October 3, 2011.

15. Nabil Sukkar, interview with the author, Damascus, October 5, 2011.

16. Dr. Bassam Barakat, interview with the author, Damascus, November 4, 2013.

17. Jason Samenow, "Drought and Syria: Manmade Climate Change or Just Climate?" *Washington Post*, September 9, 2013, http://www.washingtonpost.com/blogs/capital-weather-gang/wp/2013/09/09/drought-and-syria-manmade-climate-change-or-just-climate.

18. US Energy Information Administration, "Syria," February 18, 2014, http://www.eia.gov/countries/cab.cfm?fips=SY.

19. World Bank, "Country and Region Specific Forecasts and Data," http://www.worldbank.org/en/publication/global-economic-prospects/data?variable=NYGDPMKTPKDZ&region=MNA.

20. Rana Issa, interview with the author, Damascus, October 6, 2011.

21. Anonymous clothing store owner, interview with the author, Damascus, October 2011.

22. Hagop, interview with the author, Damascus, November 2013.

23. Loveday Morris, "Syrian Islamist Rebels Kill and Kidnap Hundreds of Civilians, Rights Group Says," *Washington Post*, October 10, 2013, http://www.washingtonpost.com/world/middle_east/syrian-islamist-rebels-killed-or-kidnapped-hundreds-of-civilians-rights-goup-says/2013/10/10/9ceaac8a-31e9-11e3-9c68-1cf643210300_story.html.

24. For further background see "Armenian Genocide," Armenian National Institute, http://www.armenian-genocide.org/genocide.html.

25. Nalbandian, interview with the author.

26. Father Simon Faddul, interview with the author, Beirut, May 31, 2013.

27. Nalbandian, interview with author.

28. Hagop, interview with the author.

29. Sheik Abdul Salaam al-Harash, interview with the author, Damascus, November 14, 2013.

30. Hagop, interview with the author.

31. Nalbandian, interview with the author.

32. Hagop, interview with the author.

33. Nalbandian, interview with the author.

34. Amira Hana, interview with the author, Damascus, November 17, 2013.

35. Nalbandian, interview with the author.

36. Nick Cumming-Bruce, "Top UN Rights Official Links Assad to Crimes in Syria," *New York Times*, December 2, 2013, http://www.nytimes.com/2013/12/03/world/middleeast/top-un-rights-official-links-assad-to-crimes-in-syria.html.

37. Maryam, interview with the author, Zahle, Lebanon, May 2013.

38. Most Reverend Archbishop Issam Darwish, interview with the author, Zahle, Lebanon, May 31, 2013.

39. Joseph, interview with the author, Zahle, Lebanon, May 31, 2013.

40. For regularly updated figures on Syrian refugees in Lebanon, see the UNHCR website, http://data.unhcr.org/syrianrefugees/country.php?id=122.

41. For updated figures on all Syrian refugees, see the UNHCR website, http://data.unhcr.org/syrianrefugees/regional.php.

42. Basem Shabb, interview with the author, Beirut, June 4, 2013.

43. Elie El Hindy, interview with the author, Lebanon, June 5, 2013.

44. Faddul, interview with the author.

45. El-Hindy, interview with the author.

46. Anonymous, interview with the author, Syria, October 2011.

47. Hugh Macleod and Annasofie Flamand, "Syria: Brutally Violent Shabiha Militia Member Tells It Like It Is," *Global Post*, June 15, 2012, http://www.globalpost.com/dispatch/news/regions/middle-east/syria/120614/syria-shabiha-thug-assad-mafia-guns-smuggling-violence-houla.

48. Ibid.

49. Michael Jansen "Russia and Iran Must Stop Enabling Syrian Government to Remain in Power, Warns Kerry," *Irish Times*, February 18, 2014, http://www.irishtimes.com/news/world/middle-east/russia-and-iran-must-stop-enabling-syrian-government-remain-in-power-warns-kerry-1.1694963.

50. Ebrahim, interview with the author.

51. Peter Beaumont, "Syria: Massacres of Sunni Families Reported in Assad's Heartland," *Observer*, May 4, 2013, http://www.theguardian.com/world/2013/may/04/syrian-sunni-families-die-in-assads-heartland.

52. Anne' Barnard and Hania Mourtada, "An Atrocity in Syria, with No Victim Too Small," *New York Times*, May 15, 2013, http://www.nytimes.com/2013/05/15/world/middleeast/grisly-killings-in-syrian-towns-dim-hopes-for-peace-talks.html.

53. Stephanie Nebehay, "Syrian Forces behind Last May's Banias Massacres as Government and Rebels Committed War Crimes, UN Reports," *Reuters*, September 11, 2013, http://www.huffingtonpost.com/2013/09/11/syria-banias-massacres_n_3906350.html.

54. Ebrahim, interview with the author.

55. "Leen," interview with the author.

CHAPTER 8. WHY IRAN BACKS SYRIA

1. For more details on the 2009 Iranian Green Movement, see Reese Erlich, *Conversations with Terrorists: Middle East Leaders on Politics, Violence, and Empire* (Sausalito, CA: PoliPoint Press, 2010), p. 93.

2. Jubin Goodarzi, "Iran and Syria," in *The Iran Primer*, United States Institute of Peace, http://iranprimer.usip.org/resource/iran-and-syria.

3. James Zogby, "The Rise and Fall of Iran in Arab and Muslim Eyes—A New Poll," Wilson Center, March 5, 2013, http://www.wilsoncenter.org/event/the-rise-fall-iran-arab-and-muslim-eyes-new-poll.

4. Mohsen Milani, "Why Tehran Won't Abandon Assad(ism)," *Washington Quarterly*, December 1, 2013.

5. Ibid.

6. Ibid.

7. Hossein Ruyvaran, interview with the author, Tehran, June 11, 2013.

8. Under Secretary of State for Political Affairs Wendy Sherman, "Testimony before the US Senate," May 15, 2013, http://www.foreign.senate.gov/imo/media/doc/Sherman_Testimony.pdf.

9. Professor Foad Izadi, interview with the author, Tehran, June 13, 2013.

10. Ibid.

11. Alex Vatanka, "Syria Drives Wedge between Turkey and Iran," Middle East Institute, May 16, 2012, http://www.mei.edu/content/Syria-drives-wedge-between-turkey-and-iran.

12. Izadi, interview with the author.

13. Robert F. Worth, "Effort to Rebrand Arab Spring Backfires in Iran," *New York Times*, February 2, 2012, http://www.nytimes.com/2012/02/03/world/middleeast/effort-to-rebrand-arab-spring-backfires-in-iran.html.

14. Ibid.

15. Sayed Mohammad Husseini, interview with the author, Tehran, June 12, 2013.

16. Izadi, interview with the author.

17. This story first appeared on the public radio program *The World* in June 2007.

18. Ruyvaran, interview with the author.

19. Fadi Burhan, interview with the author, Tehran, June 12, 2013.

20. Farnaz Fassihi and Jay Solomon, "Top Iranian Official Acknowledges Military Role in Syria," *Wall Street Journal*, September 16, 2012, http://online.wsj.com/news/articles/SB10000872396390443720204578000482831419570.

21. Farnaz Fassihi, Jay Solomon, and Sam Dagher, "Shiite Militiamen from across the Arab World Train at a Base near Tehran to Do Battle in Syria," *Wall Street Journal*, September 16, 2013, http://online.wsj.com/article/SB10001424127887323386460457906738286180898984.htm.

22. Ibid.

23. "Iran to Sign Oil Deal with Iraq while Friendship Pipeline Still Underway," Albawaba Business, July 21, 2013, http://www.albawaba.com/business/iran-gas-export-iraq-508114.

24. Abbas Abdi, interview with the author, Tehran, June 14, 2013.

25. Transcription of mobile phone recordings of Rafsanjani's August 31, 2013, speech are available in Farsi at www.bloghnews.com/news/21183.

26. Alireza Nader, "What to Do Now? Iran Torn on Syria," *Iran Primer*, US Institute of Peace, http://iranprimer.usip.org/blog/2013/sep/11/what-do-now-iran-torn-syria.

27. Reese Erlich, *The Iran Agenda: The Real Story of U.S. Policy and the Middle East Crisis* (Sausalito, CA: PoliPoint Press, 2007), p. 28.

28. Sherman, "Testimony before the US Senate."

29. Karen DeYoung and Scott Wilson, "Goal of Iran Sanctions Is Regime Collapse, US Official Says," *Washington Post*, January 10, 2012, http://www.washingtonpost.com/world/national-security/goal-of-iran-sanctions-is-regime-collapse-us-official-says/2012/01/10/gIQA0KJsoP_story.html/washingtonpost.com.

30. "Yusuf Abdi," interview with the author, Tehran, June 9, 2013.

31. Tahereh Karimi, interview with the author, Tehran, June 9, 2013.

32. Dr. Khodadad Asnarshari, interview with the author, Tehran, June 10, 2013.

33. Siamak Namazi, "Sanctions and Medical Supply Shortages in Iran," Wilson Center study, February 2013, http://www.wilsoncenter.org/publication/sanctions-and-medical-supply-shortages-iran.

34. Ghader Daemi Aghdam, interview with the author, Tehran, June 10, 2013.

35. Asnarshari, interview with the author.

36. Mohammad Sadegh Janansefat, interview with the author, Tehran, June 10, 2013.

37. Ibid.

38. Abbas, interview with the author, Iran, June 2013.

39. Hassan Rouhani, "What Iran Wants in 2014," *Project-Syndicate*, January 8, 2014, http://www.project-syndicate.org/commentary/hassan-rouhani-on-iran-s-new-moderation.

40. AIPAC, "Congress Must Act to Ensure Iranian Compliance," AIPAC, January 14, 2014, http://www.aipac.org/~/media/Publications/Policy%20and%20Politics/AIPAC%20Analyses/Issue%20Memos/2014/AIPAC%20Memo%20-%20Congress%20Must%20Act%20to%20Ensure%20Iranian%20Compliance.pdf.

41. Scott Stewart, "The Covert Intelligence War against Iran," *Security Weekly*, STRATFOR, December 8, 2011, http://www.stratfor.com/weekly/covert-intelligence-war-against-iran.

42. Erlich, *Iran Agenda*, pp. 17–18.

43. Sayed Mohammad Marandi, interview with the author, Tehran, June 12, 2013.

44. Reza Marashi and Trita Parsi, "The Wrong Path to Peace with Iran," CNN, December 31, 2013, http://edition.cnn.com/2013/12/31/opinion/marashi-parsi-iran-peace/index.html. NIAC is the largest Iranian American political group, and it favors normal diplomatic relations with Iran.

45. Thomas Erdbrink, "President-Elect of Iran Says He Will Engage with the West," *New York Times*, June 29, 2013, http://www.nytimes.com/2013/06/30/world/middleeast/president-elect-of-iran-says-he-will-engage-with-the-west.html.

46. Izadi, interview with the author.

47. Robin Wright, "Iran's Foreign Minister Says Sanctions Would Kill Nuclear Deal," *Time*, December 9, 2013, http://world.time.com/2013/12/09/exclusive-irans-foreign-minister-says-sanctions-would-kill-nuclear-deal/.

48. Mehdi Khalaji, "Syria as a Spoiler in Iran's Foreign Policy," Washington Institute, August 27, 2013, http://washin.st/18YcyLw.

CHAPTER 9. WILL THE KURDS HAVE THEIR WAY?

1. Barkhodan Balo, interview with the author, Moqebleh Camp, Kurdish region, Iraq, September 15, 2011.

2. "The Peace Treaty of Sevres," HR-Net, Section III, Article 64, www.hri .org/docs/sevres.

3. Mufid Abdulla, "Mahabad—The First Independent Kurdish Republic," *Kurdistan Times*, June 12, 2011, http://kurdistantribune.com/2011/ mahabad-first-independent-kurdish-republic/.

4. Ibid.

5. Jordil Tejel, *Syria's Kurds: History, Politics, and Society* (London: Rutledge Group, 2009), p. 48.

6. Human Rights Watch, "Syria: The Silenced Kurds," October 1996

7. Becky Lee Katz, "Turkey: Kurdish Teenager Convicted as Terrorist for Attending Demonstration," *Los Angeles Times*, July 10, 2010, http://latimesblogs .latimes.com/babylonbeyond/2010/07/convicted-of-terrorism-a-young-kurdish-girl -is-serving-her-seven-year-and-nine-month-prison-sentence-in-turkeys-prison-e.html.

8. Reese Erlich, "Brad Pitt and the Girl Guerrillas," *Mother Jones*, March/ April2007,www.motherjones.com/politics/2007/03/brad-pitt-and-girl-guerrillas.

9. Anonymous PKK women, interview with the author, Qandil Mountain camp, Kurdish region, Iraq, November 26, 2006.

10. Soner Cagaptay, "Arab Spring Heats up Kurdish Issue," *Washington Institute*, March 2012, http://www.washingtoninstitute.org/policy-analysis/view/ arab-spring-heats-up-kurdish-issue.

11. Abdullah Ocalan, *Prison Writings: The Roots of Civilisation* (London: Pluto Press 2007), p. 243.

12. "The Kurdish Democratic Union Party," Carnegie Middle East Center, March 1, 2012, http://carnegie-mec.org/publications/?fa=48526.

13. "KNC Leader: Syrian Kurds Are Disappointed by PYD's Actions," Rudlaw online news, July 1, 2012.

14. "Can Med," interview with the author, Erbil, Kurdish region, Iraq, September 11, 2011.

15. Tejel, *Syria's Kurds*, p. 50.

16. "Annual Human Rights Report 2008," UK Foreign and Commonwealth Office, p. 167.

17. Bashar al-Assad, interview with the author, Damascus, June 14, 2006.

18. "Syria's Assad Grants Nationality to Hasaka Kurds," *BBC*, April 7, 2011, http://www.bbc.co.uk/news/world-middle-east-12995174.

19. Christian Sinclair and Sirwan Kajjo, "The Evolution of Kurdish Politics

in Syria," Middle East Research and Information Project, August 31, 2011, www
.merip.org/mero/mero083111.

20. Balo, interview with the author.

21. Tejel, *Syria's Kurds*, p. 116.

22. "Factbox: Why Small Producer Syria Matters to Oil Markets,"
Reuters, August 27 2013, www.reuters.com/article/2013/08/27/us-syria-oil
-factbox-idUSBRE97Q0JW20130827.

23. Stanley Reed, "Iraqi Government and Kurdistan at Odds over Oil Production," *New York Times*, November 14, 2012, http://www.nytimes.com/2012/
11/15/business/global/delicate-balancing-act-for-western-oil-firms-in-iraq.html.

24. Julian Borger and Mona Mahmood, "EU Decision to Lift Syrian Oil
Sanctions Boosts Jihadist Groups," *Guardian*, May 19, 2013, http://www.the
guardian.com/world/2013/may/19/eu-syria-oil-jihadist-al-qaida.

25. "Ciwan Rashid," interview with the author, Erbil, Kurdish region, Iraq,
September 13, 2011.

26. Mohammad Farho, interview with the author, Erbil, Kurdish region,
Iraq, September 11, 2011.

27. Hassan Saleh, interview with the author, Erbil, Kurdish region, September 10, 2011.

28. "Interview with Syrian Kurdish Politician Mish'al at-Tammo," *Kurdwatch*, July 21, 2011, www.ekurd.net/mismas/articles/misc2011/7/syriakurd342
.htm.

29. Ibid.

30. Farnaz Fassihi, "Kurds Look beyond Assad, with Dream of Autonomy,"
Wall Street Journal, September 29, 2011, http://online.wsj.com/news/articles/
SB10001424053111904491704576572114191429564.

31. "Interview with Syrian Kurdish Politician Mish'al at-Tammo," *Kurdwatch*.

32. "Iraqi Kurds Blame Syria for the Death of Kurdish Figure Mish'al
Tammo," CNN, October 11, 2011, www.ekurd.net/mismas/articles/misc2011/
10/syriakurd367.htm.

33. "Can Med," interview with the author.

34. "Liberated Kurdish Cities in Syrian Kurdistan Move into Next Phase,"
Rudlaw, July 25, 2012, http://www.ekurd.net/mismas/articles/misc2012/7/
syriakurd554.htm.

35. Wladimir van Wilgenburg, e-mail interview with the author, September
25, 2013.

36. "Mr. Saleh Mohammed the Head of the Democratic Union Party Said
in an Interview with *Al Jazeera*," official PYD website in English, www.pydro
java.net/en/index.php?option=com_content&view=article&id=94:mr-saleh

-mohammed-the-head-of-the-democratic-union-party-said-in-an-interview-with-al
-jazeera&catid=34:news&Itemid=53.

37. Mustafa Karasu, "The Third Way in Syria," Official PKK, www.pkk
online.com/en/index.php?sys=article&artID=196.

38. "Davutoğlu Says Turkey Not against Kurdish Autonomy in Post-Assad
Syria," *Today's Zaman*, August 29, 2012, www.todayszaman.com/news-289023
-davutoglu-says-turkey-not-against-kurdish-autonomy-in-post-assad-syria.html.

39. Ibid.

40. Ben Hubbard, "Kurdish Struggle Blurs Syria's Battle Lines," *New York
Times*, August 1, 2013, http://www.nytimes.com/2013/08/02/world/middle
east/syria.html.

41. Erika Solomon, "Special Report: Amid Syria's Violence, Kurds
Carve out Autonomy," Reuters, January 23, 2014, http://www.reuters.com/
article/2014/01/22/us-syria-kurdistan-specialreport-idUSBREA0L17320140122.

42. "Interview: Rights Official Speaks of Situation in Rojava, PYD Chal-
lenges," Rudlaw, March 2, 2014, http://rudaw.net/english/interview/02032014.

43. Solomon, "Special Report."

44. Saba, interview with the author, Zahle, Lebanon, May 31, 2013.

45. Tracy Shelton, "Kurds in Syria: A Struggle within a Struggle," *Global
Post*, March 25, 2013, www.globalpost.com/dispatch/news/regions/middle-east/
syria/130324/kurdish-forces-syria-war-third-party.

46. Ibid.

47. C. J. Chivers, "Defying Common View, Some Syrian Kurds Fight Assad,"
New York Times, January 22, 2013, http://www.nytimes.com/2013/01/23/world/
middleeast/some-syrian-kurds-resist-assad-defying-conventional-views.html.

48. "Rebels Team up with Nusra Jihadists against Syria Kurds," *Middle East
Online*, August 12, 2013, www.middle-east-online.com/english/?id=60674.

49. Ibid.

50. "Among the Kurds," Syria Comment, August 2, 2013, www.joshua
landis.com/blog/problems-for-syrians-in egypt/.

51. Omar Mushaweh, interview with the author, Istanbul, August 8, 2012.

52. Emrah Ulker, "US Warns Kurdish Autonomy in Syria Could Be Slippery
Slope," *Today's Zaman*, July 30, 2012, www.todayszaman.com/news-288108-us
-warns-kurdish-autonomy-in-syria-could-be-slippery-slope.html.

CHAPTER 10. ISRAEL, PALESTINE, AND SYRIA

1. Chris McGreal, "Revealed: How Israel Offered to Sell South Africa
Nuclear Weapons," *Guardian*, May 23, 2010, www.theguardian.com/world/

2010/may/23/israel-south-africa-nuclear-weapons. See also: "How Israel Helped Apartheid South Africa Build Nuclear Weapons," War in Context, April 5, 2013, http://warincontext.org/2013/04/05/how-israel-helped-apartheid-south -africa-build-nuclear-weapons.

2. In 1993, as part of the Oslo peace process, Israel recognized the Palestinian Liberation Organization and the right of Palestinians to their own state. The PLO recognized the Israeli state. Years later, Prime Minister Benjamin Netanyahu insisted that the Palestinians must recognize Israel as a Jewish state. Hussein Ibish, "Should the Palestinians Recognize Israel as a Jewish State? *Foreign Policy*, May 25, 2011, www.foreignpolicy.com/articles/2011/05/25/should_the _palestinians_recognize_israel_as_a_jewish_state.

3. Syrians argue the commonly used term *Golan Heights* is a misnomer because the area consists of rolling hills, some of which lie below Israeli territory. Israelis argue that *Golan Heights* is accurate because they occupy a strategic position overlooking Israel. In this chapter I use the neutral term *Golan*.

4. Maryam Ajami, interview with the author, Golan, October 23, 2013.

5. Akba Abu Shaheen, interview with the author, Golan, October 23, 2013.

6. Dr. Ali Abu Awad, interview with the author, Golan, October 23, 2013.

7. Eyal Zisser, interview with the author, Tel Aviv, October 22, 2013.

8. Mark Heller, interview with the author, Tel Aviv, October 22, 2013.

9. "Barak: End of Syria's Assad Would Be 'a Blessing for the Middle East,'" *Haaretz*, December 11, 2011, http://www.haaretz.com/news/diplomacy-defense/ barak-end-of-syria-s-assad-would-be-a-blessing-for-the-middle-east-1.400850.

10. "Senior Member of the SMC Defects to ISIS and Details Foreign Involvement in the Opposition," *Brown Moses Blog*, December 2, 2013, http://brown -moses.blogspot.com/2013/12/senior-member-of-smc-defects-to-isis_2.html.

11. Associated Press, "Israel Sends Humanitarian Aid to Syria," *New York Times*, December 3, 2013, http://www.nytimes.com/2013/12/04/world/middle east/israel-sends-humanitarian-aid-to-syria.html.

12. Anne Barnard, Michael R. Gordon, and Jodi Rudoren, "Israel Targeted Iranian Missiles in Syria Attack," *New York Times*, May 4, 2013, http://www .nytimes.com/2013/05/05/world/middleeast/israel-syria.html.

13. Anne Barnard, "Syria Condemns Israeli Assault near Damascus," *New York Times*, May 5, 2013, http://www.nytimes.com/2013/05/06/world/middle east/after-strikes-in-syria-concerns-about-an-escalation-of-fighting.html.

14. Michael R. Gordon, "Some Syria Missiles Eluded Israeli Strike, Officials Say," *New York Times*, July 31, 2013, http://www.nytimes.com/2013/08/01/world/ middleeast/syrian-missiles-were-moved-before-israeli-strike-officials-say.html.

15. Anne Barnard, "Israeli Warplanes Strike near the Border of Syria

and Lebanon," *New York Times*, February 24, 2013, http://www.nytimes
.com/2014/02/25/world/middleeast/israeli-warplanes-strike-near-the-border-of
-syria-and-lebanon.html.

16. Herb Keinon, "Israel Wanted Assad Gone since Start of Syria Civil War,"
Jerusalem Post, September 17, 2013, http://washingtonpac.com/Articles%20
of%20Interest/israel_wanted_assad_gone_since_s.htm.

17. Jodi Rudoren, "Israel Backs Limited Strike against Syria," *New York
Times*, September 5, 2013, http://www.nytimes.com/2013/09/06/world/middle
east/israel-backs-limited-strike-against-syria.html.

18. Jodi Rudoren and Isabel Kershner, "Lobbying Group for Israel to Press
Congress on Syria," *New York Times*, September 9, 2013, http://www.nytimes
.com/2013/09/10/world/middleeast/lobbying-group-for-israel-to-press-congress
-on-syria.html.

19. AIPAC, "Our Mission," AIPAC home page, http://www.aipac.org/
about/mission.

20. Mark Landler, "Pro-Israel Group Finds Its Momentum Blunted," *New
York Times*, February 3, 2014, http://www.nytimes.com/2014/02/04/world/
middleeast/potent-pro-israel-group-finds-its-momentum-blunted.html.

21. Mustafa Barghouti, interview with the author, Ramallah, West Bank,
October 24, 2013.

22. Ron Kampeas, "Coalition Brings Together Groups Opposing New
Iran Sanctions," Jewish Telegraphic Agency, January 28, 2014, http://www
.jta.org/2014/01/28/news-opinion/politics/coalition-brings-together-groups
-opposing-new-iran-sanctions.

23. Chemi Shalev, "Israel, Saudi Sheikhs and Congress Isolated in World
Arena," *Haaretz*, November 24, 2013, http://www.haaretz.com/blogs/west-of
-eden/.premium-1.559850.

24. UN Security Council Resolution 242, November 22, 1967, http://
unispal.un.org/unispal.nsf/0/7D35E1F729DF491C85256EE700686136.

25. United Nations Resolution 497, December 17, 1981, http://unispal.un
.org/UNISPAL.NSF/0/73D6B4C70D1A92B7852560DF0064F101.

26. "Golan Heights Profile," *BBC*, May 21, 2013, http://www.bbc.com/
news/world-middle-east-14724842.

27. Heller, interview with the author.

28. David W. Lesch, *Syria: The Fall of the House of Assad* (New Haven, CT:
Yale University Press, 2012), p. 36.

29. Jay Solomon and Bill Spindle, "Syria Strongman: Time for 'Reform,'"
Wall Street Journal, January 31, 2011, http://online.wsj.com/article/SB20001424
05274870483270457611434073503236.html.

30. Shimon Shiffer, "Netanyahu Agreed to Full Golan Heights Withdrawal," *Y Net News*, October 12, 2012, http://www.ynetnews.com/articles/0,7340, L-4291337,00.html.

31. Heller, interview with the author.

32. Zvi Hauser, "No Peace without the Golan," *Haaretz*, December 13, 2013, http://www.haaretz.com/opinion/.premium-1.563291.

33. Hannan Ashrawi, interview with the author, Ramallah, October 24, 2013.

34. Barghouti, interview with the author.

35. Ashrawi, interview with the author.

36. Ziad El-Zaza, interview with the author, Gaza City, June 8, 2011.

37. "Preliminary Statement of the NDI/Carter Center International Observer Delegation to the Palestinian Legislative Council Elections," Carter Center, January 26, 2006, https://www.cartercenter.org/news/documents/doc2283.html.

38. Khaled Meshal, interview with the author, Damascus, December 18, 2008.

39. Robert Tait, "Iran Cuts Hamas Funding over Syria," *Telegraph*, May 31, 2013, http://www.telegraph.co.uk/news/worldnews/middleeast/palestinian authority/10091629/Iran-cuts-Hamas-funding-over-Syria.html.

40. Ibid.

41. Rick Gladstone, "Large Truck Bomb Reported to Kill 60 Syrian Troops," *New York Times*, June 17, 2013, http://www.nytimes.com/2013/06/18/world/ middleeast/large-truck-bomb-reported-to-kill-60-syrian-troops.html.

42. "Palestinian Public Opinion Poll No. 45," Palestine Center for Policy and Survey Research, September 30, 2012, http://pcpsr.org/survey/polls/2012/p45e .pdf.

43. Professor As'ad Ghanem, e-mail interview with the author, October 16, 2013. The poll was conducted in 2012.

44. Naela Kahil, "Syria War Polarizes West Bank Palestinians," *Al-Monitor*, September 13, 2013, http://www.al-monitor.com/pulse/originals/2013/09/syria -war-palestinians-baath.html.

45. Barghouti, interview with the author.

46. Bruce Stokes, "Little International Support for Arming Syria Rebels," Pew Research Center, May 2, 2013, http://www.pewglobal.org/2013/05/02/ little-international-support-for-arming-syria-rebels/.

47. Khaled Abu Toameh, "Rival Palestinian Factions Hamas, Fatah Unite against Western Attack on Syria," *Jerusalem Post*, August 29, 2013, http://www.jpost.com/Middle-East/Palestinians-Hamas-Fatah-voice -opposition-for-Western-attack-on-Syria-324709.

48. Ibid.

49. Zisser, interview with the author.

50. Barghouti, interview with the author.

CHAPTER 11. UNITED STATES, RUSSIA,
AND OUTSIDE POWERS

1. State Department spokesperson, interview with the author, Washington, DC, April 16, 2012.

2. "Kathy," State Department source, interview with the author, Washington, DC, April 2012.

3. State Department spokesperson, interview with the author.

4. "Clinton: SNC No Longer Leads Syrian Opposition," *Voice of America*, October 31, 2012, http://www.voanews.com/content/brahimi-seeks-chinese-support-for-syria-solution/1536429.html.

5. "Kathy," interview with the author.

6. State Department spokesperson, interview with the author.

7. Peter van Buren, interview with the author, Washington, DC, April 17, 2012.

8. Henry Precht, interview with the author, Washington, DC, April 16, 2012.

9. "Remarks by President Obama in Address to the United Nations General Assembly," September 24, 2013, http://www.whitehouse.gov/the-press-office/2013/09/24/remarks-president-obama-address-united-nations-general-assembly.

10. John J. Mearsheimer, "American Unhinged," *National Interest*, January–February 2014, http://nationalinterest.org/article/america-unhinged-9639.

11. "Remarks by President Obama in Address to the United Nations General Assembly."

12. Jonathan Watts, "NSA Accused of Spying on Brazilian Oil Company Petrobras," *Guardian*, September 9, 2013, http://www.theguardian.com/world/2013/sep/09/nsa-spying-brazil-oil-petrobras.

13. "Snowden: NSA Conducts Industrial Espionage Too," *CBS News*, January 26, 2014, http://www.cbsnews.com/news/snowden-nsa-conducts-industrial-espionage-too/E.

14. Mearsheimer, "American Unhinged."

15. Sammy Ketz, "Moscow Rejects Saudi Offer to Drop Assad for Arms Deal," *Agence France Press*, August 8, 2013, http://www.google.com/hostednews/afp/article/ALeqM5jhPTvibpnk98IR09Amuc5QzWQsIQ?docId=CNG.c0b07c0fd43690568ae07ab83f87f608.6d1&hl=en.

16. Pepe Escobar, "Syria's Pipelineistan War," *Al Jazeera*, August 6, 2012, http://www.aljazeera.com/indepth/opinion/2012/08/201285133440424621.html.

17. Nafeez Ahmad, "Syria Intervention Plan Fueled by Oil Interests, Not Chemical Weapon Concern," *Guardian*, August 30, 2013, http://www.theguardian.com/environment/earth-insight/2013/aug/30/syria-chemical-attack-war-intervention-oil-gas-energy-pipelines.

18. Rhonda Roumani, "Four Armed Men Attack US Embassy in Damascus," *Washington Post*, September 13, 2006, http://www.washingtonpost.com/wp-dyn/content/article/2006/09/12/AR2006091200345.html.

19. Peter Grier, "Why It Took so Long for Obama to Say Syria's Assad Must Go," *Christian Science Monitor*, August 18, 2011, http://www.csmonitor.com/USA/Foreign-Policy/2011/0818/Why-it-took-so-long-for-Obama-to-say-Syria-s-Assad-must-go.

20. Ahmad Bakdouness, interview with the author, Damascus, October 5, 2011.

21. "Leen," interview with the author, Damascus, October 2011.

22. Thom Shanker, "General Says Syrian Rebels Aren't Ready to Take Power," *New York Times*, August 21, 2013, http://www.nytimes.com/2013/08/22/world/middleeast/general-says-syrian-rebels-arent-ready-to-take-power.html.

23. Mark Mazzetti, Robert F. Worth, and Michael R. Gordon, "Obama's Uncertain Path amid Syria Bloodshed," *New York Times*, October 22, 2013, http://www.nytimes.com/2013/10/23/world/middleeast/obamas-uncertain-path-amid-syria-bloodshed.html.

24. Ibid.

25. Jack Keane and Danielle Pletka, "How to Stop Assad's Slaughter," *Wall Street Journal*, May 23, 2013, http://online.wsj.com/news/articles/SB10001424127887323744604578477203521015598.

26. Doug Bandow, "Choosing between Two Evils in Syria," Cato Institute, August 6, 2012, http://www.cato.org/publications/commentary/choosing-between-two-evils-syria.

27. Pat Buchanan, "Syria: Just Whose War Is It?" *WorldNetDaily*, September 5, 2013, http://www.wnd.com/2013/09/just-whose-war-is-this/.

28. Arlette Saenz, "Let Allah Sort It Out," *ABC News*, June 15, 2013, http://news.yahoo.com/sarah-palin-u-decision-syria-let-allah-sort-182044264--abc-news-politics.html.

29. Thomas L. Friedman, "A War for Oil?" *New York Times*, January 5, 2003, http://www.nytimes.com/2003/01/05/opinion/a-war-for-oil.html.

30. Thomas L. Friedman, "This Ain't Yogurt," *New York Times*, May 5, 2013, http://www.nytimes.com/2013/05/05/opinion/sunday/friedman-this-aint-yogurt.html.

31. Danny Postel and Nader Hashemi, "Use Force to Save Starving Syrians," *New York Times*, February 10, 2014, http://www.nytimes.com/2014/02/11/opinion/use-force-to-save-starving-syrians.html.

32. Danny Postel, "Syria, Russia, and What Can Be Done: Some Questions for Bob Dreyfuss," *Nation*, February 24, 2014, http://www.thenation.com/article/178517/syria-russia-and-what-can-be-done-some-questions-bob-dreyfuss.

33. "Security Council Approves 'No-Fly Zone' over Libya, Authorizing 'All Necessary' Measures to Protect Civilians, by Vote of 10 in Favour with 5 Abstentions," UN Security Council, March 17, 2011, https://www.un.org/News/Press/docs/2011/sc10200.doc.htm.

34. Reese Erlich, "Militias Become Power Centers in Libya," *Progressive*, September 2012, http://www.progressive.org/libya_militias.html.

35. Stephen Zunes, "Despite Horrific Repression, the U.S. Should Stay out of Syria," Foreign Policy in Focus, May 15, 2013, http://tpit.org/despite_horrific_repression_the_us_should_stay_out_of_syria/.

36. "War in Syria," American Friends Service Committee, May 10, 2013, http://www.afsc.org/story/war-syria.

37. Friends for a NonViolent World homepage: http://www.fnvw.org/index.asp?SEC=F2DC5E79-EB52-4C39-BA7A-A80ACCF39803&Type=B_BASIC.

38. Michael R. Gordon, David E. Sanger, and Eric Schmitt, "Russia Scolded as US Weighs Syria Options," *New York Times*, February 17, 2014, http://www.nytimes.com/2014/02/18/world/middleeast/russia-is-scolded-as-us-weighs-syria-options.html.

39. Nicholas Blanford and Fred Weir, "Why Russia Is Blocking International Action against Syria," *Christian Science Monitor*, September 19, 2011, http://www.csmonitor.com/World/Middle-East/2011/0919/Why-Russia-is-blocking-international-action-against-Syria

40. Howard Amos, "Billions of Dollars of Russian Business Suffers along with Syria," *Moscow Times*, September 2, 2011, http://www.themoscowtimes.com/business/article/billions-of-dollars-of-russian-business-suffers-along-with-syria/443078.html.

41. Fred Weir, "Why Russia Is Willing to Sell Arms to Syria," *Christian Science Monitor*, January 19, 2012, http://www.csmonitor.com/World/Europe/2012/0119/Why-Russia-is-willing-to-sell-arms-to-Syria.

42. Ibid.

43. Russian diplomat, interview with the author, November 2013.

44. Blanford and Weir, "Why Russia Is Blocking International Action against Syria."

45. Aaron Zelin, phone interview with the author, March 11, 2013.

46. Mohammad Fahd al-Qahtani, interview with the author, Riyadh, February 2, 2013.

47. "Saudi Arabia Punishes Two Activists for Voicing Opinion," Amnesty International, March 11, 2013, https://www.amnesty.org/en/news/saudi-arabia-punishes-two-activists-voicing-opinion-2013-03-11.

48. Ben Gilbert, "Saudi Arabia Walks a Fine Line in Backing Syrian Rebellion," *Al Jazeera America*, January 20, 2014, http://america.aljazeera.com/articlcs/2014/1/20/saudi-arabia-walksafinelinkinbackingsyriarebellion.html.

49. Abdurrahman al-Talq, interview with the author, Saudi Arabia, February 3, 2013.

50. Mansour al-Turki, interview with the author, February 5, 2013.

51. Randa Slim, phone interview with the author, Washington, DC, March 11, 2013.

52. Qahtani, interview with the author.

53. Eric Schmitt, "CIA Said to Aid in Steering Arms to Syrian Rebels," *New York Times*, June 21, 2012, http://www.nytimes.com/2012/06/21/world/middleeast/cia-said-to-aid-in-steering-arms-to-syrian-rebels.html.

54. Vali R. Nasr, "Islamic Comrades No More," *New York Times*, October 28, 2013, http://www.nytimes.com/2013/10/29/opinion/international/nasr-islamic-comrades-no-more.html.

55. "Saudi Arabia Designates Muslim Brotherhood as Terrorist Group," *Reuters*, March 7, 2014, http://www.reuters.com/article/2014/03/07/us-saudi-security-idUSBREA260SM20140307.

56. Reese Erlich, "Do Lebanon's Taif Accords Offer Lessons for Syrian Peace?" *Global Post*, August 2, 2013, http://www.globalpost.com/dispatch/news/regions/middle-east/lebanon/130801/syria-peace-lebanon-taif-accords.

BIBLIOGRAPHY

Aldington, Richard. *Lawrence of Arabia: A Biographical Enquiry*. Westport, CT: Greenwood, 1976.

Barr, James. *A Line in the Sand: The Anglo-French Struggle for the Middle East, 1914–1948*. New York: W. W. Norton, 2012.

———. *Setting the Desert on Fire: T. E. Lawrence and Britain's Secret War in Arabia 1916–1918*. New York: W. W. Norton, 2008.

Borne, John E. *The USS Liberty: Dissenting History vs. Official History*. New York: Reconsideration Press, 1995.

Chomsky, Noam. *The Fateful Triangle: The United States, Israel & the Palestinians*. Boston: South End Press, 1983.

Choueiri, Youssef M. *Islamic Fundamentalism*. Boston: Twayne Publishers, Division of G. K. Hall, 1990.

Collins, Larry, and Dominique Lapierre. *O Jerusalem!* New York: Simon & Schuster Paperbacks, 1972.

Commission of Inquiry into the Actions of Canadian Officials in Relation to Maher Arar (Arar Commission). Canadian Government Publishing, 2006.

Crooke, Allistair. *Resistance: The Essence of the Islamist Revolution*. New York: Pluto Press, 2009.

Erlich, Reese. *Conversations with Terrorists: Middle East Leaders on Politics, Violence, and Empire*. Sausalito, CA: PoliPoint Press, 2010.

———. *The Iran Agenda: The Real Story of US Policy and the Middle East Crisis*. Sausalito, CA: PoliPoint Press, 2007.

Fisk, Robert. *Pity the Nation: The Abduction of Lebanon*. New York: Nation Books, 2002.

——— *The Great War for Civilization: The Conquest of the Middle East*. New York: Alfred Knopf, 2005.

Gould, Elizabeth, and Paul Fitzgerald. *Crossing Zero: The Afpak War at the Turning Point of American Empire*. San Francisco: City Lights Books, 2011.

Graves, R. Perceval. *Lawrence of Arabia and His World*. London: Thames and Hudson, 1976.

Hashemi, Nader, and Danny Postel. *The People Reloaded: The Green Movement and the Struggle for Iran's Future*. Brooklyn: Melville House, 2010.

———. *The Syria Dilemma*. Cambridge, MA: MIT Press, 2013.

Ingrams, Doreen. *Palestine Papers 1917–1922: Seeds of Conflict*. London: John Murray, 1972.

Kaplan, Robert D. *The Arabists: The Romance of an American Elite*. New York: Free Press, 1993.

Landis, Joshua. "Syria and the 1948 War in Palestine." In *Rewriting the Palestine War: 1948 and the History of the Arab-Israeli Conflict*. Edited by Eugene Rogan and Avi Shlaim. Cambridge: Cambridge University Press, 2001.

Lawrence, T. E. *Seven Pillars of Wisdom*. London: Wordsworth Classics, 1997.

———. Introduction to *Travels in Arabia Deserta*, by Charles Doughty. http://zineb-returns.blogspot.com/2012/05/te-lawrence-on-englishmen.html.

Lesch, David W. *Syria: The Fall of the House of Assad*. New Haven, CT: Yale University Press, 2012.

McBride, Sean, et al. *Israel in Lebanon: Report of the International Commission to Enquire into Reported Violations of International Law by Israel during Its Invasion of Lebanon*. London: Ithaca Press, 1983.

Ocalan, Abdullah. *Prison Writings: The Roots of Civilisation*. London: Pluto Press, 2007.

Oren, Michael. *Power, Faith, and Fantasy: America in the Middle East, 1776 to the Present*. New York: W. W. Norton, 2007.

Pargeter, Alison. *The Muslim Brotherhood: From Opposition to Power*. London: Saqi Books, 2010.

Provence, Michael. *The Great Syrian Revolt and the Rise of Arab Nationalism*. Austin: University of Texas Press, 2005.

Redd, Adrienne. *Fallen Walls and Fallen Towers: The Fate of the Nation in a Global World*. Ann Arbor, MI: Nimble Books, 2010–2011.

Rogan, Eugene. *The Arabs: A History*. New York: Basic Books, 2011.

Sennott, Charles, M. *The Body and the Blood: The Middle East's Vanishing Christians and the Possibility for Peace*. New York: Public Affairs, 2001.

Starr, Stephen. *Revolt in Syria: Eye-Witness to the Uprising*. New York: Columbia University Press, 2012.

Swanson, Bill, ed. *Encarta Book of Quotes*. New York: St. Martin's Press, 2000.

Tabler, Andrew. *In the Lion's Den: An Eyewitness Account of Washington's Battle with Syria*. Chicago: Lawrence Hill Books, 2011.

Tejel, Jordil. *Syria's Kurds: History, Politics, and Society*. London: Rutledge Group, 2009.

Thomas, Lowell. *With Lawrence in Arabia*. 16th ed. London: Hutchinson, n.d.

United Nations. "Final Report, United Nations Mission to Investigate Allegations of the Use of Chemical Weapons in the Syrian Arab Republic." December 12, 2013. https://www.un.org/apps/news//story.asp?NewsID=46730&Cr=syria&Cr1=.

United Nations Office for Human Rights. "UN Issues First Report on Human

Rights of Gay and Lesbian People." December 15, 2011. http://www.un
    .org/apps/news/story.asp?NewsID=40743#.UyCUyfrn_gg.

Wright, Robert. *Our Man in Tehran: The True Story behind the Secret Mission to Save
    Six Americans during the Iran Hostage Crisis and the Foreign Ambassador Who
    Worked with the CIA to Bring Them Home.* New York: Other Press, 2011.

INDEX

Pages in *italic* indicate subject was interviewed.